my point…
and I do
have one

E L L E N
DEGENERES

my point...
and I do
have one

BANTAM BOOKS
New York   Toronto   London   Sydney   Auckland

This edition contains the complete text
of the original hardcover edition.
NOT ONE WORD HAS BEEN OMITTED.

MY POINT . . . AND I DO HAVE ONE
A Bantam Book

PUBLISHING HISTORY
Bantam hardcover edition published October 1995
Bantam paperback edition / October 1996

ISBN 0-553-57361-6

Published simultaneously in the United States and Canada

Bantam Books are published by Bantam Books, a division of Bantam Doubleday Dell Publishing Group, Inc. Its trademark, consisting of the words "Bantam Books" and the portrayal of a rooster, is Registered in U.S. Patent and Trademark Office and in other countries. Marca Registrada. Bantam Books, 1540 Broadway, New York, New York 10036.

PRINTED IN THE UNITED STATES OF AMERICA

OPM   0 9 8 7 6 5 4 3 2 1

Table O'Contents

Acknowledgments

I wish to thank a few people for their support and love, which are two of the most important things in my life: Betty DeGeneres, Elliott DeGeneres (or Mom and Dad), Vance DeGeneres, Arthur Imparato, Rob Weisbach, Alex Herschlag, Sue Rose, Lisa Phillips, J. J. Harris, Jeremy Zimmer, Ted Harbert, Stu Bloomberg, Renee Kurtz, Michael Eisner, Rich Frank, Dean Valentine, Jan Nash, Karen Kawahara, and Eric Bilardi. And all of the people who come up to me on the street and tell me nice things. Thank you.

A Note from the Author

Hello and welcome to my book (and now yours). Thank you for your interest in my thoughts, my words of wisdom, and my recipe for French toast. Throughout the year it took me to write this, I wrote in solitude, recording my thoughts as they came to me, digging up old memories, pouring out my heart and soul. Then, at the end of the process, I hoped and prayed to God that there were a few people out there who would enjoy it.

As you may have noticed, my mind does not work the same as most. That is to say, I'm sort of, well—different—and yet it seems to have worked for me. So as you read this, I hope it does what I intended it to do when I decided to write it. I hope it entertains you, inspires you, makes you laugh, makes you think, makes you smile, makes you feel better about yourself, makes you more aware of your feelings, makes you love your brothers and sisters, makes you more successful in life, makes you wealthier, makes you exercise more, makes you eat healthier, makes you stop smoking, makes you taller, thinner, more beautiful, more fluent in Spanish! Or at least makes you not regret buying it.

Ellen DeGeneres
June 1995

thanks for no

memory

....

That's not my life...

Who am I? How did I get to be me? If I wasn't me, who would I be? How can you mend a broken heart? These are all good questions. Well, almost all good questions—I'm pretty sure the last one is just a Bee Gees song.

Anyway, what I'm trying to say is who I am now is what I was then, plus all the stuff in between, minus a few years during the seventies. Actually, that might not be what I'm trying to say. Here's what I really mean: When you start to write a book, you begin at the beginning; when you start to examine your life, you begin with childhood.

I try to work on my memory. A few things come back to me when I concentrate. Like, I'm now pretty sure I had parents. I have these two old people who are my parents now, and they say they were also my parents then. I'm thirty-six. I *was* a little girl. I know because my parents say I was.

I was born in Jefferson Parish, Louisiana, at Ochsner Hospital, January 26, 1958. I lived in a house on Haring Road in Metairie until I was . . . oh, let's say eight or nine—maybe ten . . . could've been seven or six, I don't know.

I don't think I remember my first memory. Actually, I suppose I would have to remember my first memory. If I didn't remember my first memory, then it couldn't in all honesty be my first memory. It could, however, be the first thing that I forgot. Do I recall the first thing that I forgot? I don't remember. Maybe.

I am amazed when people tell me that they remember things like lying in their cribs or getting their diapers changed (these are things they remember doing as infants not as adults—that would be an entirely different story and probably not a very pleasant one). Some people even remember learning how to walk, which I find especially surprising since I just barely remember learning how to drive.

Sometimes my lack of memory (or, to put a positive spin on it, my surplus of forgetfulness) worries me, especially since it's not limited to my early childhood. I don't remember huge portions of my life. Maybe something big (i.e., an anvil or France) fell on my head and gave me a slight form of amnesia. Maybe a lot of things have fallen on my head. I just don't know.

My parents have tried to help me out, but they remember even less about me than I do. They hardly took any pictures of me. But my brother—who was four years older than me (and still is, as a matter of fact)—they took so many pictures of him that you can flip through his photos and it's like one of those animation books; it looks like a movie where he's walking and riding a tricycle and running around. They must have taken a picture of him every ten seconds.

After four years of that, my parents must have gotten tired. I came along and they said, "We don't have to take any pictures. We'll remember." But they don't. It was ridiculous. There were statues of my brother around the house, but nothing of me. They tried to fool me and show me pictures they said were of me. But I'd say, "That's not me. Those are pictures you cut out of a magazine. I know, because I'm neither Elizabeth Taylor nor a member of England's royal family."

So I decided to do something to fill in these great gaps in my memory. I set out to interview people who knew me through various stages of my life. Most of those I interviewed didn't look familiar, but I'm sure they were telling me the truth. Otherwise they wouldn't have answered the ads or accepted the money I gave them. What follows are the transcripts of some of those interviews.

. . . .

My Investigation Notes:

I was born, bred, and lightly sautéed in and around New Orleans, a city steeped in tradition and marinated in history. During those formative years, a trusted family friend and neighbor was Miss Selma Clanque (pronounced Klan-kay), a woman who earned her living making decorative jewelry out of crawdads.

I interviewed Miss Selma, now a feisty spitfire in her early seventies, on the fire escape of her apartment (which she insisted we call a lanai). Throughout, she chain-smoked clove cigarettes and drank a mixture of Ovaltine and vodka, a cocktail she calls chocolate thunder.

What do you remember most about me as a baby?
You were fat. Oh lordy, were you fat! You didn't walk for the longest time, 'cause you were so fat. They just rolled you wherever they wanted you to go.

Anything besides that?
I think your parents just kept feeding you. They were happy you weren't walking. They already had your brother, a very handsome boy—no fat on him—so they figured, might as well let you take your time.

Do you remember anything not having to do with my being fat?
Well . . . you had a big old head, too, and not a lick of hair on it. Bless my corns, you were one ugly baby. Now you know that Miss Selma Clanque's mother didn't raise her to say nothing mean about no one. But your mama dressed you in the most hideous clothes—flowery frocks and bonnets and the like. Now when you've got a bone ugly child, you don't want to bring more attention to it. Am I right?

Let's move on. Do you have any memories of me from when I was in grade school?
I recall you coming home all upset because there was a cloakroom in your class and you didn't own a cloak. In fact, none of the little boys or girls had a cloak. I don't think any of them even knew what a cloak was. For some reason this scared you.

Do you remember my being good at anything?
You would nap better than anybody else, and your parents would brag on you being good at recess. You were quite a good tetherball player, probably because you were so aggressive.

I remember tetherball. A ball would be attached to a pole by a rope and you'd try to whack the ball hard enough to wrap the rope around the pole. It was violent. You'd either hurt your hand on the metal thingee holding the rope and ball together or you'd be on defense, standing in front of the ball, and get hit in the face. Somebody would always end up crying.
Well, crying's good. It prepares you for life. The more often I see children crying, the more often I think, "That's gonna be a healthy adult." That's what life is all about. There's a lot of crying involved. So you'd better cry now and get used to it.

Well, it's nice to know that I was good at something.
Oh my, yes! You were so good at tetherball that I bet someone $100 cash that you would become a professional tetherball player.

I guess you had to pay up?
Why? You ain't dead yet. There's still time. Everybody's always trying to get Miss Selma Clanque to give them

$100, just like it grew on trees. Look at me, I ain't Rocke-feller, am I?

No, you're not. Thanks for the time. I've got to go.

I moved to Atlanta, Texas, in my second year of high school. When Columbus came to the New World, he thought he was in India so he referred to the people he met as Indians. When the first settlers came to Texas, they thought they were in Georgia, so they called the place Atlanta. It was a culture shock moving from New Orleans (The French Quarter, jazz, great restaurants) to such a small town as Atlanta (Dairy Queen). So, I learned a different way of life.

My high school guidance counselor in Atlanta was Mr. Bowden Lamar, a man rumored to have a wonderfully infectious laugh; rumored, because no one living had actually ever heard him laugh. We spoke in his office at Atlanta High where, though he appeared to be some-where in his early hundreds, he still doles out advice as a guidance counselor.

Mr. Lamar, was I a good student here?
Well, the teachers here remember you very fondly. They all say you were very bright.

Why, thank you. I guess that's . . .
But they're just saying that because you're famous now. I know because I've seen your records.

What do those records say?
That the only reason you passed any class was because your teachers gave you very broad clues. For instance, if the answer to a question was Thomas Jefferson, your teacher would say, "The answer to that rhymes with

Bhomas Hefferson." If you still couldn't guess, she'd start singing, " 'Movin' on up, to the East Side. We finally got a piece of the pie.' "

The theme from "The Jeffersons"?
Exactly. Sooner or later—usually later—you'd end up getting the answer.

Was I good at anything?
Athletics, I suppose. You were on the tennis team. And you started the girls golf team. You were the only one on the team, playing every day by yourself. You would whack the ball very aggressively then acknowledge the applause of a crowd that only existed in your mind. Very strange and more than slightly disturbing.

Do you remember what I looked like?
Well, you were a little hefty. Yup, you were a little hefty girl who'd drive to school each day in a canary yellow Vega. But then again, everybody here is a little hefty. That's because the only kind of food you can get around here is chicken-fried. Chicken-fried steak, chicken-fried broccoli, chicken-fried sushi, chicken-fried whatever.

What sort of career do your records say I was best suited for?
Let me see. Oh here it is. "Ellen DeGeneres might be good at making caramel candies of some kind, either chewy or hard. Not the wrapping, just the candy."

Just one last question. How come this school didn't have a drama department?
Oh, we had a drama department. We all just thought it was best for everybody involved that you never knew about it. Whenever we wanted to put on a play, we'd just

send you golfing somewhere. Ha, ha, it's kind of funny, isn't it?

Yeah, hilarious.

As soon as I graduated from high school, I moved back to New Orleans. I had no plans to go to college and no idea what I was going to do, but I don't remember caring either. After all, it was the 1970s, and the country was tapping its platform shoes to the sounds of K.C. and the Sunshine Band.

I worked at a series of places including a restaurant (where I shucked oysters) and a law firm (where I shucked lawyers). A friend of mine during that time was Rita Bangs, an aspiring coffee importer. I interviewed Rita at a Renaissance Faire called "Ye Olden Dress Up in Funny Clothes Thymes" where she was employed as a wench.

When you think of me in New Orleans during the 1970s, what comes most to mind?
Your older sister was prettier than you and a lot more popular. But you were smarter.

I don't have an older sister. I have an older brother.
Whatever. Anyway, your father took your family on a trip to a resort. You were his favorite. He always called you Baby.

Really?
Oh yes. The waiters at the resort were all these good-looking college guys. But you fell in love with the dance instructor, even though your father hated him because he thought he got some girl pregnant. But your father ended up liking him when he saw the two of you dance at the big show at the resort.

That's not my life. That's the movie Dirty Dancing.
No, I'm pretty sure it's your life.

Really?
No. But it was a good movie.

Do you even know me?
Not in so many words. But I'm a big fan. Do you know how I can meet Patrick Swayze?

No. Thanks for meeting with me. You were no help at all.
You're welcome.

The last person I spoke to was Dr. Max Fenetre. He wouldn't say how I knew him but assured me he could supply a missing piece of the jigsaw puzzle that is my life. We spoke at his Beverly Hills office once he was assured that I had health insurance.

So, what would you like to tell me about myself?
I'll tell you, but only if I can be the person in italics.

No. The person who asks the questions is in italics. That's how it's done.
But I'm a doctor and therefore have much more authority than you. Ergo, I should be in italics.

I did all the other interviews in italics. I'm not going to change now.
HOW ABOUT IF I'M IN BOLD AND ALL CAPITALS, LIKE THIS?

No, it would be too distracting.
That's it, interview's over. Get out of my office, you italics hog.

YEAH, WELL GOOD-BYE TO YOU, TOO. HA, HA, HA.

Hey! I just remembered my first memory. I'm eating eggs and toast and feeling a little bit grumpy. Then I take a sip of strong black coffee and read my horoscope in the newspaper. Wait a minute. That was just an hour ago at breakfast. I guess it's possible that that's my first memory. Perhaps my philosophy is "Don't hold on to things, it will only bring you pain." Or that might not be my philosophy. I just don't remember.

a letter to my friend

or ....
a frog in a sombrero does not a
party make

I didn't know it was a
party for your grandmother's
90th birthday.

In digging through my old photos and letters for this book, I've discovered correspondence that brings back wonderful old memories. And, well, some not-so-wonderful memories.

Dear Morgana,

I just wanted to drop you a quick note to thank you for inviting me to your party last week. I'm not very good at parties. But I guess you know that by now. I feel awkward at them and tend to overcompensate by acting in a way that others who don't know me well might consider a tad weird. However, you know me well and besides, you're a very perceptive and, I might add, very *forgiving* person.

I guess what I'm trying to say is I'm really really really sorry for what happened. Maybe it was good, though. Maybe this will be one of those things that a little while from now you'll look back on and laugh at. Okay, maybe it will be longer than a little while. Eventually, though, after at most a few decades, there's bound to be some laughter. Isn't there? Oh God, I'm so sorry.

I know that we're good enough friends that I could just call you on the phone, but I thought a letter would be preferable for two reasons. One, often it's easier to say things in a letter than it is to say them in person. And two, you don't seem to be answering my phone calls anymore.

Sometimes nobody answers the phone—even if I let it ring over five hundred times (I've counted). At other times, somebody who sounds like you (but I'm sure isn't) answers and asks who it is. When I say "Ellen," that person (who, as I said before, I'm sure isn't you, because you are much too compassionate) immediately develops an obviously fake Russian accent and says, "She not home. She move far away to place with no phone. I begging you, please leave alone."

All that being said, let me begin my apology.

I think a lot of what happened can be traced back to the rum cake I brought over. I just looked over the recipe, and I see now that it called for two table-spoons of rum. For some reason, maybe because I was nervous because I don't cook that much, I misread that as two *bottles* of rum. It's an honest mistake, and your little nephews were eventually going to find out what a hangover is anyway.

I had at least two slices of the rum cake, and I believe that's why I blurted out that your real name is Marge. I thought everybody already knew. I also thought that everybody would find your old nick-name, "Large Marge," funny. I understand now that it isn't funny. Anyway, it shouldn't bother you because you're not heavy anymore. Oh yes, I'm also sorry that I told people about your liposuction. But at least I didn't tell anybody about your breast enlargement surgery. Oh, that's right, I did. Sorry.

As for what I call "the Charades incident," for some reason I get a little competitive (okay, way too com-petitive) playing party games—once again, to make up for my own insecurities. That's why when Rever-end Green couldn't figure out I was doing *Fried Green Tomatoes* and kept on guessing *Two Mules for Sister Sarah* (which, you have to admit, isn't even close—it doesn't even have the same number of words!) I got mad.

That in no way excuses my calling him a God damned rat @+%ˆ#$%, *%$@–eating moron. Isn't it cute when you write curses out that way? It's too bad I didn't say it like that. Also, when I jokingly implied that he was a child molester, I had no idea about the recent trial (though I am happy to hear that all the charges have been dropped).

Now, the gift. I was under the mistaken impression (boy, hindsight is always twenty-twenty, isn't it?) that the party was for your wedding shower. That's why I got what I considered to be a gag gift. I didn't know it was a party for your grandmother's 90th birthday. Otherwise, I never would have gotten her the crotchless underwear and the coupon for a free nipple piercing.

I admit I laughed pretty hard when your grammy opened the present (sorry about the wine coming out of my nose onto your new rug—club soda should get out that stain, not cola like I tried), but I thought she was laughing, too. Now I know she was hyperventilating. I swear I've never seen anybody's face turn that red before. That is why I shouted out, "Look at her, heh heh. She looks like a big tomato!"

Not funny.

I am glad to hear that your grammy is out of the hospital. I'm the one who sent the big basket of muffins. Nobody told me she was diabetic. She only ate a few of them, and when I called the hospital they said that at most that added three days to her stay there—maybe four.

This part is the hardest to explain. I know that when you opened the door to your bedroom it looked like I was shaving your dog. Well, I was shaving your dog . . . but not for the reason you might think. I didn't say, "Hmmm, I think Marge's dog—I'm sorry, *Morgana's* dog—would look better with less hair." Though, you have to admit, the cut does give Colonel Chompers an interesting look and makes him seem quite distinguished (I don't care what the judges at the dog show say).

What happened was, in trying to spit my gum across your kitchen and into the trash can (a trick I do remarkably well, usually) I missed, and the gum landed in Colonel Chompers' fur. I tried to pull it out, but it just made matters worse. So I snuck him into your bedroom with the hope of finding some scissors and cutting the gum out. I didn't locate scissors, but I did find your Lady Gillette and thought, hey, this might work—which eventually it did. The gum came out. I am sorry that some got on your drapes. I thought they were tissue paper.

But, you have every right to ask, why was I wearing your bathing suit while shaving your dog? Good question. In looking for the scissors, I found the bathing suit in the third drawer of your bureau (I didn't look in your second drawer, so you have no reason to be embarrassed). I had seen that suit in a store that day and thought it might look good on me. So, I figured this was a good opportunity to try it on.

I believe you see now that there was a logical explanation for everything that happened at your otherwise very successful party.

I hope that you find it in your heart to forgive me, and we can be as good friends as we were before last weekend.

Love,
Ellen

P.S. Oh yes, I almost forgot. I'm also sorry that I bit your fiancé, I mean ex-fiancé, on the ass. Oops.

daily
affirmations

or ....
a cup of pudding a day is the
way to stay o.k.

I will wake up.

I will brush my teeth.

A Poem

Death, disease, famine
homelessness, abuse
I can't even watch
the 5 o'clock news
When did we lose control
and how do we rebel
Take a look around
we're on a rocket ship to hell
There could be an answer
it may not be too late
but it involves a transfer
try love instead of hate
All you can do
is be good to people
and hope that those people
will be good to you too
but good luck
I doubt it

When your life gets to be overwhelming, when you feel like too much of the world is depressing, there are two things you can do: One, sit in your house and feel the doom and gloom and continue to watch the news, shaking your head in resignation and saying to yourself, "Oh no, my life sucks. The world is ending, there's nothing I can do." This is one way to go. I, personally, wouldn't recommend it.

"Well," you say, "what's the *other* option?"

Here it is: If you must watch the news, turn the sound off and imagine the news anchor people are telling you all about your day. Make up happy events, adding your name into the report every third or fourth sentence.

Sing loud with wild abandonment as you get dressed in the morning (any cheery song will do).

And most important, get yourself some daily affirmations.

I do daily affirmations every day—hence the word "daily." I guess, if you're lazy, you can do weekly affirmations or monthly affirmations or even yearly affirmations. Actually, I suppose New Year's resolutions are yearly affirmations. But if you're making the same New Year's resolution every year (e.g., "I will be more popular"), and it's still not happening (e.g., "Nobody ever calls me. I'm all alone. Boo hoo."), it may be time to change your strategy. Your next yearly affirmation should be to do daily affirmations.

Daily affirmations are an important way to pick yourself up. We all have bad days and you can't always count on other people to make things better. For instance, you might say to someone, "I'm a bad person," expecting them to say in return, "Oh, no, you're not, you're one of the kindest, most thoughtful people I know." But nine times out of ten, they'll say instead, "Really. Hmmm. Hey, could you pass the Chee-tos?" And sometimes you're not even eating Chee-tos, you're eating barbecue potato chips or some weird flavored popcorn!

So, because you can't rely on other people, for your own ego you need daily affirmations. Some obvious affirmations are: "I am a good person" or "I love myself" or "I matter." But I think it's a good idea to start small. You should say things that make you feel good because they are easy to accomplish. ("I will wake up." "I will brush my teeth.") Don't push yourself. Those can be very good morning affirmations. I guess, though, if you're really depressed, and it's 8 o'clock at night, "I will wake up" would technically be an evening affirmation.

The more depressed you are, the simpler the affirmation should be. Under the right circumstances, "Who cares if I'm drunk?" is a perfectly reasonable affirmation.

Sometimes the only way you can make yourself feel better is by putting other people down. And that's okay.

There is nothing wrong with that—whatever gets you through. "I'm not as fat as she is." "I have more teeth than he has." "Thank God I'm not as bone ugly as they are." These are all fine affirmations. However, it's best that when you're in public you say this kind of affirmation to yourself. It can save you embarrassment and a black eye. These are silent affirmations.

You probably do affirmations without even knowing it. Every time you drive over the speed limit, you're saying, "No copper is gonna catch me speeding." And when you put that ski mask over your head, you're saying, "Nobody is going to recognize me while I rob this gas station." You're pumping yourself up and telling yourself you can succeed.

Here are some affirmations that have helped me. Use them if you'd like. They're yours free (except for what you paid for the book; if you borrowed this book from a friend or the library and you feel you should send me a few bucks, that's fine, too).

I am the world's tallest midget.

I'm a little teapot, short and stout. Here is my handle, here is my spout.

I bet nobody knows I'm crazy.

I look good in bell bottoms.

Archie would rather date me than either Betty or Veronica.

I can walk through walls. Ouch! No, I can't.

I mean for my hair to look like this.

The Great Spirit smiles on me. On me and only me. The Great Spirit hates everybody else. We're best friends.

I don't need to exercise. I have the perfect shape.

I'm smarter than my dogs. Well, smarter than one of my dogs.

I look good with back hair.

Being grubby equals being cool.

I sing better than Bonnie Raitt. I have as many Grammys as Bonnie Raitt. I am Bonnie Raitt.

It's not important to know what everybody else seems to know. I don't care how much they laugh at me.

La la la la la la la la la la la la—Talk all you want, I can't hear you—la la la la la la la la. La la la.

If I put my mind to it, I could do anything. I just don't feel like putting my mind to something. So there.

I have X-ray vision. Wait a minute. I don't. These glasses are a rip-off.

I meant to get ripped off.

I've fallen and I can get up.

I'm good at watching TV.

I can come up with better affirmations than these.

ellen

degeneres:

road warrior

or ....

sometimes you need a map,

sometimes you need a globe,

sometimes you need a map and a

globe—but not very often

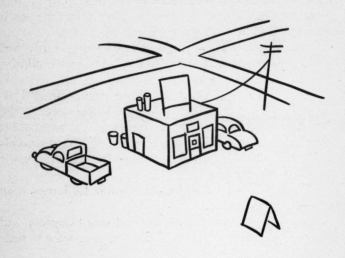

It was the mid-80's
when it wasn't considered "cool"
to know where you were.

"**A**unt Ellen, tell us a story." It's so cute when the kids from the neighborhood drop on by.

They just love to hear me spin a tale. It's either that or they love that I buy liquor for them no matter how young they are. You've got to learn to drink sometime, so it might as well be with someone you can trust.

"Please, Aunt Ellen, please tell us a story," Little Tori pleaded between sips of her Margarita. Then suddenly, "Ahhhhhh! My head hurts."

"You've just got an ice-cream headache, dear," I assured her. Then I told her that it would go away if she pressed her tongue to the roof of her mouth and held it there for a little bit. (This really works.) Within seconds her headache was gone. "I feel so much better. You know so much, Aunt Ellen."

"Well, I've been drinking for a whole lot longer than any of you," I quipped.

We all laughed at that. After we stopped laughing and I freshened everyone's drink, I said, "So, you want to hear a story, eh?"

"Yes, yes we do, we surely, surely do! Oh yes, indeedy, doddy, duddy, we do, Aunt Ellen," Tori, Tony, Toni, Tone, Toby, Terry, and Pedro said in unison. "We want to hear a scary story."

"How about if I tell you how I broke into show business? I originally wanted to be a singer. I used to perform with the Judds. In those days we were known as Two Judds & A DeGeneres. And, well, I was always known as the funny one." I laughed.

"That's not a story!" the children cried. "We want a *scary* story, Aunt Ellen, not some old joke from your stand-up."

Kids are so cute. I have no idea where they get their ideas. I never did that joke in my stand-up. I may have mentioned it on Leno or *Regis and Kathie Lee*, but I'm pretty sure I didn't do it in my stand-up. Well, not more than once or twice.

"I'll tell you the scariest story I know. It's about bad gigs that I've had." Gigs, for those of you who don't know, is plural for gig. I lit a cigarette and started my story.

"There have been many, many bad places that I have played. One of the worst was a long, narrow, dingy restaurant that may have had fifteen tables (or, if you only counted tables that didn't wobble . . . no tables). There was no way that it was created for any type of art form, whether music or comedy or anything. It was barely created for the consumption of food. I don't remember what town this was in. It could have been any town. Though, on second thought, I don't think there is a place called Anytown. I'm pretty sure it was either in the Midwest, the South, or on the East or West Coast. Or it could have been in Canada. I was traveling. I was on the road. It was the mid-eighties, when it wasn't considered 'cool' to know where you were.

"I was with some comedian, and I didn't know who he was either, even though we were doing fifteen dates together, driving from city to city. When we got to the restaurant, there was a chalkboard sitting on the street out front. It said: Soup of the Day—Cream of Asparagus. Ellen DeGeneres.

"That's when I had the Funniest Person in America title. That's the only reason I got top billing over the comedian I was with, who was the opener. He didn't even get on the chalkboard. And soup of the day had top billing over me. People would really have to want cream of asparagus soup—that would lure them in. And while they were there for the soup, well, I was just there. Nobody knew who I was. And, I'm sure my name was misspelled. My name was never spelled right. And even if it was spelled right, what did that mean to anybody? That's pretty scary right there, isn't it?"

The kids stared at me, which I took to mean, "Yes, that is pretty scary." Just then, who should come in the door but little five-year-old Mercedes and her twin brother, Oldsmobile. I had forgotten that I gave them the keys to my car to drive down to the neighborhood mart for some salted nuts and a two-pound bag of swizzle sticks. My grandmother used to say, "What's a party without swizzle sticks?" And, even though I still have no idea what she was talking about, I'm never without them.

As we were passing out the nuts and the sticks, little Toby, remembering that I was in the middle of a story, asked without a hint of sarcasm, "Aunt Ellen, how did you get to be the funniest person in America?"

"This is how I got the title 'The Funniest Person in America,'" I continued, leaning back in my BarcaLounger, remembering it as if it were either yesterday or over ten years ago. "I performed stand-up comedy in New Orleans for about a year, and then the club I worked at closed down. This was through no fault of my own, but since then my philosophy has been it's just as easy to be funny without a flamethrower as it is to be with one. After that I was working in a law firm as a court runner. I worked there for about a year (until I was so out of breath I had to quit) and then I entered the Funniest Person in New Orleans contest.

"The contest was at a club before a panel of judges, and about fifteen other people competed, a lot of whom had never even been on stage before. I had a 102° fever—I was really, really sick. I almost went home, but I decided to stay. I was the last person onstage, and I won.

"They taped the show that night, and my tape was sent to the contest for the whole state of Louisiana. I won and became the Funniest Person in Louisiana. I don't even think anyone else entered (maybe Al Hirt or Archie Manning). Then my tape was sent to New York—it was put up in a fine hotel and given one hundred dollars a day spending money, which is a lot for a tape—to compete against the tapes from the other forty-nine states. Well, to make a long story short . . ."

"It's a little late for that," one of the children murmured. I couldn't tell who it was since all of them are trained ventriloquists. I decided to continue.

"So, my tape, representing Louisiana, made it to the top five from all the states. Then all five tapes went to Pee Wee Herman, Harvey Korman, and Soupy Sales—those were the judges—two of whom, if I'm not mistaken, are now on the Supreme Court. And they all picked me as the winner. So I won Funniest Person in America for Showtime based on that one 102° fever performance.

"After I won, I started traveling with that title. Showtime started taking me around to find the next year's winner. I played parking lots, supermarkets, and other places looking for next year's winner (most funny people will eventually wind up in parking lots or supermarkets). I traveled in a van with a big nose and funny glasses (on the van, not me). They wanted to make sure I didn't have too much dignity. I was on the road all the time.

"Having that title and being on Showtime got me a lot of attention. And at that time there wasn't comedy everywhere and there weren't that many comedians, so to be on television was sort of a big thing. Club owners could say, 'As seen on Showtime,' 'As seen on TV.'

"I moved to San Francisco, and suddenly I was getting jobs middling and headlining with the title The Funniest Person in America. Comedians who had been working a long time and had a lot more material and a lot more stage time and just education in general in how to handle themselves in front of an audience were a little bit peeved. And they were right to be: I was constantly blown away by the act who came before me.

"A title like that really sets you up. You know how people try to pick fights with The Heavyweight Champion of the World? People try to pick fights with The Funniest Person in America, too. And they're usually a lot easier to beat up.

"My Uncle Punch would use the title sarcastically. 'Well, if it isn't The Funniest Person in America sitting with us for Thanksgiving.'

"Or, 'Well lookie here, it's The Funniest Person in America visiting me in the hospital. I guess you wanna apologize for hitting me in the head with that turkey drumstick.'

"I don't think they have the contest anymore. They stopped after a couple of years. Where are the other people who won? I don't know. Maybe some of them are in Congress. Who knows?"

"Aunt Ellen," Tony asked as he scratched the cobra tattoo I had gotten for him that day at a cute little parlor frequented by longshoremen, "was it like winning the Miss America contest?"

"It wasn't like Miss America." I laughed. "There were no tough questions like 'How would you use your title as The Funniest Person in America to help world peace?' And the talent portion of the show was . . . being funny. Clearly that was my talent as The Funniest Person in America. There was no bathing-suit portion, funny or otherwise, and I very rarely wore the crown, except when I was at home. Sometimes, I'd wear the banner and the crown, but not out. There was no song, 'There she goes, the funniest person in America.' Some people may have sung that song, but I didn't hear it. The tape from Georgia did win Miss Congeniality, but I don't think it did the comic from Georgia—a very nice man—any good."

I realized then that I had gotten away from the scary part of my story. To quiet the children down, I spent about an hour teaching them to blow smoke rings from their cigarettes. Then I turned off all the lights in my house (it took just a second; all I had to do was clap loud twice), held a flashlight under my chin, and said, "Now that you have some background, here are some really scary stories of bad gigs.

"One bad place I played was a marine base in front of three hundred marines. It was all men. I walked onstage and they were all screaming. They wanted me to take my clothes off, basically. They were naming parts of my body they wanted to see (some parts I hadn't even heard of). They would not shut up, and I was trying to talk to them. 'Hey, how is everybody doing?' I was trying to gain control. But these marines were just screaming at me. And I stayed up there for maybe three minutes. I realized that they were never going to shut up, and I walked offstage.

"I told the guy in charge, 'I can't do this.'

"He said, 'Whoever booked you was stupid because these men are animals, and we want them to be animals. We train them to kill. We don't want them to like art. We don't want them to appreciate art.'

" 'I just want my hundred dollars. I just want to go home. But, thank you for calling what I do *art.*'

"He kept telling me how stupid it was that I was there. Naive me, I thought these guys would be happy to see a woman, happy to hear comedy. They should have booked some stripper or something. They didn't want to hear 'The Phone Call from God,' or 'Aren't People Stupid?' or 'Don't You Hate It When You Taste Something That Tastes Bad . . . and People Want You to Taste It?'

"They'd yell, 'I'd like to taste something.' They were just horrible. No matter what I said, everything was a sexual connotation. They weren't clever. There were no double entendres. They were barely able to master the single entendre.

" 'Who here is from out of town?'

" 'I've got your out of town.'

" 'What do you mean by that?'

" 'You want me to be mean?!'

" 'You don't know what you're talking about, do you?'
" 'No.'

"But you learn from these situations, you grow from them. You learn that no matter how good you are, there are certain places you walk into and there's a certain energy in that room that you cannot change. It's like having Guns 'N Roses open for Perry Como. There's no way that the audience is going to say, 'Well, this is sort of good.'

"Like in Vegas, I would open for the Pointer Sisters or Dolly Parton or Smokey Robinson. And the audience would just be waiting for them. So, while I was on, people would be eating or talking or turned around or just still being seated right in front of me. And I'd be onstage trying to do my act.

"The worst gig was the first time I played a casino. It was in Atlantic City. I opened for Lola Falana. Most of the people in the audience were between seventy and eighty. I walked out, and, needless to say, my stuff was not going over at all. I was supposed to do twenty minutes. There were no laughs and I was going faster and faster, trying to fill in the dead air. I did about ten minutes, then I walked offstage. The union guys were screaming at me, 'We have this timed so that the curtain goes up when Lola comes out. You've got to go back out there.'

" 'I can't get back out there. There's nothing else for me to say. That was the safest stuff, the easiest stuff I have.' It was a huge fight and I almost got fired. But the next day, over a pot of tea and some scones, the union guys convinced me to come back and find a way to do twenty minutes.

"So that night I had to talk slower and stall. I used this whole analogy of how, when you order the barbecued chicken entrée at a restaurant, you're choosing it because you really want the barbecued chicken. But the waitress tells you, 'Well, you know, cole slaw comes with that barbecued chicken.' And you say, 'Well, I'm not interested in the cole slaw. I just want the barbecued chicken.'

"I told the second-night audience, 'This is sort of what I am. I'm the cole slaw. Maybe you didn't really want the cole slaw, but I come with the barbecued chicken. Lola Falana is the barbecued chicken, I'm the cole slaw. If you taste the cole slaw, you may enjoy it. I know you don't really want it. And you can have your barbecue; it's not like you're not going to have your chicken. But just taste the cole slaw and see if you enjoy it. And even if you don't enjoy it, it's on the plate. It's gotta be there.'

"And that would take up a little bit of time; nobody would laugh, but it would take up time. People would sometimes yell out, 'Is it the type of cole slaw with mayonnaise or the vinegar kind? Because I'm allergic to mayonnaise.'

" 'Well then maybe you're allergic to me, ma'am. Or, maybe I don't have to be cole slaw. I could be baked beans. What wouldn't you mind so much?'

" 'I don't know. Hon,' she says, turning to her husband, 'when we're at the Kentucky Fried Chicken, what do we usually get with the chicken?'

" 'Cole slaw.'

" 'No, I'm allergic to cole slaw!'

" 'Beans?'

"Everybody broke into conversations.

" 'I don't like cole slaw.'

" 'Well, she's not saying she's cole slaw, she's saying she's something else made out of cabbage. Like, for instance . . . cole slaw.'

"And I'm going, 'Now wait a minute. Everybody listen to me. I'm just making an analogy. I'm not really cole slaw.'

"And the audience went, 'Ohhhhh,' then after a beat, 'We want Lola! We want Lola!'

"It's really scary when you have a whole room full of

people seventy years old chanting, 'We want Lola.' Oh yes, I can't think of anything scarier. So, my little friends," I addressed the moon-eyed children looking up at me, "was that a scary story or what?"

The children looked at each other, then they started to chant, "We want Lola! We want Lola! We want Lola!"

And they wouldn't be quiet until I called Lola Falana and had her come over and entertain us.

But that's a story for another day.

the plane

truth

or ....
dem ain't goobers, dem's peanuts!

I never thought 3/4 of an inch
could mean so much.

I know that experts say you're more likely to get hurt crossing the street than you are flying (these, of course, would be the street-crossing experts), but that doesn't make me feel any less frightened of flying. If anything, it makes me more afraid of crossing the street. As soon as the light turns green, I run across the street as fast as I can, screaming like a madwoman. I arrive on the other side out of breath, wheezing, and clutching my stomach (or if I'm in a whimsical mood, the stomach of the person standing next to me).

So, to conquer my fear of flying, I decided to write down my feelings on a recent trip. I kept an in-flight journal (which is like an in-flight movie—but without anyone standing up in front of you so you miss the good parts, and with better sound).

I felt edgy the moment I stepped into the aircraft. That could be why I snapped at the woman in front of me. In my defense, she did ask the flight attendant a pretty stupid question: "Excuse me, where is seat 27-B?" I mean, really. But I see now that I overreacted when I screamed at her, "Well, moron, you walk in the only direction you can, and it's the 27th row, seat B—next to seat A. All righty?!" That sort of response is probably one of the many reasons why I'm not a flight attendant.

It was only when the woman (27-B) turned around to look at me that I saw she was a nun. I guess that sort of hatlike thing she wore on her head should have given me a clue, but sometimes I don't have that good an eye for details.

I tried to apologize by smiling and giving her a playful punch on the arm to let her know I was joking. Well, either my playful punch carried more of a wallop than I intended (due to the tension I feel about flying), or her advanced years made her frailer than she appeared, or she was just a big old ham (which is my theory), but the nun shouted out, "Owww!" and rubbed her arm like she was in pain. She rolled up her sleeve and . . . You know, that bruise could *easily* have been there before I hit her.

My good friend Jasmine (at least I think that's her name; I'm so scared that it's affecting my already rattled memory; I know that it's the name of a tea, so if it's not Jasmine, it's either Earl Grey or Hibiscus) told me that a good way to combat fear is to chant. So all the way to my seat I was chanting, "I'm going to die, I'm going to die, oh sweet Lord, I'm going to die." It didn't work. If anything, I was more petrified when I got to my seat (27-A). Even seeing the familiar face of the nun in 27-B (who seemed to flinch when she saw me) didn't calm me down.

So here I am, sitting in my seat, working on my journal. Hey, there's a fly on this plane. I am so scared of flying, I can't imagine how flies do it all day, every day. But, then again, that's what a fly does, fly. It's his job. What's going through that fly's mind? He's looking out the window and probably saying to himself, "Wow, look how high up I am. I've never gotten up this high, I am going very, very fast, and I'm not really working any harder than I usually do."

This fly just happened to wander onto a plane in Los Angeles. Several hours later it is going to get off in New York City. I'm concerned it will be disoriented, and not just from jet lag and being improperly dressed for New York, but more in a *Home Alone* 2 kind of way.

A bunch of flies will probably be waiting as it gets off the plane. They'll all be hugging, blocking the way. Nobody will get by. There will even be a chauffeur holding a tiny sign that says FLY. I'll be relieved to see he has friends there. Well, I'm assuming it's a *he*. It's so hard to tell unless you hold them really still and look closely, and I don't want to do that on the plane with people around. That's something you should do at home—alone.

Aghhhhhh! What was that? "Fuck, we're going to crash!!!"

Oh, I wish I hadn't shouted that out loud. It was just the beverage cart rumbling by. Being on a plane just freaks me out. Any little movement, and suddenly it's like I have Tourette's syndrome. Anything at all—"Fuck! Shit!" I don't even curse. I never curse. It's so embarrassing. "Pardon me, Sister, I am sorry, I . . . I was frightened. Pray for me."

Now she's going to turn on that little air thing above her. Maybe I'm paranoid, but I think it takes power away from the plane somehow. I get mad if people next to me use theirs.

"Sister, don't use that, that's . . . Dang! Shut it off! I'll hit ya! Shut it off!!"

The nun just left to find a different seat. Some people are so touchy. I'm sure she didn't learn that little hand gesture in her convent, either.

As scary as this flight is, it's nothing compared to those tiny Buddy Holly planes that I've had to fly in to get to different stand-up performances. Oh God, those little propeller planes, those little eight-seater tiny planes where you can actually see the pilots in the cockpit. They're reading through some manuals like *So You Want to Be a Pilot*. They're just flipping through the pamphlet trying to figure out which buttons to push to land the plane.

I've got to relax somehow. Why didn't I think of this sooner? I'll recline my seat. Oh, that makes all the difference. That ¾ of an inch between upright and reclined is the difference between agony and ecstasy. I never thought ¾ of an inch could mean so much. *Now* I can sleep. When I get home, I'm going to put some gizmo in my chairs so that they go back ¾ of an inch, too. I wouldn't overdo it like the guy sitting in front of me. His seat goes so far back that his head is practically in my lap. I can pretty much read his newspaper.

I'd better not get too comfortable in my ¾ of an inch recline because toward the end of the flight, the flight attendant is going to say, "You're going to have to put your seat in the upright position for landing." They're so adamant about that every single time, like that's gonna make a difference. Because if we crash, the investigators are going to say, "Oh, that's a shame, her seat was reclined ¾ of an inch. When will they learn? What was that— thirty thousand feet? She could have made that. Sheesh. If only she'd been upright."

Being reclined isn't working. I'm still freaking out. I know what I need. "Oh, flight attendant. Oh, ma'am." You have to talk nice to the flight attendants because they're all arrogant little bitches. Unless, of course, you happen to be a flight attendant or are related to or are friends with one—then you are the absolutely lovely exceptions to this rule. But the rest of them, they have this attitude. And they can afford to have the attitude, because they have the power—they have the peanuts.

They have these six peanuts that we need. Six peanuts. Somebody could offer that to you on the street, and you'd say, "I don't want that shit—get that away from me. Six peanuts? No-oh." Somehow they've done research. They know that the higher we go, the more we need nuts. And we go crazy if we don't get them.

"Miss, I didn't get my, uh—my peanuts. And I'd really appreciate it if you gave me some. They're good, aren't they? I've never been able to get them on the ground either. At least not ones this good. Thank you. Oh, thank you."

Fuck, what was that! "We're going to crash!" Oops, false alarm. It's just the food cart coming down the aisle.

I think they only give you six peanuts so that you don't spoil your appetite for the disgusting meal that's soon to follow. You never hear anybody say, "You know, I can't finish that. Could you wrap that up for me please? That was delicious. It's just too much. I'm stuffed! What was that, pigeon?"

But we do get excited about it, don't we? "Oh, here comes the cart, put down the tray! La la la la. Put down your tray! They're starting on the other side first. Hurry! Hurry! Those people over there—they're eating. Those people are eating."

This is the tiniest food I've ever seen in my entire life. I guess they figure everything's relative. You get that high up, you look out the window, "Well, it's as big as that house down there. I can't eat all that. Look at the size of that. It's as big as a house. Me thinking I could eat all that! Ha! Split that steak with me. Now *that's* a steak." Any kind of meat that you get—chicken, steak, anything—has grill marks on each side, like somehow we'll actually believe there's an open-flame grill in the front of the plane.

Salads are always two pieces of dead lettuce and salad dressing that comes in that astronaut package. As soon as you open it, it's on your neighbor's lap. "Could I just dip my lettuce, ma'am? Hm, that's a lovely skirt. What is that, silk?" But you know, should that happen, club soda's gonna get that stain out immediately.

That's the answer to anything you ask up there, I don't know if you've noticed that.

"Excuse me, I have an upset stomach."
"Club soda, be right back."
"Excuse me, I spilled something."
"Club soda, be right back."
"Ooh, the wing is on fire!"
"Club soda, be right back."

I thought the food would make me feel less frightened. But it didn't. Maybe if I stretch my legs and go to the restroom it will help.

That was the tiniest bathroom I've ever been in. I guess they figure since the food is so tiny, the bathrooms should be minuscule, too. I read a book once where two people had sex in an airplane bathroom. I don't see how that's possible. I barely had enough room to sit down. There is a lit sign in there that reads: "Return to Seat." "Return to Cabin." Why do they think that needs to be lit? Because we'll relax in there for a little while? "Miss, bring my peanuts in here, please. This is *beautiful*. The water is so blue, it reminds me of the Mediterranean. I don't ever want to leave."

You have no concept of time when you're in there—it's like a casino: no windows, no clocks. I could be the only one to get up out of my seat to go to the bathroom—everybody else is sound asleep when I go—but after I've been in there for what I think is thirty seconds, I open the door and everyone in the plane is lined up, looking at their watches, making me feel like I've been in there forever.

And now I've got to explain the smell that was in there before I went in there. Does that ever happen to you? It's not your fault. You've held your breath, you just wanna get out, and now you open the door and you have to explain, "Oh! Listen, there's an odor in there and I didn't do it. It's bad. You might want to sprinkle some club soda, if you uh . . ."

I think my only hope of escaping my mind-numbing fear is to sleep; to sleep and perchance to dream. The only trouble is when I fall asleep on a plane, I always have a nightmare. . . .

I'm in a department store walking through the area with the makeup counters—then all of a sudden I'm a penguin on ice skates—Florence Henderson is cooking macaroni and cheese in my kitchen and my brother has gained 200 pounds and is being fed by three Haitian women wearing disco clothes and in the background the Bee Gees are arguing over what outfits to wear for their big comeback.

Then I turn into myself again and Bruce Willis calls me up and asks me to go out with him and drink some wine coolers. So, we're sitting in an outdoor cafe in Italy called Louis'. He's telling me his life was meaningless until I came into it. I tell him I'm not ready to make a commitment. Just then I give birth to three sets of twins: they're nine years old, one has false teeth, two are great dancers. The rest move to South Dakota for schooling.

Now I'm dancing with Lewis and Clark (my two children) and an iguana who's making eyes at me (he's not that good of a dancer). Bruce punches him in the nose. The iguana turns into Sean Penn, who knocks Bruce unconscious. Sean and I start walking, and he tells me his life has been meaningless up until he met me, then we see one of those photo booths, four for a dollar. He urges me to pose with him. So we get in and have our pictures taken. He covers his face for all of them. He asks me to keep them. He beats up the machine.

I fly back to the States alone. The pilot announces, "Ladies and Gentlemen, we'll be landing in ten minutes. Ellen, I just want to say my life has been meaningless until you came into it." We land. I go to the baggage claim, and my bag comes out first. I think to myself, "Ellen, you must be dreaming—that's impossible. . . ."

"Fuck, we're going to crash!!"

False alarm. The plane just landed. I guess I'm alive. Oh well, that wasn't so bad. But what about that dream! I don't know what it means. I'm pretty sure it's sexual.

Maybe it just means I shouldn't be flying.

ellen's new

hobby

....

You can do it, Ellen.
Get out of the house, find your
path and follow your heart.

JOURNAL ENTRY

I need a hobby. Something to pass my time—a goal I can work toward. I've tried knitting, square dancing, social work. I need to have passion about something. Here I am, sitting at my kitchen table, staring at my pancakes and coffee, feeling the emptiness of a life with no meaning.

It's like I'm sitting in a car but the engine is idling. I'm not even on the road—just off to the side. I see the others swoosh by me. I can recognize the shapes of the cars but not the direction they're going. I'm alone, all alone in a car on the side of the road.

My dogs are staring at me, trying to give me hope. "You can do it, Ellen," they say. "Get out of the house, find your path and follow your heart." I want to find it so bad, I do. But all I can do is turn on my TV and watch *Regis and Kathie Lee*. I can answer those trivia questions. Maybe they'll call me and put a pin in my city. I want a pin; I want to share a hot-air popcorn popper with number 35. That's who I would pick.

I just saw a flash of a woman with dogs on the screen. She races or something; she used the word *Iditarod*. I looked it up in the dictionary, but it wasn't there. I was so upset, I started to cry and scream, "Why—why—why?" I was pounding on the table with my closed fists. I was filled with anger—raging with fury—I was a wild stallion rearing up on its hind legs, snorting and whinnying and kicking and . . . Wait a minute. Hold on just a cotton-pickin' minute. This is passion I'm feeling. This word *Iditarod* has moved me. I must find out what this *Iditarod* is and do it—I will *Iditarod* and I will win.

JOURNAL ENTRY

I am beginning to feel frustrated. It is my fourth week of training for the Iditarod and I am seeing very little progress, if any at all. The big race is two months away, and I worry I won't be ready. I already have one strike against me: My sled barely moves along the concrete-paved roads.

Having only two dogs is also not helping. Since I don't believe in hitting, I certainly won't strike my dogs just to make them pull me. So I encourage them strongly. "Please, let's go, come on." But they come toward me and get in the sled. Seems they're conditioned to come *to* me when I speak, not away. I've tried dog biscuits, but as I place them down several yards ahead of the dogs, by the time I run back to get in the sled, they've run to get the biscuits without me in it. Also, one of my dogs is rather small so the times we do move at all, it's in circles—the larger one sets our course off balance.

I am sweating so much in those big Eskimo clothes because of the warm California climate. I should warn others to wear a cooler version here. Ah, well, I must not give up. It's a dream. I will race! I can't let the neighborhood children's silly taunts stop me. Let them laugh all they want. I will race in the Iditarod one day.

JOURNAL ENTRY

I've given up returning phone calls. I've given up my so-called "normal" life. I can't be bothered. The race is but a month away. I eat, drink, and sleep Iditarod.

I've begun to question aspects of my training. I had heard that carbo loading was good, but now I am not so sure. My dogs have gotten fat and lethargic. I may need to change their diet of spaghetti, potatoes, pound cake, and ice cream. Now, when I bring them to the sled, they just roll over and fall asleep. Sometimes, to my eternal shame, I do the same.

Perhaps I should quit. No, no, no!! I cannot allow a negative thought. My will cannot be broken or bent. I must continue chanting my mantra:

Icanarod, Iwillarod, Iwinarod, Iditarod.

Icanarod, Iwillarod, Iwinarod, Iditarod. Icanarod, Iwillarod, Iwinarod, Iditarod. If I chant loudly enough, I can barely hear the jeering from the neighborhood children. They are ignorant philistines. No matter how many times I correct them, they get it wrong. I scream to deaf, uncaring ears, "It's pronounced *Iditarod*, not idiot!"

I have ended my quest for corporate sponsorship. The only offer came from a place called Uncle Huey's Dry Cleaning and Donut Shop and only if I wore a vest with their motto: "If you get some jelly donut on your clothes, we'll clean it before you're finished with your second cup of coffee." I have too much pride. I will not look ridiculous, so I turned them down. They can keep their $35.

JOURNAL ENTRY

I do worry that I will not be ready in time to race the Iditarod after all. It is only two weeks away, and I have made little progress. The dogs sense when we are about to begin training. They watch me get dressed and know that when the big boots come out, we are headed for the sled. It's 87°, unusually hot for this time of year. I have lost fifteen pounds just from wearing these big bundly clothes and sitting in my sled, but I must get used to the bulkiness.

I have made some progress, though. Last Thursday, Bootsie, Muffin, and I were out in the street sitting there, same as every morning—we've chosen to go out at 3:00 A.M. to avoid both traffic and cruel neighborhood children. Suddenly, Bootsie and Muffin took off with a start that caught me unawares (I had dozed off). I was thrown from the sled and the dogs ran for a half a mile or so. I caught up to them and encouraged them profusely. "Good doggies," I said. "Good dogs—two good girls." I'm not sure, but I think they saw a squirrel or something. It's too bad there wasn't another squirrel to get us back home. We walked; I carried the sled. I sure hope we'll be ready. Maybe there are squirrels in Alaska.

JOURNAL ENTRY

Well, we're in Alaska and I'll tell you something, it's *cold*. It's so cold it's snowing—looks like it has been for a while. The dogs are not taking to the snow the way I'd hoped they would. Muffin, the smaller one, is being downright stubborn, refusing to step foot (or paw) in the snow. I can't really blame her—she sinks into it so far, her ears are barely sticking out.

I feel we are in trouble with both dogs pulling—and there's no way to try with only Bootsie. Also, Bootsie has, it seems—and this is terrible timing—just gone into heat. I was debating whether I should neuter her before the race and then I totally forgot. You can imagine the scene she's causing. I've never seen her act this way. I keep apologizing to all of the other contestants.

So far, no one is talking to me. They're kind of snobbish folks. And real serious about this race. I think some are cheating, too. Some have as many as eight dogs. They must all know each other—all of the dogs look alike and are well-behaved. They look at my dogs a lot—probably very curious about the breed. It's hard to tell what they are with their little sweaters on.

Uh-oh, I hear a ruckus outside. Sounds like Bootsie is into some trouble with other dogs. I'll sign off for now. The big day is soon upon us.

JOURNAL ENTRY

Anchorage, Alaska. Five A.M.

I haven't been sleeping well. I'm very worried about the race. It starts tomorrow, and since arriving here I've learned a lot more about this event. For instance, you're supposed to have somewhere between fourteen and twenty dogs per sled. Wow! That's crazy. I mean—where do all of these people live that they're allowed to own that many dogs? I know for my own neighborhood there is a zoning law that prohibits a person from having any more than three dogs. Nevertheless, I must adapt to the circumstances and move forward. I will go to the local animal shelter today and get more dogs. Since Bootsie and Muffin are somewhat familiar with the routine, I won't need the full twenty dogs. I'll just get fifteen. A nice seventeen will do just fine. I figure these dogs will be so grateful to be adopted they'll do anything I ask of them. After the race I'll simply find good, loving homes for them.

JOURNAL ENTRY

Uh-oh. I think I'm in trouble. For some reason the shelter didn't have that many dogs. I got seven—that's all they had—and eight cats (I was desperate). I see no reason why I can't train the cats to pull. I've seen movies and TV shows where they use cats (for what exactly I don't remember). Besides, with the nine dogs total, they should be able to get it going, and once we have momentum it should be easy pulling for the cats (well, kittens—they're ten weeks old). Maybe I'll just keep the kittens in the sled with me. They can't add any weight. I wonder if I can push the sled in addition to the dogs pulling or at least just run alongside. I've picked up a pamphlet on the race— hopefully I will get a little more insight on this Iditarod.

Bye for now.

JOURNAL ENTRY

Oh my— Maybe this wasn't such a good idea. I'm afraid I'm not as prepared as I would like to be. My intentions were good, but Bootsie is having a problem with the kitties. I've tried to introduce them slowly so as to avoid the problem we had the first day. I've never seen Bootsie so aggressive. Luckily, I got there in time to stop her violent charges at the poor kitties. I can't imagine why she hates them so!

The race started yesterday. I hope I can catch up. It shouldn't be that hard. I've attached a small motor to my sled, which should help matters somewhat. I plan on leaving tonight.

Over and out.

JOURNAL ENTRY

Things have gotten worse and worse. All the other racers are two days ahead of me. I hate them. They are a distasteful group whose juvenile jeering made me yearn for the taunts of my neighborhood children. I dream of wiping the smiles off their smug, pudgy faces. How dare they call me a Sheila Disco Musher?

But I fear that my dreams of revenge will just be dreams. The motor on my sled didn't work, probably because it wasn't attached to anything. All it did was make a lot of noise, weigh down the sled, and scare the cats.

I must keep my spirits up. Not so much for myself as for my team. I must not give up hope. If we do not feel like winners, we cannot win. To that end I will head to downtown Anchorage today to get the three poodles on my team pedicures.

Whenever I ask myself, "Why go on?" I must answer, "Why not." Miracles do happen.

Icanarod, Iwillarod, Iwinarod, Iditarod.

JOURNAL ENTRY

I won! I won! They say I didn't. They say I cheated. They say I've been disqualified. All I know is I finished first. My team and I were the first ones to get from Anchorage to Nome.

They can bitch and moan as much as they please. Nowhere in the rules does it say you can't use a Winnebago. It was a stroke of genius and a bit of luck. Who would have guessed that there was an auto dealership across the street from the dog groomer? With the sled and dogs and cats in the back, we just took off down the freeway. We beat the nearest racer by two days and we rarely went over fifty-five miles an hour, mainly because Muffin gets nauseous if I drive any faster.

As for the other Iditaroders, I have never seen such a group of sore losers in my life. But I pity them more than hate them. They're just jealous.

I can't get rid of my posse (that's what I've started calling my team). To hell with neighborhood rules, I'm keeping them all. Maybe I'll return to defend my title next year. Back to back!

JOURNAL ENTRY

Life has no meaning again. I gaze into the abysmal void that is my soul and all that is reflected back is my own emptiness. I am bored and restless. The high of being the Iditarod champion did not last long. I need a new challenge. But what?

My posse, my team, my cats and dogs: They're listless as well. I try to maintain a happy exterior for their sake, but they're not fooled.

Once again I'm watching *Regis and Kathie Lee*. Even Kathie Lee's stories about Cody fail to cheer me up. Before I turn off the set and do God knows what, I see an image: a boat skating across the sea. A woman mentions the America's Cup, the world's premier yacht race. Yes!!!!

I bet there are no rules about having pets as part of your crew. Me and my posse start training tomorrow. Until I get a yacht, we'll just use an inflatable raft in my pool.

The dream lives.

ellenvision

·····························

Nuns were very popular
in the 60's.

I feel extremely lucky to have my own TV show. Every day I pinch myself because I'm sure I must be dreaming. Actually, I don't pinch myself. It's one of my manager's jobs to pinch me and say, "You ain't dreamin', kid!" Then I pinch him, he pinches me back, and it usually ends up in a slap fight. Sometimes the slap fight lasts until midnight. Then we call it a day, go to sleep, and repeat it all again the next morning.

I guess what I'm trying to say is that I'm so happy that my show is as good, and as based in reality, as it is. You wouldn't believe some of the shows that were offered me by network executives before I accepted *Ellen* (which, by the way, is named for Ellen Burstyn).

In one show presented to me, I was going to be a single news producer for a small TV station in Minneapolis. I said, "That sounds an awful lot like *Mary Tyler Moore.*" They replied, "Who's going to remember?"

Other shows I was offered included *Hello Ellen* (with MacLean Stevenson), *Ellen the Chimp Lady,* and a sitcom version of *The Piano*—I was going to play the Holly Hunter part, and either Siegfried or Roy was going to play the Harvey Keitel role.

I think the worst idea I was subjected to was a show called *Inky Dinky Do.* "*Inky Dinky Do,*" I said, "what's it about?" The network executive said, "We don't know yet. All we've come up with is the title."

I don't mean to imply that I haven't gotten weird notes from the network about my show now. They'd like me to develop some magic powers, like the ability to see through lead or bend spoons with my mind. But no matter how weird my show—*Ellen*—might get, nothing compares to how weird TV was during the sixties.

Not that there aren't bad shows on now, but at least they kind of have a base in reality. Well, okay, *Melrose Place* doesn't.

The sixties were when hallucinogenic drugs were becoming really, really big. And I don't think it's a coincidence that we had the type of shows that we had then, like *The Flying Nun*.

If you think about it, nuns were very popular in the sixties. They must have had a good publicist then. They had *The Sound of Music*, about a nun. They had *The Singing Nun*—remember her? "Dominique a nique a nique a Dominique . . ." So they figure, "Hey, the nuns are popular, let's do a TV show." But I think it was just about nuns until they got the Network Notes. "Nuns are good. People will watch. But, couldn't they fly or something? People like flying."

I'm just surprised there were no copycat shows, like *The Swimming Rabbi* or *The Leaping Episcopalian*. Because, no matter how bizarre a show is, if it's popular, someone is going to try to imitate it. *Bewitched* came on and one year later it was *I Dream of Jeannie*. "No, they're different. On one she twitches her nose, on the other she blinks. But the most important thing is, one's a witch and the other's a genie. It's so different it's not even funny."

Other similar shows were *The Addams Family* and *The Munsters; Gilligan's Island* and *Lost in Space; Mr. Ed* and *My Mother the Car* (one is a talking horse, the other a talking car—they're both transportation); *Gunsmoke* and *60 Minutes* (well, they both have a bunch of guys and one girl).

My Mother the Car has to be the weirdest show ever. It even tops *The Flying Nun*. A man's mother dies and is reincarnated as a car. It *could* happen. I mean, a talking toaster or talking can opener, an ironing board or a Ping-Pong table—*those* would be ridiculous. But a talking car? That's much more likely.

Somewhere along the way to putting this show on the air, drugs had to be involved. It was the sixties. To me it sounds like the last idea you have, and you mention it, kind of embarrassed, after all your other ideas have been rejected. "I came up with this one at 3:00 in the morning. I don't know . . . Well, it's a talking car—you know, like they have—and it's this guy's mother . . . I guess."

Now he might not have been zoned out on boo or goofballs, but the network guy who bought it, man, *he* had to be on something. "Right, it talks. Just like a person talks. I dig it. Write it up. I'll give you more notes after I tie-dye my shirt and drive up to San Francisco to see the Grateful Dead. Wow. Look at my fingers. They're funny."

I saw Jerry Van Dyke, the star of *My Mother the Car*, in person around the time that show was on the air, but it's kind of embarrassing how I saw him. The only major trip that my family ever took was to Los Angeles, Disneyland, and Anaheim. We took a train and that was kind of fun. My parents told my brother and me that it was an airplane, but we figured out after the first thousand miles that they were lying. We went to Hollywood and saw the set where *Gilligan's Island* was shot. That was every bit as exciting as you could imagine.

While we were in Hollywood, my mom spotted Jerry Van Dyke walking down some street. It was a big deal for us to see a celebrity, so, when my mother saw him she screamed, "There's Dick Van Dyke's brother!" He looked around kind of uncomfortably. Even as a child, I was humiliated. I just knew that that wasn't a good thing.

I don't remember how old I was at the time. Maybe my parents would remember or perhaps even Jerry Van Dyke.

I guess they had another talking-car show in the eighties: *Knight Rider*. That was much different, though. It was a drama and not a comedy.

Actually, of all those odd shows, *Mr. Ed* doesn't sound so weird. I guess that's because my Uncle Cookie had a talking horse. Well, it was really a dog with a saddle on it, but my Uncle Cookie thought it was a horse. He was blind and a little loopy.

We didn't want to break his heart. It was all he had,

that horse. Or dog. It was a small dog. But he never saw a horse, so he didn't know how big it was supposed to be.

Nobody heard him talk but my Uncle Cookie. The dog would be lying on the floor (actually it was dead) and my Uncle would say, "That's a good one, Spot. He's telling a joke now."

That's right, Uncle Cookie.

I went to a
psychic

or ....

baloney is just salami with an

inferiority complex

You have a brother or a sister
or you are an only child.

A lot of people who know I'm writing a book ask me, "So, do you think it's going to be any good? Well, do you?"

It's hard to tell how successful or good anything is going to be. And, to be honest, it makes me a little nervous. That's why I decided to do the only rational thing: go to a psychic. I mean, what's the use of putting in a lot of hard work if this book is going to be a flop? I could better use my time doing other stuff, like becoming a professional ballerina or flossing.

The first psychic I went to wasn't that good. Do you know how some people go to student beauticians to save a little money? I went to a student psychic. There was a little psychic academy in a mini-mall between a video store and a frozen-yogurt place. It was called Gus's Psychic School.

My student psychic was named Chuck. He was an ex-soldier who was going to psychic school on the GI Bill. The first thing he said to me was "You are at a crossroads and confused. There are questions you want answered." "Well, yeah," I said, "that's why I'm here. Why else would I go to a psychic?" I should have gotten suspicious when he said, "How am I supposed to know? What am I, Kreskin?"

Chuck said "Oooooooo" and raised his hands in the air every time he made a prediction. I guess he thought it looked like he was communicating with powerful entities in the spirit world, but to me it looked like he was auditioning for a minstrel show. I knew he was bad because he wouldn't say anything without first consulting his Time/Life book on unexplained phenomena.

His predictions were kind of vague, to say the least. "I see you pouring some kind of liquid into your mouth out of a cylindrical object. This object, it's made of . . . glass. After you pour the liquid into your mouth, you will no longer be thirsty."

"There is someone important in your life whose name

starts with either the letter E . . . C . . . B . . . F
. . . or M through W."

"You have a brother or a sister. Either that or you are
an only child." I told him I had a brother; he seemed
proud of himself, then went back to psychicing.

"Your brother knows how to drive." As a matter of fact
he does. He drives an ambulance. He's not a paramedic or
anything, he just got a good deal on it. It doesn't get very
good mileage, but the upside is he's never late to meet-
ings.

"On Letterman tonight, Dave's guests will be Angela
Lansbury and Sting." I had to tell him that wasn't a prediction, it was a blurb from *TV Guide*. He tried to cover by
saying he has never read *TV Guide*, even though there was
one on his desk with the crossword puzzle half done.
Then he said that so much came to him, he couldn't
remember if it was a prediction or if he read it somewhere.

I asked him about my past lives, hoping that I had
been Cleopatra or, at the very least, someone who once
had lunch with Cleopatra. He told me that once I had
been a monkey, but that in my last life I was a spring roll
at a Chinese restaurant. Now that's ridiculous, even
though it does explain a recurring nightmare where I'm
held upside down over a dish of hot mustard sauce.

At a beautician school, there is a teacher present at all
times to advise the student and make sure things don't get
too out of hand. At the psychic academy, the psychic
teacher wasn't there. He would just call in by phone now
and then from his condo in Hawaii to tell his students he
knew they were doing a good job. Or he would call and
say things like "Tell that woman there's something caught
in her teeth."

The student psychic finally admitted that he wasn't
very good. He was, however, able to predict where I
would find a good psychic. The session wasn't a total

waste because he gave me a dollar-off coupon for the frozen-yogurt place next door.

You could tell the woman he referred me to was good because she opened the door before I rang the bell. Then she said, "You must be Ellen." Well, that was the capper. Because Ellen is my name and all. Sure I had an appointment, and she could have been looking through the keyhole, but I prefer to think she had finely honed psychic powers.

It seems most psychics have names like Esmerelda or Cassandra—spooky kinds of names. Mine was named Shari Lewis. Not the woman with Lambchop the puppet, just somebody with the same name. I wouldn't trust a psychic who used a puppet. I don't think it's because I'm prejudiced or anything. It's just that it would disturb me to have a little puppet voice say, "You will be successful as long as you never get up on stilts. Avoid *Circus of the Stars*—don't even watch it."

The psychic knew that I was nervous about writing a book. This might be because the first thing I said to her was "I'm nervous about writing a book." She looked me in the eye (or possibly both eyes, I don't remember) and without raising her arms or saying, "Ooooooooo," she made her predictions. The good news, she said, was that my book is going to be on best-seller lists for over twenty-five years and win a ton of awards (literally a ton; they'll actually weigh them at one point). The bad news, though, was that I was going to have to sit down and actually write the book. I was kind of hoping that elves would come in the middle of the night while I was sleeping and write a best-seller for me; the psychic told me that though this wasn't impossible (she claimed one or two of Danielle Steel's books were written this way) in my case it was highly unlikely. Bummer.

Then she took out her tarot cards. She wasn't able to get a very good reading, so then she took out a deck of regular cards. An hour and a half later she had won $150 off of me playing gin rummy. So you can see, she's a very good psychic, even though what she really wants to do is deal blackjack in Vegas.

The good psychic would pick up the phone before it rang. Of course, it's possible there was nobody on the other line. Once she said, "God bless you." I said, "I didn't sneeze." She looked deep into my eyes and said, "You will, eventually." And, damn if she wasn't right. Two days later I sneezed. It felt eerie. Not the sneeze, just that she predicted it.

It sounds like a real L.A. thing to do, going to a psychic. I was thinking this as I drove away from her home in my Mercedes convertible on my way to pick up my dog from his personal trainer. What's great about this trainer is that she also does my dog's colors. It turns out my dog is an Autumn, which explains why he looks so good in an olive green sweater.

Well, as I was driving, the phone rang. This was weird in itself, because the psychic had predicted that I would get a phone call later in the day. As it turned out, it was my psychic calling. While we were chatting, I got a fax reminding me to call my bird psychiatrist.

Now a bird psychiatrist isn't an actual bird; that would be ridiculous. He's a human psychiatrist that deals with my bird's problems. You just call him up on the phone, tell him what's bothering your bird, and he tells you how to deal with it. He's a bit cheaper than an actual psychiatrist —no pun intended—so sometimes I call him up with one of my problems and pretend that it's one of my bird's problems. Actually, I don't even own a bird.

"Well my bird is thinking about starting a new relationship. The problem is that this other bird reminds him of somebody else, somebody who had hurt him in a previous relationship. My bird had been rejected and didn't take it well. He drank a lot of fermented seed juice and didn't go out much for a long time. And when he did, he took out his pain on other birds.

"Also, my bird, Paco, who has a sitcom that's called *Paco* (he's a very funny bird), is worried about a book he's supposed to write. So, he's not sure this is the best time to start a relationship.

"Paco had an interesting dream recently. I sensed the dream. I know him well enough to pick up the dreams, but not well enough to actually help him. That's why I called you. He had this dream that he was being held upside down and dipped into a dish of hot mustard sauce . . .

"Oh, I see, he probably was a spring roll in a past life."

I put on the answering machine, so I wouldn't get any more phone calls as I drove. I felt content. So, I guess what I'm trying to say is that I have a good feeling about this book. That's what you asked, right?

how to

explain sex to

a child

or ....

where there's a corn chip, there's
bound to be hot sauce

Oooo baby, I feel lucky tonight.

Hey, Debbie, this is Ellen. That's a real cute phone message. You sounded just like Elmer Fudd. Geez, I hope you were trying to sound like Elmer Fudd. If you weren't, I'm terribly sorry. Thanks for saying that you'd watch my house while I'm gone next week on vacation to the Luxembourg Soft Cheese and Jazz Festival. I know you said you would water the plants, bring in the mail, and turn some lights on so that it looks like somebody is home. But if it's not too much of an imposition, could you also make sure that the mobile over the crib isn't tangled? Otherwise, the baby is just going to get bored. I never knew having a kid was so much responsibility! Bye bye.

I'm just joking. I don't have a baby. I do, however, have a mobile and a crib. I enjoy those things, so I have them. And, even though I don't have a baby, I have hired a nanny. In case I decide to have a baby, it's nice to know that Bok Choy is there. (To keep him in practice, I have him read me a bedtime story every night and occasionally I let him burp me.)

I want to have a child. I really do. I think about it every day—and every day I change my mind: I want one now. I'll wait a year. I want one now. I'll wait a year. Well, you get the idea.

I think that part of my dilemma is that even though I want to have a baby, I don't want to *have* the baby. I can't imagine *hav*ing the baby. Giving birth is just so much pain. I know it's a beautiful child you end up with. I'm aware of that. But if I want a new washer and dryer, I wouldn't necessarily want to *have* a new washer and dryer, if you know what I mean (and if you don't, I really don't care to explain it in any more detail).

I don't think I could go through that pain (having the *child*—let's just forget the washer and dryer now, okay?). A lot of women I know believe in natural childbirth. No matter how much discomfort they're in, they refuse to take drugs. Mercy, mercy me! Just thinking about that pain makes me want to take drugs (sometimes I even drive down to the hospital and demand an epidural).

I don't need a baby growing inside of me for nine months, either. For one thing, there's morning sickness. If I'm going to feel nauseous and achy when I wake up, I want to achieve that state the old-fashioned way: getting good and drunk the night before. I know that a woman glows when she's pregnant, and that sounds neat. But, I can get a pretty good glow by enjoying a steam bath followed by some assorted skin creams. The thing that I don't understand most is when a pregnant woman joyfully talks about feeling her baby kick. To me, getting kicked isn't as big a thrill as others make it out to be. I've never liked getting kicked from the outside, why should I feel any different about an inside kick?

But I would like to have a child. So, one day I'd like to adopt a baby who needs a loving home and be a mother who will adore him or her and teach it important things. I think I'd make a great mother. I'm great with kids. I know this because I'm the godmother to a precious little two- or five-year-old boy or girl (I'm not sure of the specifics). I probably would be overprotective of my child, though. She (if it's a girl) or he (if it's not a girl) would always have to wear a helmet (even if it's just to eat cereal; those spoons can be mighty dangerous!); would be on one of those protective leashes until, at least, senior year of high school; and would, in general, be raised like people raise veal—confined to a crate by itself somewhere.

I think my best quality as a mother would be the ability to communicate complex ideas simply. I think all parents dread the old "How are babies made" question. I know my parents had a problem explaining this to me.

"Mommy, Daddy—how are babies made?"

"Well, Ellen honey, there's an egg."

"Like a chicken egg?"

"No, smaller."

"Like a robin's egg?"

"No, much smaller—it's very small. And Daddy gives Mommy . . . Well, there's a Papa Bear and a Mama Bear and the Mama Bear has the baby in her tummy—"

"So I grew in a bear's stomach?"

"No, but if you were a bear you would've."

"But I'm not a bear?"

"No, you're a little girl."

"So, where did I grow?"

"In Mommy's tummy."

"How did I get there?"

"Daddy gave her special sauce."

"Like McDonald's?"

"Who knows? Maybe."

"How did he give it to her? In a hamburger?"

"Okay. Yes."

"I like hamburgers. Good night."

"Good night, sleep tight."

I know that I could do a much better job answering that question than my parents. Other people sense this, too. In fact, hardly a day goes by when somebody doesn't ask me, "Ellen, how can I explain sex to my children?" Unfortunately, it's always the same person who is asking me that question. He's the man who runs the cheese shop I go to—Cheeses 'N' Things it's called (I've always been afraid to ask what the 'N' Things are). Anyway, this man's only child works in the store with him, is in his mid-twenties, and from the way he handles a sharp cheddar, can probably explain more about sex to his father than vice versa.

Whatever the case, I'm sure there are many other reasonably sane people who are troubled by this problem. And the more children there are (and I'm not sure where these children are coming from), the more explaining about sex there is to be done.

By sex I mean, of course . . . sex. You know what I'm saying. There are many different types of sex, but for the purpose of this explanation I'm just talking about . . . you know, sex. In other words, you might have two consenting adults, a coconut, a pound of confetti, and a very thirsty yak. What they do may be very beautiful and spiritual and fulfilling, but it's not necessarily something you'd care to explain to a child. Okay, I think we've defined our terms, so let's get on with the explanation.

If you're nervous about explaining sex to a child, a good technique is to imagine that the child is not a child but is instead an alien from another planet. If it makes it easier for you, paint the child green and put a fake eye on its forehead. When the child asks you about sex, you can then say, "That sounds like English, but it's probably some weird alien language I'll never be able to understand. You're probably asking me to take you to my leader."

So you take the child to Washington, D.C. and insist that the President meet with the child. Then the President can explain sex to the child. I mean, what else has the President got to do? On second thought, this might not be such a great technique.

Okay then, what you've got to do is just explain sex simply and to the point. You just say, "When you get older you're going to meet somebody that you really, really, really like. Well, if you're lucky you're going to like that person. Maybe you don't even like 'em a lot, but at least they don't bug you too much. Or, okay, it's, let's say, closing time at the bar—it's really late and you've been knocking down quite a few Rusty Nails. And you know how the lighting is at those bars. I mean, everybody looks good. But then the next morning you look at the person next to you, and you're like, 'Argghhhh! Help me!' "

Maybe it's better to be a bit more allegorical. Tell a

little story. You could say that there's a Papa Bear and a
Mama Bear. And the Mama Bear says, "Where is that Papa
Bear? He hasn't been home in a long time. He says he's
working late at the pretzel factory, but I don't believe that
lying grizzly bastard." So she hires another bear to follow
the Papa Bear—a Detective Bear (or, if you prefer, a
detective goat—don't be afraid to add your own spin to
the story).

Well, the Detective Bear shadows the Papa Bear for a
week. Then he tells the Mama Bear that every night, after
work, Papa Bear goes to the same hotel room in the Poco-
nos. Well, Mama Bear decides that she's going to give
Papa Bear a big surprise. So, she goes to the hotel, kicks
down the door, and there in the heart-shaped tub, sipping
champagne, as naked as the day they were born are . . .
No, this isn't a good way either.

There is a big fat queen bee, and she likes her honey.
So, she's in her hive and all these male bees are just
buzzing around saying, "Oooo baby, I feel lucky tonight."

Or you take a big tub of butter, some milk, two or
three eggs, a dash of vanilla . . . No, I'm sorry, that's not
sex, that's my recipe for French toast. At least I hope that's
not sex.

You know, I think the best idea is just to let the child
watch cable TV. Or go out and rent 9½ Weeks. When I was
in school, they showed us a sex education film about a boy
calling up a girl on the phone and asking her out on a
date. Nowadays, I'm sure they show 9½ Weeks or something starring Sharon Stone.

So, in conclusion, that's how I would talk to a child
about sex. I sincerely hope that I've been of help. Excuse
me, but I've got to go out for a short walk. All of a sudden
it has gotten very hot in here, and I've developed a craving for French toast.

in the kitchen
with ellen

or ....

as tasty as poison and just as

deadly

How did people ever figure out
that eggs were edible?

When I wasn't famous, nobody cared about how I ate or how I cooked or how I did my laundry or how I communicated telepathically with animals. But ever since becoming well known through my appearances on television, people seem to be a lot more curious about those things. Seems kind of funny to me, but, hey, if the public wants to know some of these things, I don't think I have the right not to tell them.

Well, I guess I do have the right to not tell. I mean, there's no law that says any person of famous or semifamous stature or reputation shall find it incumbent upon said person or personage to divulge eating, cooking, laundry, or animal-telepathy habits to the general public at large, or even in small groups. This is strictly a matter of choice for me, and I choose to say, "Yes. Yes, I *will* tell you what you want to know about me." And one of the things you seem to want to know most about me is my recipe for French toast.

It is one of my favorite recipes, and I bet dollars to donuts that after you try it out, it will be one of your favorites, too. Come to think of it, I'm not exactly sure I know what the saying "betting dollars to donuts" means. Maybe it used to be "betting donuts to donuts," but then . . . no, that still doesn't make sense. I don't even know when people started betting donuts. I do know that if you're in Las Vegas, you can't just go up to the roulette table, put a jelly donut on number 17, and shout out, "C'mon. Mama needs a big mess o' crullers!!" Believe me, I've tried. Oddly enough, you can put a chip down on any number. But it's a plastic chip and not the kind that you eat. So maybe it isn't all that odd after all.

But I digress.

Anyway, this is something that I cook up whenever people drop by, whether it's invited guests (Gus, my mailman), or tour buses filled with screaming fans (who tell me that I serve better food than Kevin Costner or Madonna).

Believe it or not, Ellen's Real Frenchy French Toast is also a great alternative to candy for trick or treaters on Halloween. Ah, the look on the little children's faces when I drop the still-steaming hot bread into their bags followed by a generous dollop of butter and a splash of maple syrup. You can see their faces because in Hollywood children don't wear masks on Halloween. They usually dress up as agents, valet parkers, or second-unit directors instead.

Now, on with the recipe.

Ingredients

BREAD

"What kind of bread should I use?!" you might say, panicking a wee bit early. Well, there are many types of bread: wheat, rye, white, Italian, Swiss, Dopey, Doc, pumpernickel . . . Do you know if you took every type of bread there is and laid them end to end—and I'm not counting crackers—well . . . Sorry, I'm not exactly sure of the point I'm trying to make. Maybe, just that it would go really really really far.

In the 1960s, bread was slang for money, as in "Hey, man, gimme some bread so I can buy a psychedelic headband." I don't know why that was. Maybe it's because in the 1940s, dough was slang for money, as in "Excuse me, Mister, can I borrow some dough so that I may purchase a spiffy fedora." One theory is that dough rose and eventually became bread. My point being that you shouldn't put money into this recipe.

EGGS

How did people ever figure out that eggs were edible? Did they see something come out of a chicken and think, "Boy, I bet that would be tasty?" There had to be a first person who ever ate an egg. I'm sure it wasn't pleasant. In fact, there are pictures in a cave in the south of France showing a Neanderthal crunching into an egg and getting a big mouthful of egg shells; to the side there are other Neanderthals pointing at him and laughing. But who got the last laugh? I don't really know, I wasn't there. Also, this might not be true. It's possible it's just a dream I had one night after eating a bad clam.

People probably started eating some foods because they saw other animals eating them first. For instance, somebody saw a pig digging up truffles and eating them and said, "Say, that pig must know what he's doing. Otherwise he wouldn't be a pig. Hey, I can talk. Listen, everybody, I've invented language."

There had to be a first person who ate beets. Why why why didn't that person tell everybody that it wasn't worth the bother? To this day, people are still eating huge forkfuls of beets and asking God in Heaven how anybody decided that this could be food. Or, maybe that's just me.

SQUID

Actually there is no squid in this recipe. I was just thinking about them. I wonder what happened during their evolution to allow them to shoot out ink behind them. Some people think they developed this talent to avoid predators. But maybe it's just a neat magic trick: the squid squirting out the ink and when the ink disperses, the squid is gone. He's like the David Copperfield of the ocean. I'm not saying that a squid is married to a supermodel like Claudia Schiffer, but I'm not saying that he isn't, either.

BUTTER

If you have a moral or health reason for not using butter, then you can substitute some other lubricant, such as margarine, oil, or Vaseline. In a pinch you can rub a peanut really hard and fast over your pan. I've never tried this, but it's possible that you could squeeze out a drop or two of oil.

I probably should have mentioned earlier that you are going to need a . . .

PAN
You probably are also going to need a . . .

KITCHEN
I suppose you could cook the French toast over a heat source not found in a kitchen. You could try the cable box over your TV, but that doesn't give off much heat. It might take a year or two to cook the Real Frenchy French Toast properly. The same holds true for a candle. You'd need seventy or eighty candles to do the job right. You'd have to wait for your Uncle Hank's birthday party and cook over his cake. But, if you're doing this, you're just being obstinate. Go to the kitchen, use the stove, and stop being such a big baby.

SALT AND PEPPER (TO TASTE)
If you can't taste it, then it ain't salt and pepper! That's an old cooking joke. For the life of me, I've never been able to figure out what it meant.

VANILLA
If you don't have vanilla, you can substitute chocolate, butter pecan, or fudge ripple.

LAIT
That's french for milk. Calling it lait is what makes ordinary French toast Real Frenchy French Toast. You could call all of the ingredients by their french names, but then you'd run the danger of making Really Pretentious Frenchy French Toast.

To Cook
Now, do what I do. Give all the ingredients to your housekeeper, sit down with a . . .

COLD FROSTY BEER
in front of the TV, and before you can say Gerard Depardieu, your housekeeper will be bringing out a piping hot bushel of the tastiest French toast you've ever had.

Now, enjoy and bon appétit.

things that

sound like a

good idea at

first, but

really aren't

....

A. Taking a shower with someone.

B. Pet sitting.

C. Pie eating contests.

D. A mud bath followed by a shiatsu massage.

E. Having somebody read to you.
   1. Reading to someone else.

F. Writing a book.

ellen

degeneres is

a man!

or ....
ellen degeneres is a man!

WARNING!!!

ANOTHER POEM

I wish I were taller
And had perfect legs
And had easier hair to fix
And was a man
Sometimes I do
But not really
But sometimes
But not a lot
Just a little
Once in a while
O.K. only once
When I had to use the restroom
And somebody was in the ladies' room so it was locked
And the men's was open but I was too chicken to go in
So I wished I was a man then
Just that one time

Someone recently wrote a letter recently to a national magazine recently (and you know it must really be recently since I've mentioned it so many times) asking, "Why does Ellen DeGeneres always wear pants and never skirts?"

I'm guessing that the person who wrote that letter meant skirt, a noun signifying an article of clothing, and not skirt, a verb defined as, "to evade or elude (as a topic of conversation) by circumlocution." Because, if they mean the *verb* skirt, well, they're dead wrong. I'm always skirting. I skirt so much that it would not be inappropriate for someone to call me Skirty, though I can guarantee that I will never answer to that nickname.

But it's probably pretty safe to assume that the person who wrote that letter wanted to know why instead of wearing skirts, I wear pants.

First, let me just say, Wow! Some people have a lot of free time! I mean, it's one thing to wonder that to yourself.

But to actually take time to write to a magazine about it? I have to conclude, however, that if one person wondered that, probably others have too. So, once and for all, here's the reason.

If you must know, years ago when I was young and impressionable, after eating some fermented berries at Camp Tatchey-Too Too, I had both my legs completely tattooed with designs of bougainvillaea. Now, if I wear a skirt, I am constantly bothered by bees.

I hope that clears that up. Thank you for your curiosity.

All kidding aside—actually, I change my mind. I don't want to put all kidding aside. I want the kidding right there in front where we all can see it. The main point of this book is kidding. If I put all kidding aside, there would be nothing left but nonkidding, and believe me, that wouldn't make a very interesting book. So forget that: the kidding stays (or I go).

Now, where was I? Oh yeah. Some people probably think that you're less of a woman if you wear pants, and that's just not fair (unless you're a man, in that case you might like being thought of as less than a woman . . . or at least less womanly—or maybe not). So, what am I trying to say? Probably something about how unfair it is to be judged by appearances. Yeah, that sounds right.

It is unfair to be judged by appearances. Even though I don't wear skirts, I know I'm a girl. Of course, I forget that sometimes. Wait a minute, I should clear that up. I can already see some reviewer singling that quote out. I don't forget that I'm a girl—I know I'm a girl (I've got two x chromosomes and I'm not afraid to use them)—but I think of myself as a human being first, just a person.

I'm a person who's a woman, and I don't like dresses or panty hose or heels. I guess you could chuckle and say that I'm just a woman trapped in a woman's body. But, if you did say that, nobody would know what you meant, and probably more than one person would ask you to kindly stop chuckling.

High heels should be outlawed (at the very least there should be a five-day waiting period before you can buy them). They destroy your feet. It should be mandatory that the Surgeon General print a warning label on high heels like they do on a package of cigarettes (i.e., Warning: These shoes can lead to lower back pain, aching toes, and the illusion that you're taller than you actually are).

Anyway, just to reiterate, I do know I'm a girl. As proof (and I don't know why you want proof all of a sudden), when I'm out in public and I have to use the restroom, I head straight for the ladies' room or the door with a stick figure wearing a dress (even though I'm not wearing one myself) or, if it's a seafood restaurant, the door marked "Gulls" and not "Buoys."

I guess the bigger point, though, is that fairly or unfairly (and sometimes both at the same time), we are judged by the way we look. And, more often than not, we're the ones who are judging ourselves.

I'm sometimes—by which I mean most of the time—insecure about the way I look. But, then again, I believe most people are insecure about their looks (though I'm not sure enough of myself to ask them). I'd bet even supermodels sometimes look at themselves in the mirror and say, "Oh, look. There's a part of me that's less perfect than the other parts of me that are more perfect."

I know that I'm being too critical. I know that I should just accept the way I look. I know that my appearance isn't as important to me as my thoughts and creativity and energy and relationships with people: that's what I thrive on. But none of this knowledge stops me from spending hours in front of the mirror looking for what I've been told (by the people waiting in line behind me at the Gap) are imaginary imperfections.

Doesn't it seem that when you look in the mirror, the tiniest imperfections seem huge? And you know that that's all people are going to be staring at all day: a blemish, a rebel strand of hair that refuses to behave, a flaming arrow in your forehead (this may not be a good example of a tiny imperfection).

So that I don't spend most of my day looking in the mirror consumed with self-doubt, I've developed some basic grooming and fashion tips that help me get started each day. And, on the small chance that they may help you, too, here they are.

There is only one rule: You've got to have nice shoes —that'll get you by. (Remember the saying: "I felt bad because I had no shoes, then I saw someone with really ugly shoes?") Well, unless you're wearing ratty old socks with holes in them. That would be stupid. So, nice shoes *and* nice socks are all you need.

And, of course, there's your hair. That's important, too. It should be well-groomed—be it long or short. Here's another tip: If you've ever had spaghetti in your hair, you know it's hard to tell because, of course, it's long and stringy. Now if your hair *isn't* long and stringy, it's easier to tell. But, just in case, always check your hair every morning for spaghetti.

Any type of pasta aside, your hair should be trimmed regularly and have a clean, fresh appearance. Well, that goes for your overall body really—it should be clean and fresh. You should try to not have any perspiration (or very little) and smell good. Nice odor is important.

Now makeup, in my humble opinion, is optional. But that's just me. I've *never* understood the concept—except in movies and TV, where without makeup you look like a zombie; though, not enough like a zombie to get away without wearing any if you're playing a zombie in a movie. It's what we in L.A. call a vicious circle. Or maybe it's something else we call a vicious circle. Either way, makeup is optional.

Why must women wake up and paint their faces? Who came up with this idea? What's wrong with washing and moisturizing? So, if you wash and moisturize, if you care to wear makeup, go right ahead. No one's stopping you. I only suggest reconsidering. Is it totally necessary? If you are a man the same rule applies. Also if you care to shave, go ahead and shave.

So, now that the grooming part is taken care of, we'll move on to clothing. I won't go so far as to pick out your outfits, but they should be stylish—not trendy—classic clothes. They should be comfortable, not stifling or too conservative. Hats are optional, although it's a risk. It is definitely making a strong statement that others may react negatively to. So bear that in mind, won't you? Also remember, you're eventually going to take off your hat. And, there's no telling what your hair is going to look like. It may have given up hope and be lying dead on your scalp. Or, craving oxygen, it might be jutting out in surreal spikes. There may also have been spaghetti in your hat before you put it on. In that case, go back to the earlier tip.

Speak clearly and directly in an even tone, loud enough to be heard but not so loud as to be annoying. Have you put on those good shoes? Now you're ready for the day.

And remember, don't let anyone—not me, not even the great pasta chefs of Europe!—tell you how you *should* look.

chapter 13

....

See Chapter 14.

chapter 14

Regarding Chapter 13: I realized it's bad luck to have a thirteenth anything. Most hotels don't even have a thirteenth floor—they just go from twelve to fourteen. But you realize that fourteen is actually thirteen, so what good does it do? You can't eliminate the actual floor—it is, after all, thirteen—but they call it fourteen. So we all know that this is really Chapter 13 even though it says Chapter 14. I think I'll skip this one, too, and go on to Chapter 15, which will really then be fourteen.

the scariest

thing

....

CREAK...

Whoever started all
those boogeyman stories
is a horrible person.

REAL FEARS VS. RIDICULOUS FEARS

Fear of earthquakes.	Fear of a pack of wild baby kittens dropping on your head as you are sleeping soundly in your bed at night.
Fear of flying.	Fear of losing control of the volume of your speech while saying something rude about someone sitting in front of you while at church.
Fear of speaking in public.	Fear of combing your hair so hard your head bleeds while your date is waiting in the front room.
Fear of high places.	Fear of having the uncontrollable urge of shaving not only your head, but the heads of everyone you meet.
Fear of dying.	Fear of eating way too many oranges for no apparent reason.

When you're a grown-up and you're up really late, it's still scary, isn't it? No matter how much you try to convince yourself it's cool, it's okay, you're imagining those little noises. It's scary. Whoever started all those boogeyman stories is a horrible person. It had to be started, obviously, by one guy—one guy telling a little kid a bedtime story. He just threw in the boogeyman. Clearly it caught on. I doubt there are royalties involved—if there are, he's probably feeling ripped off. Who knew it would turn out to be such a big hit? Maybe he could try to sue K.C. and the Sunshine Band. Although it's a different boogeyman, the song still scares me. Don't get me wrong—I danced to it just as much as the rest of you in 1975—but come on, someone sat down and wrote those lyrics. But I digress. My point . . . and I do have one, is that I still get scared at night. Every tiny creak, every little noise, I open my eyes real wide and listen with them. Have you noticed that? When it's dark and you can't see a thing, you open your eyes really wide and glance back and forth, like your eyes become your ears? Maybe it's just me.

You can tell a lot about a person by looking at the things that scare her or him (actually, I'm not really sure that's true, but since it's the premise of this story, I'll write it down and hope that nobody reads it too carefully). Sometimes what a person fears is actually the thing that they desire. For instance, if somebody is afraid of ice cream it could mean that they desire ice cream (hence the saying, I scream, you scream, we all scream for ice cream). However, if that person is allergic to ice cream, it probably means that they desire hives or some other type of rash.

Some people believe that it's a good idea to face your fears. I usually feel that it's much healthier to tie them up in a bag, drive out to the country, chuck them out your window, then drive home as fast as you can. But at the moment, I'm lying in bed in the middle of the night. I'm too tired to take a long drive. So, I will try looking into my heart to see what frightens me.

Ghosts. I'm afraid of ghosts. Do I really believe in ghosts? Sometimes I do. I watch these supernatural phenomena shows about people who have seen doors and windows open and close and furniture move around the room. Sometimes I think, "Cool, I'd love to see that." But, most of the times, I wouldn't. I'd get kind of freaked out if a coffee table started dancing around, even if it was a goofy dance like the hokey-pokey.

The house I live in now might have a ghost. I think I've seen the guy. When I first moved into this house, strange things happened. I'd lock a door and a few minutes later I'd see that it was unlocked. A sliding door opened. It could've been the wind, you say. Well then, my skeptical friend, explain why there was a man standing in the middle of my bedroom dressed in some turn-of-the-century attire. Actually, it turns out that the man was my neighbor who got lost coming home from a costume party at Ernest Borgnine's house. But it could have been a ghost.

I'm also afraid of space aliens and spaceships. I'm scared that I'll be abducted by some UFO and then poked and prodded, which, from what I read, is what space aliens mostly do. Or what if they put some sort of chip in your brain that made you kill at their command or, even worse, made your favorite radio station the easy-listening one? What would be frightening, then, would be to come back and know that if you told anyone what happened to you, they'd think you were a nut. The only thing that scares me more than space aliens is the idea that there aren't any space aliens. We can't be the best that creation has to offer. I pray we're not all there is. If so, we're in big trouble.

Let's see, what else frightens me. Oh, I know. The scariest thing in the world almost happened to me the other day. Just thinking about it makes me break into a sweat (or maybe it's the hour and a half that I just spent on my treadmill that has caused me to break into a sweat; the important thing is that I'm sweating). Let me tell you about it. But first, a warning: If you are faint of heart, it would be a good idea to have a registered nurse nearby while you read this tale of near-terror. On the other hand, if you are a registered nurse, there's no need to have a faint-of-heart person with you. All they'd do is fidget around a lot and make you nervous.

I was at home, I was barefoot, I was about to put my shoes on . . . (Have I set the mood, is your heart beating fast?) Like a fool, I was just going to slip my foot into my shoe without looking. Luckily, at the last second I glanced down. In my shoe was . . . a huge spider—a big black-and-orange, hairy, crunchy spider. I almost put my foot right on it. Isn't that scary? Isn't that like something Stephen King would write? Stepping on a spider has to be the scariest thing in the world.

Actually, do you know what would be scarier? If, after putting on the one shoe I then recklessly put my foot in the other only to discover that it was teeming with . . . *hundreds* of spiders! All the babies were in there, a whole— let's see, it's a gaggle of geese, a school of fish, what is a group of spiders called? Oh, now I remember: a whole *snorkel* of spiders. That would be the scariest thing ever.

Unless, let's say you're out camping in the woods, or not even camping, or even in the woods; you're sleeping in your backyard. I don't know why. Maybe you like the great outdoors, but you want to be close to home in case somebody calls. Or maybe you had a fight with the person you live with, and you ended up yelling, "Okay, that does it. I'm sleeping in the backyard tonight!" It's only when you get back there that you realize it wasn't much of a threat. But you have too much pride to go and sleep inside (even though your dogs look at you from inside through the picture window with an expression that's a mixture of pity and confusion).

So (and this is the scary part), you're in the backyard and you're just about to doze off when you start feeling something kind of funny—not ha ha funny, but creepy, weird funny. So you look inside your sleeping bag and there's . . . a snake crawling up your leg. Aghhhhhhh!

That just blows the spider thing away. It is not possible for there to be anything scarier than that.

Wait, I just thought of something more frightening. What if you're playing Frisbee on the beach and the person you're playing with (either a friend or someone kind of attractive who just happens to have a Frisbee, and you're flattered when they ask you to play with them—this part isn't important so you shouldn't be dwelling on it) throws the Frisbee way past you and you're furious because it's their fault, but you smile and yell, "I'll get it," and they say, "Okay." (Notice how I've managed to build up the suspense with some terse dialogue?)

Anyway, it turns out that the Frisbee has flown into one of those caves that you see at most beaches. Well, you go to get it and you realize that the Frisbee has gone farther down into that cave than you had thought. So you have to spelunk down into the abysmal depths of the pitch-black cave.

Finally, you reach what you assume is your Frisbee and you grab it, but it feels weird so you say, "Why is my Frisbee squishy?" So you squeeze it harder and you realize, "Hey, this isn't a Frisbee . . . it's a bat!"

Well, the bat starts making that *wee-bee-bee-bee* bat noise that bats make when you're squeezing them a little too hard (for more information on this read *Bats and the Sounds They Make When You Squeeze Them*, by Carney Pheek). So you start running as fast as you can out of the cave, but your screaming sets off thousands of bats—not a snorkel, that's only for spiders—a whole *Nipsy Russell* of bats, which start flying out after you. Now you're running through the sand, which is even harder than it sounds because you're wearing high heels (they look good with the swimsuit and slenderize your hips). So you're heading for the water thinking you'll be safe from the bats. But just before you submerge, a bat bites you on the ear. Oh man, those sharks can smell blood from miles away. So now you can see the shark fins swimming toward you. But you can't get out of the water because of the Nipsy Russell of bats. What a dilemma. It's like *The Pit and the Pendulum*, only different. I defy you to come up with something scarier than that. It's impossible.

Unless, say you're on a farm visiting your aunt . . . or whomever . . . and she calls out to you through the kitchen window, "Ellen, Ellen honey—would you mind going to look for that thing I misplaced?" And you don't even care what the thing is—because that guy's inside and he wants you to call him Uncle Larry and he's not your uncle and he's drunk all the time and he always wears those weird pajamas—but it's her life. So you go to look for that thing, and you think you see it in some bushes. You reach in to grab it, and you think you have it, but what you realize you're grabbing instead is (Oh my God!!!) a . . . lamb.

Okay, I admit that's not too scary by itself. But what if it's not just one lamb? What if it's a lot of lambs? What if it's a rack of lambs? That's pretty scary, huh? Because a lot of anything is scarier than one something.

Am I right? Think about it. One hundred poodles are scarier than one leopard. That's assuming, of course, that the leopard has no legs. You could come home, open the door, and see a leopard with no legs sitting in your living room. So what could it do? It's got no legs. It would be growling away, and you could sit right in front of it and make faces and touch its nose and "Woo" at it.

The only way a no-legged leopard could hurt you is if it fell out of a tree onto your head. I don't know how it got up the tree; maybe some of the other animals lifted it up there. But you have to admit when that leopard fell on you and clamped down on your head with its teeth, it would be pretty bad. You'd start running down the street yelling, "Help, help me, please."

And more often than not, you'd run into a big group

of animal-rights activists, a *Naugahyde* of animal-rights activists. And, instead of helping, they'd probably throw red paint at you. You would scream out, "It's not a hat, it's a live animal! It's got no legs. I would never wear fur. I am wearing it against my will."

So now you've got a live leopard on your head and paint all over you as well. That is pretty darn terrifying. But you know, I don't want to diminish the spider in my shoe. Believe me, looking back, that was scary enough. I guess all I'm trying to say is you don't have to make stuff up; there are enough scary things in real life.

the time ellen

degeneres had

an emergency!

....

Just flap, flap, flapping
in the breeze...

Once I had to be taken to the emergency room of a hospital. It was an experience I wouldn't wish on my worst enemy. Actually, I don't have a worst enemy or even a best enemy. I've never taken the time to rank my enemies. I'm afraid of hurting somebody's feelings. "Hey, I thought I was your worst enemy," one of my lesser enemies might complain. I sort of wish I did have a worst enemy, though. Because, come to think of it, having them go to the emergency room is exactly the sort of thing that I would wish on them. I mean, what's the point of having a worst enemy if you can't take enjoyment from seeing them suffering and in pain? It would be kind of fun. As it was, it was me suffering and in pain.

I got hurt in a real stupid way. Before they tape my sitcom, I go out and warm up the audience a little bit. Usually I tell jokes, but sometimes I perform feats of strength. You know, like pulling a jeep across the stage using my teeth. Well, this time I had people come up from the audience; I would tense my stomach muscles and they'd punch me as hard as they could. Everything was going fine until I relaxed for just one second. Out of nowhere this huge teamster ran over from the donut table and socked me in the gut. It was either a teamster or Dom DeLuise dressed up like a teamster.

That's not really what happened. I just don't care to tell you why I really went to the emergency room. Okay, I had a cyst. See, it's not quite as interesting as getting socked in the gut by Dom DeLuise. But still, it did hurt like hell.

I was in bed doubled over in pain. It really confused my dogs. That's not saying much, though. It doesn't take a lot to confuse my dogs. Ringing the doorbell does the trick.

My manager, a man who told me that it was in my best interest that I don't know his name, so I refer to him always as "my manager," drove me to the hospital. I would have taken an ambulance, but when I called on the phone they told me that you had to book one two weeks in advance. It's just as well. I never know how much to tip the drivers of those things anyway.

We picked up my mother on the way. She wanted to come because that way we could ride in the car pool lane. Also, she works as a speech pathologist at the hospital I was going to. She figured since she was an employee she could make things easier for me. You know, like getting me a good table and giving me the skinny on how things work there. "You see that man in the white coat with a stethoscope? He's a doctor." (Thanks, Mom.) "If you were to speak to him you would call him Dr. Jones and not Mr. Jones. That is, assuming that his last name is Jones."

When you're in terrible pain, you don't care about the way you look; you're not embarrassed by your facial contortions and grimaces; you don't care if you're wearing plaids with stripes, which, thank God, I wasn't.

I was doubled over in the car, my face pressed against the window (the passenger window, not the front window), crying out in pain. When we were stopped at red lights, people would look over from the next car. They'd see my manager driving and me sitting next to him crying. You could see on their faces what they were thinking. First they'd think that I was in an abusive relationship and had just been hit. Then they'd slowly recognize me, honk their horns, and give me a big thumbs up. My manager would never hit me, but while I was groggy from the pain he did have me sign something that gives him 50 percent of whatever I make.

They rushed me into the emergency room: doors slamming, voices overlapping, people running—a flurry of activity. But as soon as I got in, I had to sit and wait and wait and wait. It's not fair. It's not like the bakery where you take a number and it's first come first served. Here they have this crazy idea of bringing you in based on how serious they feel your illness or injury is. I knew I was in for a long wait when I saw a guy sitting next to me with his arm falling off and his head in his lap. As it was, he was only there for the happy hour. If you're admitted between five and six there's a buffet table with cocktail franks and nachos.

The first thing I had to do, besides proving that I had insurance, was tell them what my symptoms were. Unfortunately, they recognized me as a comic, so they thought I was trying to be funny, that I was trying out a new part of my act.

I said, "I have this sharp intense pain in my lower abdomen. I started feeling it about two hours ago. . . ."

And the admitting nurse would interrupt me, barely able to control her giggling, "Yeah, yeah. . . . Then what happened? Wait! Mary, Stan, come over here, she's really funny. Start from the beginning."

"I was hurting so much I couldn't move," I continued.

The admitting nurse started laughing hysterically. "Oh yes. That's great, it's hilarious. Oooooo, I've got an idea. Tell the rest of it like you're on the phone with God. That would make it really funny."

So after I made it past the admitting nurse, they had me sit on these extremely uncomfortable plastic chairs (they were rejected by Greyhound bus stations for being too painful) in the waiting area again until they could find someone to help me. Everybody else there was watching TV. They finally wheeled me in to see a doctor because my crying and screaming in pain was ruining people's TV-viewing experience. "Keep it down, we're trying to watch Jerry Springer!"

They gave me a number of tests to try to figure out what was wrong: blood tests, X-rays, ultrasound, temperature, algebra. Some tests seemed valid; others seemed to serve no purpose at all. Like when one doctor had me sit on a pony and whistle the theme song from *Mission Impossible*. "Why do I have to do this?" I said between whistles.

"We just want to rule out whistling pony disease," he replied, "and anyway, Dr. Jones brought the pony in so we figured we might as well use it."

What was really bad was when this guy tried to hook me up to an IV. He kept on missing my vein. He'd stab at me and miss; there was blood everywhere. I got really nervous when I looked down and saw his Seeing Eye dog.

I told the nurse I didn't think this guy knew what he was doing and I'd prefer it if she put in the IV. She looked at me surprised. "I'm sorry, I thought you wanted him to do it. I have no idea who this guy is."

The doctor came in later. He said that my blood looked good and that my urine was clear and looked good too. That calmed me, until I realized that I hadn't even had a urine test. Either he had looked at somebody else's urine or he found me attractive and this was one of his pick-up lines. Maybe I was supposed to tell him that his urine was clear and looked good also.

I was tested until midnight. Everybody looked at me. At one point, a doctor's neighbor's nephew's son was examining me. If that isn't wacky, I don't know what wacky is. Eventually, by doing an ultrasound, they discovered that I had a cyst that the doctor said was the size of a really, really big cyst.

Finally, at midnight, I was wheeled into my hospital room. It was a little disappointing. No mint on the pillow, no view, no HBO. And believe me, this place wasn't cheap either.

Shortly afterward they brought me my first meal. Now the food in hospitals is the stuff that's so bad that it doesn't even make it onto airplanes. They brought me broth and Jell-O, which ironically is one of my favorite meals. If it's fixed right, it's great. I think it's bad when broth and Jell-O taste exactly the same.

Another thing that's awful is the gown they make you wear. It doesn't fit right, and it's completely open in the back, leaving exposed an area of my body that I traditionally keep covered with clothes. You walk down the hall and it's just flap, flap, flapping in the breeze—the gown, that is; the part of my body I traditionally keep covered wasn't flap, flap, flapping. If it was, I'm sure I'd be one of the first people to know. All I'm saying is that the gown was humiliating. But, on the bright side, since the hospital is in Beverly Hills, my gown also had shoulder pads. So, it was slimming and degrading at the same time. I think Cher wore one to the Oscars last year.

I was depressed when I woke up the next morning. Because besides being sick, it was my birthday. There's nothing like spending your birthday hooked up to an IV and trying to keep your gown closed in the back to make you aware of the aging process, the inevitability of death and decay, and countless other happy, carefree thoughts.

They did cheer me up, though, when they brought me my breakfast: broth and Jell-O. Somebody must have known it was my birthday because they put a candle in the broth.

It wasn't my worst birthday, though. That would have to be either the year I decided to eat my age in hard-boiled eggs, the year I thought I had gotten tickets to see the musical *Tommy* but instead ended up seeing a one-man show based on the life of Tom Bosley, or when I turned twelve and fell off my pony while whistling the theme from *Mission Impossible*.

On the other hand, I did lose five pounds a lot quicker than I would have by dieting, and I had someone cute tell me that my urine looked good.

Luckily I was able to go home after just one day. But I had to rest for a long time. We lost a week of production on my show. And, to be honest, the first week or two that I was back I don't think we made the best episodes. My character was always lying in bed with her feet slightly elevated. Every now and then they would cut to me and I would just react to whatever action was taking place and say something like: "Wow, that's crazy" or "You don't say" or "You learn something new every day, don't you?"

It was heartwarming going back to the set for the first time after recuperating. Everybody was so happy to see me. Well, everybody but Erik Estrada. He had been promised my role if I didn't make it back and had already started rehearsing. I think it would be a completely different show, him playing Ellen instead of me. I'm not saying worse, just different.

The whole experience of being sick and going to the emergency room has really made me value how good life is without a cyst. It has also made me appreciate the little things in life. Like . . . Actually, I can't think of anything right now. All that popped into my head was "mashed potatoes." And, well, I like mashed potatoes, but I can't honestly say I appreciate them more than I ever did. Oh, I guess I do appreciate having clothes that aren't open in the back.

On the down side—if there can be a down side to having a ruptured cyst—I'm now much more of a hypochondriac than I ever was. For instance, just the other day I was sure that I had an awful stomach ulcer. It turned out that I had just left one of the pins in my new blouse.

So, my advice to everybody reading this is simple: Don't have a cyst. Believe me, it's not all the fun and kicks it's made out to be.

one step

closer to god

or ....

one step back,

you do the hokey-pokey

and you turn yourself around

Hey, what's a matter,
were you born in a barn?

Like most of us humans (if you're a nonhuman and are another species of animal instead, like a llama, screech-monkey, or whatever, then congratulations on learning how to read), I am always searching for answers. Sometimes I don't even know the question, and yet I need answers. Sometimes I know the answer and I need the question, but that's only when I'm watching *Jeopardy!*

Some of the answers I search for are to questions like: What is the meaning of life? How did it all begin? Is there such a thing as infinity? (It boggles my mind that there is no beginning or end to the universe, only a big middle that's probably the result of too much starchy foods.) Now, don't get the wrong idea. I don't think about this stuff constantly. Sometimes I just sit in my den and watch *Wheel of Fortune.* That Vanna White sure seems like a sweet girl—so happy and upbeat.

But right now I am thinking about those big questions, because right now I'm thinking about God. That's because there's a woman, who by the looks of her is either from India or Sweden, about one hundred yards away from me (I say one hundred because I'm sitting under one field goal and she's under another; so I'm guessing one hundred). She has been sitting on a tree stump rocking back and forth with little beads and a tiny book in her hands for two hours—praying sort of out loud. I can't really hear what she's saying, but man oh man, two hours? What could you possibly pray about for two hours?

I'd like to tell her, "Excuse me, Miss, but he's busy—or she or whoever. Keep it short. There are people in Yemen who would like to talk."

I think that when you pray, it's like you're leaving a message for God. You don't want to have God check her answering machine, hear your rambling prayer, and say, "Two hours, two hours?! There will be no time for miracles today. That's for darn sure."

I try to keep my prayers simple, like: "Hey, God,

what's up? Thanks for everything in my life. I'm so grateful. Thanks especially for helping me find that parking space today. That was sweet of you. Hope you're doing okay. Sorry for the mess we're making here blah, blah, blah." (I literally say, blah, blah, blah—don't ask me why, it just feels good.) I'm finished in less than five minutes (saving God time so that she can have a personal life).

Sometimes when I'm driving I get so angry at inconsiderate drivers that I want to scream at them. But then I remember how insignificant that is, and I thank God that I have a car and my health and gas. That was phrased wrong—normally you wouldn't say, thank God I've got gas. I meant gasoline for my car. But some people who have strange diseases may actually be thinking "Hey, if I only had gas, I'd feel lucky." So, like most things in life, it's all relative.

I was raised a Christian Scientist and was taught to believe that we could heal our bodies through prayer, that sickness was an illusion that could be defeated by the power of the spirit. Since my family were Christian Scientists, we probably saved a bundle: no aspirin, no medicine at all. I didn't take my first aspirin until I was in my teens and even now I feel a twinge of guilt when I go to the pharmacy—I feel as if I'm in an opium den. (Though, to be fair, I've only been to an opium den twice and I was so stoned I barely remember what it was like.) We never had to buy any of that stuff. Also, we didn't need medical insurance. It would have been a waste of money because we never went to the hospital.

I don't recall much about my religious upbringing. I remember I wore a bonnet to church, but I don't think it was a Christian Science thing to wear bonnets. It was just me and maybe a few other girls (and this guy named

Owen who wore a bonnet because he burned easily and was allergic to all other kinds of hats).

Sometimes I wonder what God is like. We picture God to look like us. Not exactly. I mean, I don't think we picture God to look like Wink Martindale, for instance. More like Bob Barker. But we assume God has some human form. Maybe God looks more like those drawings of aliens that people have supposedly seen with large heads and huge, black eyes. Maybe God is a huge sphere with millions of ears or antennas like a satellite dish for excellent reception. Maybe God is a giant bug, and when we die we're going to have to account for every cockroach and ant we've killed. Maybe God does look like Wink Martindale.

I believe that there is a lot to be learned from the Bible. But I don't believe all the stories can be taken literally. Because nobody was writing things down as they happened. Instead, one person told somebody else, who then told someone else, who told Shem, who told Hosea, who told Sinbad, who told Fabio, who told somebody else. So, what started out as a story about Moses going to the beach to get a little sun and maybe go snorkeling became the Red Sea parting and all that stuff.

That being said, here are two of my favorite Bible stories:

God is in a department store and he asks a woman where the hat section is. I don't remember the woman's name, so I'll call her Linda, because I have a friend named Linda who works in a department store. Now this story took place a long time ago—when department stores had huge hat sections. I don't remember what kind of hat God was looking for either. Probably something with a snap brim. So Linda tells God, "Go to the . . ." I'm sorry.

Linda tells God "*Thou shall go* to the third floor. The hats are right next to the Laura Ashley accessories."

You know, that might not be a Bible story. It might just be a boring story that Linda told me once. (I think it was about her selling a scarf to Charles Nelson Reilly. I kept falling asleep, so I must have dreamed the God part.)

This, however, I'm pretty sure is a Bible story. Jesus enters the temple and he's steaming mad because there are moneylenders in there. I forget what they were doing, probably lending money. Well, Jesus turns over their tables and exits in a huff, leaving the door to the temple wide open. So, one of the moneylenders yells out, "Hey, what's a matter, Jesus, were you born in a barn?" Which is ironic, because he was.

Note: I wanted to put a story here that I used to do in my stand-up act about a phone call to God. It was a signature piece of mine, meaning that when I would sign a check I'd write out the entire routine instead of my name. It would take about a half hour, so it was usually better for other people to pay my bills.

The piece is very funny. I start off saying how I feel that everything on this earth is here for a reason, that there are no mistakes. If you don't understand why one thing is here, you find out later that it works with the ecosystem somewhere else. (In case you're wondering, this wasn't the funny part, this was just the setup.)

I went on to say that I don't understand why we have fleas here, because fleas do nothing at all beneficial. I thought it would be great to be able to call up God and ask, "Why fleas?"

What followed was my imaginary phone call to God. I would say my lines and hopefully you'd be able to imagine God's. God and I would chat, he'd tell me a few jokes (e.g., Knock, Knock. Who's there? God. God who? Godzilla), and explain to me why there are fleas (to support people in the flea-collar industry). This was the funny part. If you've never heard it, take my word: huge laughs every night.

So why aren't I writing it out here? There are two reasons. One, as funny as it is to see and hear (If you don't believe me, maybe this note from my editor will change your mind. EDITOR: *She's right, it's very funny!*) it doesn't read well on the page. So much of the routine depends on nuances of timing and my delightful facial expressions (EDITOR: *She's right, they're delightful*). (Why, thank you.)

The second reason is that I got a letter from God, well, actually from God's lawyers, saying that if I printed the routine, they'd sue my ass (their words, not mine) from here to Jerusalem.

So, that's why I'm not even going to mention my phone call to God.

the ellie-gellie

Cleanliness is next to
Godliness, but dancing is
next to cleanliness.

If you know me personally, or watch my television program, then you know I love to dance. I really do, y'all. (Y'all is a New Orleans expression that I felt obliged to include at least once in this book to show that I haven't "Gone Hollywood." There, I've used it. Now no highfalutin' critic can say that I've forgotten where I came from.)

Anyway, like I said, I love dancing. You know that expression, "Cleanliness is next to Godliness"? Well, I believe that, but *dancing* is next to cleanliness, and singing along to the radio in a convertible with the wind whipping through your hair is next to dancing, and walking down a country road at sunset is next to singing along with the radio with the wind whipping through your hair, and walking down a country road at dawn is next to walking down a country road at sunset. Actually one is virtually indistinguishable from the other, but the dawn one requires getting up really early, so I'd rather just walk down the country road at sunset, unless I had to be up anyway, say if I had to pick up an old friend from the airport or I had to take somebody to the hospital or even if I just couldn't sleep. Then I guess I'd prefer walking down that country road at dawn and just getting it over with.

I have a good dance background. I've probably got a more extensive dance background than a lot of people, just to tell you something about my skills. I rarely missed *Soul Train* while growing up. And although I was never actually what you might call "on" the show itself, my friends all said that I "could've been" if I hadn't been born quite so "white," as they put it.

Since I feel blessed in this area, I think it's only right that I share my gift with you, the people who may *not* have been born with the same sense of rhythm. I'm going to teach you a simple yet hip dance I invented. I call it the Ellie-Gellie.

Alrightee, first thing we have to do is get into our

dance gear. That could be a leotard, sweats, glittery tights, whatever . . .

Hey, I like that. It looks good on you, accentuates your body in just the right way. It'll work perfectly.

Next we need to do some stretching. . . . Good. You don't want to overdo it.

And now you'll need to send away for my song, "The Ellie-Gellie Song." I wrote it specifically to do the Ellie-Gellie to. It works better than any other song for this dance, and although you *can* do the Ellie-Gellie to some other song, I can't guarantee the results. And you'll probably look rather silly doing the Ellie-Gellie to another song.

But if looking asinine doesn't bother you, then, hey, it's your life, you're obviously Mr. or Ms. Big Stuff, so go right ahead. You probably can't dance anyway, so it wouldn't make any difference either way if you used "The Ellie-Gellie Song" or some other stupid song. I don't even know why I bother trying to do something nice for someone like you. Even if I *could* teach you the Ellie-Gellie, which I highly doubt, you'd probably screw it up while dancing at some club and everyone would see you and say, "Man, the Ellie-Gellie is really a bad dance. That Ellen DeGeneres is sure a terrible dance inventor." So, it's just as well that you don't send away for "The Ellie-Gellie Song." And if you did send away for it, I'd send your money back. You couldn't get my song now no matter *how much* you paid for it.

All right, everybody else except for that creep ready? . . . Good, let's get started. Hit *play* on the CD player, tape player, record player, or whatever kind of player you happen to be using, and crank up the volume!

Not quite that loud. Turn it down just a bit. . . . There, much better. Now we're ready to D-A-N-C-E!

First, throw your left arm up in the air and shake your head up and down, but not too much. Still too much . . .

still too much . . . what are you, stupid? Stop all that ridiculous shaking! I said to shake your head *mildly!* . . . There, that's better.

Next, with arm still up in the air, do something with one of your legs. There, very good. I like that.

Now, do a *different* movement with the *other* leg. . . . No, no! What're you doing?! Is that supposed to be cool or sexy or something? You look like one of those big ol' ostriches at the zoo, flopping around all gangly and everything! Just stop it and start "The Ellie-Gellie Song" over again.

You know what? Just forget it. You've got me too riled up to be able to teach effectively now. Maybe I'll try it again in the next book. By then my nerves will be calmer, and I'll probably have several more dances for you to screw up.

See you on *Soul Train!*

things to do

if you're stuck

in an elevator

to help you

pass the time

1. Don't panic—being alone with yourself can be a healthy thing.

2. Try to whistle as many television theme songs as you can remember.

3. Think of your family—the ones you don't hate —and all of the fun times you've had.

4. Think of your favorite foods and how they are prepared (try not to think of corn on the cob or other foods that would require flossing).

5. Make pancakes (this only applies if you've got a hot plate, pancake mix, and an electrical outlet).

6. Count your arm hairs.

7. Think about giraffes giving birth and how they don't injure the baby when it drops.

8. Prepare your grocery lists for the year.

9. This is a perfect time to reflect on your childhood and who hurt you.

10. Scream.

ellen's wild kingdom

or ....

you can put high heels on a poodle, but that won't make it a hooker

I do believe that most
animal testing is improper.

KNOWN HORRIBLE EXPRESSIONS

1. Curiosity killed the cat.
2. No sense in beating a dead horse.
3. A bird in the hand is worth two in the bush.

LESS-KNOWN HORRIBLE EXPRESSIONS

1. Why put a weasel in the blender when you can chop it up by hand?
2. When you see a chipmunk, poke it in the eye— hard.
3. More than one way to file a kitten's tooth.

I went camping recently for the first time. It was a fantastic experience. I went to an amazing place: Montana. I don't know if you've been there, but it is gorgeous. I've never seen any place so spectacularly beautiful as Montana. Or was it Maine? It *was* Maine. Anyway, it is beautiful, and I've never seen any place like it. It is so special.

The important thing is that I went camping. Now, I normally don't wake up that early, but I woke up to watch the sun set. I was sitting in front of my tent, and eating breakfast—some type of Mueslix, or some other kind of outdoorsy stuff, just eating it right from my hand. I didn't even have a bowl. I just had milk and the Mueslix and my hand.

Anyway, so I'm enjoying my Mueslix (that may be an exaggeration—let's just say I was *eating* my Mueslix), when suddenly I hear some kind of noise. Since I'm alone in the middle of the woods, I'm a little bit scared. But I gather my courage, look up, and . . . Awww, how cute! Only ten feet away from where I'm sitting there's a family of deer drinking from a little, babbling brook thing (I'm not sure of the technical outdoorsy term). Just the mother, father, and two little baby deer lit by the reddish glow of the setting sun. It was so beautiful, so perfect, so wonderful,

and I thought, "Oh, I wish I had a gun." I could've just
. . . *BANG BANG BANG BANG BANG!* I could have shot
'em, gutted 'em, skinned 'em, then sprinkled 'em on my
cereal.

Actually, none of that story is true. Well, some of it is
true. I did go camping in Maine.

No, that's not true either. The closest I've come to
camping in Maine is spending a few nights at the Hilton
on Maui (come to think of it, that's not very close). My
point . . . and I do have one, is that I was being sarcastic. I don't understand hunting at all.

My cousin Archie is into hunting, and he knows that I
hate it, but that just makes him want to talk about it to me
more. He called me the other day and said, "You should've
seen it, Ellie. Heh, heh, heh. I got myself an eight-point
duck." Well, I don't know the terminology, but it was
something like that.

Archie told me all the details, ending with him drag-
ging the deer up to his car. Luckily, he got his license
back; before, he would have had to drag it up to the
highway and hitchhike. Not many people will pick up a
man and a deer—maybe one or the other, but not both.

All through Archie's story all I could think about was
that poor little innocent animal just standing around
thinking little deer thoughts: "I wonder where the berries
are. What's this on my hoof?" Whatever they're thinking.
Then Archie killed him and put his head (the deer's, not
Archie's) on the wall of his living room. "Heh, heh, heh,
heh, heh. I shot it. Heh, heh, heh. I killed it. No, it wasn't
doing anything to me, just standing there. What's your
point?"

I can see if it was something that you hated, just
something that you were so proud that you killed. Like a
burglar. Get his last expression of surprise before you shot
him. "Heh, heh, heh, heh, heh. Shot him. Heh, heh. I
killed him. He was coming in. Going for the Sony."

I ask people why they have deer heads on their walls, and they say, "Because it's such a beautiful animal." There you go. Well, I think my mother's attractive, but I have *photographs* of her. "Wasn't Mom pretty? She had great legs, too. They're in the next room, come on."

I tell you, the deer heads that I feel sorry for the most are the ones on the walls of bars or restaurants. They have the silly party hats on them, silly sunglasses, streamers around their necks. These are the ones I feel sorry for. I mean, obviously, they were at a party having a good time. They were in there dancing to their little deer music, "A crossbow will make ya *JUMP—JUMP!*" Then, all of a sudden . . . *ker-plow!* . . . the party's over.

Now, I don't want you to get the wrong idea. I'm a strong supporter of animal rights, but I do feel that some activists go a little bit too far. For instance, going up to Alaska and throwing paint at the Eskimos because of the fur coats they wear seems wrong to me. Some activists even eliminate the middleman; they throw paint right on the animal itself (I suppose that would really be the middlemink and not the middleman). The activist says to the mink, "Why wait? You're going to end up on somebody eventually." But the mink is still pissed off. "Hey! I just had a bath. How am I going to get this red paint off? And don't go telling me about club soda—that won't work."

I do believe, though, that most animal testing is improper. If you want to test cosmetics, why do it on some poor animal who hasn't done anything wrong? They should use prisoners who have been convicted of murder or rape instead. So, rather than seeing if some perfume irritates a bunny rabbit's eyes, they should throw it in Charles Manson's eyes and ask him if it hurts.

Another type of animal testing that I think is really wrong is having animals take the SATs. Their scores are always so low, and it's just not fair. It makes them feel stupid, but that's only because the tests are biased toward humans. Because if you asked a person if some type of food is edible, they might not know. They'd eat it and die. An animal wouldn't do that. But if you asked a dog, "Egg is to nest as baby is to what?" it would just stare at you. Or maybe bite your leg. Or go to the bathroom on your carpet. They feel so depressed afterward, because they just don't know. You give them their score, and they just look and say, "Huh?" Then you have to say, "I'm sorry, Mr. Doggy, but you can't go to Harvard."

Even though the animals we share this earth with don't do well on standardized tests (partially, I think, because it's hard to fill in the circles completely with their little paws), they do have an intelligence and beauty that is all their own. It's inspiring to me to be with them, watch them, and try to understand them.

So, I went to the zoo today . . . maybe it was yesterday . . . or last year. It's hard to tell when you're writing a book. I mean, I could have gone to the zoo today, but you could be reading this five years from now. You might read this same page every day for a month and think, "That's odd. Every time I read this page, Ellen says she went to the zoo. That means she's gone to the zoo every day for thirty days in a row. Boy, she must really like the zoo. Come to think of it, I must really like this page. I mean, why else would I be reading it every day for a month? I either like this page a lot or I'm going insane. Maybe I should see a doctor. Maybe I already have seen a doctor. I'm hungry. I think I'll fix myself a sandwich."

Anyway, at the zoo they're very proud about how they've managed to re-create the animal's natural habitat. I'm not exactly sure who "they" are. I just know that "they" hang around the zoo, wear funny hats, and tell everyone how proud "they" are that the zoo has re-created the animal's natural habitat. And, I must admit, the zoo has done a great job. I'm sure I've seen in those Jane Goodall chimpanzee documentaries plenty of tires on ropes swinging from trees in the jungle. And who can visualize a pride of lions on the Serengeti without imagining cages, moats, and little kids throwing marshmallows at the lions? I know I can't. Also, most animals get real ornery if they don't smell cotton candy, the natural odor of the wild.

You've got to wonder what the animals think in a zoo. The first day at school is bad enough; imagine your first day in a zoo. All these strange species staring at you, and you're saying, "What are they looking at? Is there something on my lip? Hey, you see I'm locked up; get me out of here!" I'm sure some animals go crazy in captivity and crack. "Hey, it wasn't me. It was some other polar bear who looked like me. Let me out and I'll help you find him and we can beat the crap out of him."

A lot of times at the zoo you see the monkeys throwing their own poop. I don't blame them. It must be so boring in there, you've got to do something to entertain yourself. I mean all that's there is a tire, a tree, and a few bananas. If I were in the zoo, I'm sure eventually I'd be throwing my poop. (I'm misquoted so often in the press that I'm sure this will be the one paragraph taken out of context in the reviews of this book. The headline will probably be: ELLEN WANTS TO THROW HER OWN POOP. Oh, well.)

I bet they get sick of the food they're served, too. I can just imagine some monkey saying, "Man, they see us eating bananas once and they figure that's *all* we want to eat. Geez, would it kill them to give us some Chee-tos, a ham sandwich, or some cotton candy?"

It makes me especially sad to see dolphins in captivity, because they are such incredibly smart animals. That doesn't mean that I'd want a dolphin to perform brain surgery on me. It has less to do with intelligence than one, I don't want anyone performing brain surgery on me and two, dolphins don't have any hands. It is very hard to hold a scalpel in flippers—as, I believe, Benjamin Franklin once said. Benjamin Franklin, by the way, wanted to make the dolphin the national bird of the United States, that is until he was told that the dolphin is an aquatic mammal and not a bird. He tried to cover his faux pas by quickly suggesting the turkey instead. But by that time, everyone else had voted for the eagle, mainly because it was already on the back of the quarter.

But getting back to my original point, dolphins are incredibly intelligent. They have a highly developed cerebellum, are able to learn complex tasks, and have been known to help swimmers in distress. So what do we do to reward this intelligence? We capture dolphins to put in marine shows. (Not the U.S. Marines, but water parks. I don't even know if the U.S. Marines put on shows. Well, there was *Gomer Pyle*, I guess.) It's kind of like saying, "Boy that Albert Einstein sure is smart. We should have him in a show. I wonder if he would put on a tutu and jump through a ring of fire."

Dolphins are also killed by commercial fishermen. They get caught in the nets that are used to catch tuna. I'll eat tuna, but only if it has that little sticker of the smiling dolphin with a slash through it. This means that the tuna is dolphin free. Actually, I'd like to see that sticker on other things because, frankly, I don't want dolphin in any of my food. I'd like to see that smiley dolphin sticker on Trix, chocolate cake, toothpaste, everything. They're looking for any way to sneak dolphin into our food because they're so abundant.

I was buying some spaghetti sauce and I saw something really frightening on the can: a sticker with a smiling monkey with a slash through it. I thought, "My God, what was in this stuff before?" Has animal testing become so advanced that it's now animal taste-testing?

I rest my case.

....

I have always loved animals. When I was about eleven years old, I wanted to be a veterinarian. We had a little laundry room downstairs and I made that my office. I'd sit there, take an encyclopedia, and copy from it entries about different types of cats. I'd have a separate file for each breed. So, if somebody came to my house and said, "You know, there's no difference between a Siamese and a Burmese cat," I'd reply, "Oh yeah? Come to my office and I'll show you how wrong you are, Mr. Smartypants." Unfortunately nobody ever came to my house and said that. But, if they had, I'd have been ready.

I think I realized, even at an early age, that the real beauty of pets is that they love you unconditionally. All they would like in return is a bit of attention and some food. And, the food doesn't even have to be that good. It could just come out of a can.

I try to save dogs and take them to shelters so that their owners can find them. It's because I have dogs, and I know I'd be devastated if either . . . damn, what are their names? Oh yeah . . . if either Bootsie or Lippy . . . no, not Lippy . . . Muffin. If either Bootsie or Muffin got lost . . . Bootsie is a beautiful Labrador retriever and Muffin is . . . I'm not exactly sure what Muffin is. When I got her at the shelter, they told me that she was part cocker spaniel and part terrier, but I don't think they knew. They were just making conversation. I think she's part . . . rodent. She's got hair like a possum and a snout like an anteater. But, don't get the wrong impression; she's very pretty. She's got offbeat good looks.

I'll see stray dogs wandering in front of houses and they look so sad. I just feel compelled to do something to rescue them. Sometimes it's hard because they're tied on a leash on someone's front lawn, so you've got to untie it.

Or worse, they're behind a fence, so you need wire cutters (which I always have in my car) to get them out. "C'mon, girl. I'll rescue you and find your owners."

Just last week I was driving when I saw this skinny looking stray dog out on the street. So I stopped, got out, and tried to coax the dog into my car so that I could take it to a rescue shelter. All these people on the street were staring at me like I was crazy. Well, I'm kind of used to that, so I continued, "Here boy, here Scrappy." When I don't know an animal's name, I always assume that it's Scrappy—even though I've never been right.

Then I saw why people were staring at me. It wasn't a dog, it was a coyote (who oddly enough was called Scrappy). I can only imagine what a disaster it would have been if I had gotten the coyote in my car. I was a little bit embarrassed, but I make mistakes like that often. I remember once, I met a guy while I was camping and we got along great. We were married two years before I realized he was a grizzly bear.

I don't know why I just thought of this, but, when I was a kid—younger than I am today—I had a gerbil. It was such a fun pet to have because it stayed in its little aquarium with wood shavings and a wheel and seemed to be quite content. I could go to school, go out to play as often as I wanted, and not feel guilty. I could take it out and play with it and it seemed to enjoy its little outside-the-aquarium excursions. It's a good starter pet for a kid, because it doesn't require a great deal of responsibility. You don't have to take it out on walks; that exercise wheel was a great invention. No other pet gets a little built-in gym. I wonder if they make little Stairmasters for them as well. Gerbils are the most fit of all rodents, I'd have to say.

You sometimes hear that pets eventually begin to look like their owners. I don't think that's true. We have much more of a say in how we look than a pet does. It's pretty sad if we get fashion tips from our dogs and cats. "What's that you've done to your hair? I love it. Oh . . . shedding. I'll try it."

I do dote on my dogs. I care about my dogs so much that I give them some rights that I don't necessarily advocate for all animals. For instance, Bootsie and Muffin have the right to jump up on my furniture. Also, they have the right to wake me up, clutching balls in their mouths, to see if I want to play. These are not rights I would give to a raccoon or a cougar. Though, if a cougar woke me up with a ball in its mouth, I'd probably play with him. You know, just to be safe. But the next night I would make sure all the doors were locked. I'm not crazy.

Also, I don't believe that animals should have the right to vote, but I do allow Bootsie to help me with my absentee ballot. Muffin doesn't care about politics.

It is amazing to me how perceptive pets are and how sensitive they are to their environment. Just look at how they behave before an earthquake. Before the Northridge quake, Bootsie and Muffin were very anxious. They knew it was going to happen. They were in the doorway, telling me to hurry up and join them. Bootsie had grabbed a few cans of food and Muffin had some extra batteries and a little bottle of brandy. They knew.

Though I have dogs now, for most of my life I've had cats as pets. I, personally (in some ways, but not in others), like cats more than dogs (with no offense meant to either Bootsie or Muffin). But have you ever had a cat in heat? They just change on you. Once she was my kitten, my adorable little pet. Then, she's a hooker. I went into the bathroom one night, and she was putting on mascara, "To-night, to-night, won't be just any . . . la la. Hm, hm." She didn't know the whole song. "Hm, hm." She just knew some of the words. "Hm, hm."

She was an indoor cat, but male cats knew she was in there somehow. They were just all around the house and somehow she was sneaking out because one morning I found a stamp on her paw. I wouldn't have noticed, but I had just bought this new black light, and she passed right under it. "Hey! What is that?" I said.

And the male cats, they were sneaky the way they tried to get in to see her. One of them disguised himself as a UPS man. He had the truck, the packages, everything. I said, "I'm not falling for that." The suit was just hanging off of him, his little name tag said "Fluffy." "Oh, right. I will *not* sign here. Scoot!" He went off all mad in that big truck, stripping the gears. They don't know how to drive! Cats.

He came back the next day as a cable repairman. Same outfit, little butt crack hanging out this time. So he fooled me. I let him in. He got me Nickelodeon for free, hooked that up somehow. So now I get to see all the old shows.

Smart cat—I'd like to see his test scores!

ask ellen

or ....

it might look like honey,

it might taste like honey,

and bless my corns,

it might even be honey

To chew is human,
to forgive divine.

During the early 1980s, before I became one of America's most beloved comedians (at least that's what Mom calls me; well, she either calls me that or Senorita Monkeyshines) I earned my keep by writing a column called ASK ELLEN OR DON'T ASK ELLEN, IT'S ENTIRELY UP TO YOU AND ABSOLUTELY NO SKIN OFF MY NOSE EITHER WAY, THOUGH IF YOU EVER EXPECT TO GET AN ANSWER THE LEAST YOU CAN DO IS ASK . . . ELLEN THAT IS." Most papers shortened this to ASK ELLEN since the entire title took up all my allotted space. This column, where people would ask me whatever was on their minds, ran in twenty newspapers, nineteen of which were in the Canadian province of Saskatchewan.

I have received many letters asking me to reprint some of my favorite ASK ELLENs. I have received a whole lot more letters begging me *not* to reprint them. I, however, prefer to dwell on the positive (and get away with not writing something new). So without any further ado (or to be honest with just the cutest little teeny bit of ado) here are some of my favorites. Enjoy!

Dear Ellen,
Hi, I am eight years old. The other day I went to my neighbor's house and asked him if I could borrow his toupee for Show and Tell. He told me, "Go to Heck!" I didn't know what that meant, but it sounded bad. So I told him to Fuck Himself. What is Heck?

Signed, Curious.

Dear Curious,
Many people think that Heck is just a polite way of saying Hell. Those people are as wrong as wrong can be (and believe me, wrong can be pretty damn wrong). Heck is just to the left of Hell; it's a suburb of

Hell. Heck is a little bit nicer than Hell. For instance, Heck has Dairy Queens and you don't have to pay as much for car insurance. People in Hell wish that they were in Heck.

But as nice as Heck might be (and in all honesty, it's not that nice), it is nowhere as good as being in Heaven. Oddly enough, when somebody does something nice, nobody ever says, "Go to Heaven!" I guess that's because a person would have to die before they went to Heaven. Saying "Go to Heaven" is like saying "Drop dead" but with a positive spin.

Dear Ellen,
How would I explain chewing gum to an alien? I'm just curious. There is no alien holding me hostage and making me answer stupid questions. I do not need HELP! Because, if there was an alien and he thought I was asking for HELP!, he might take me to his spacecraft, fly me to his planet, and put me in a zoo.

Signed, PLEASE HELP ME!!

Dear Please Help Me,
Good question. Chewing gum is an anomaly. I'm not exactly sure what anomaly means, but I'm sure that it could apply to chewing gum. A good rule of thumb is, whenever you don't know the answer to a question, say that it's an anomaly and then run away before anyone can ask you any more questions.

That being said, if I were to explain chewing gum to your hypothetical alien, I would say, "Well, Mr. or Ms. Alien, chewing gum is something you put in your mouth, but it's not really food. I mean, it has a flavor and everything—at least for a few minutes, then even that goes away—but there are no nutrients in it. It's not even candy. You can swallow candy, but it's probably best that you don't swallow gum. I guess humans buy it because they just love chewing; hence the saying, 'To chew is human, to forgive divine.' "

I'm not actually sure if I got that saying 100 percent right. One thing I can tell you about gum, though, is that there is no way of getting it out of your mouth that isn't disgusting. You either have to reach into your mouth with your fingers (and who knows where they've been; I suppose you probably do, unless you've fallen asleep and there's no telling where fingers go when you're sleeping) and yank out the tasteless, saliva-drenched morsel, or you have to spit it out. No matter how much you practice, you can never make spitting out gum look demure.

At some time in your life, you will step on gum that has been spit out on the street. The way to get it off your shoe is to put an ice cube on it. The gum will harden and you can scrape it off with a spatula (see last week's column: 25 REASONS TO CARRY A SPATULA WITH YOU AT ALL TIMES).

Dear Ellen,
If you ran the Academy Awards, how would you change things?

Signed, Just felt like sending a letter

Dear Just . . .
If I ran the Academy Awards (and I'm not saying that I don't, though I'm pretty sure that I don't), I would make them a lot livelier. I would assume that everybody who was nominated equally deserved to win. So, when the nominations are announced, I'd have the Oscar go to the first person from each category to arrive at the location where the announcement came from (it would be a secret and change each year). You

could win either by being fast or by preventing the other nominees from getting to the destination (by means of kidnapping, putting under anesthesia, etc). I think it would make for exciting television while still maintaining the dignity of the award.

Dear Ellen,
I read this saying the other day: "To know that we know what we know, and that we do not know what we do not know, that is true knowledge," Henry David Thoreau.

At first I found this very inspirational, then I realized I had no idea what it meant. What gives?

Signed, Am I an idiot or what?

Dear Am I an idiot or what?
You are not an idiot. Ipso facto you're a what. What's a what you might ask. But, you didn't ask. So I won't tell. Ha, ha.

If you're worried that you don't understand the saying, here is a simpler way of stating it: Knowing that you know that you know what you know is knowledge of that which you know. You know?

Hope that's helpful.

Dear Ellen,
I have these friends . . . well, they're not really friends, they're people I work with. I call them friends because it makes my life seem less lonely than if I call them co-workers. Anyway, these very close *friends* of mine are always gossiping. Whenever somebody leaves the room, they begin talking about that person behind his or her back (his if it's a male, hers if it's a female).

I found this very amusing until I figured out something: Hey, when I leave the room, they must be gossiping about me! How can I prevent this from happening?

Signed, Person with lots of friends

Dear Person . . .
The only way you can prevent people from talking about you when you leave the room is to never leave the room. I would recommend this course of action highly. Don't go to lunch. Don't go to the bathroom —wear a catheter if necessary. And always make sure your back is to a wall. Never let anyone sneak up on you. If a phone rings, don't answer it. Follow these simple rules and your workplace will be fun to work in again.

Dear Ellen,
Whenever I'm walking my dog, people bend down and talk to her, saying things like, "You're a cute doggie. How old are you?" Is this weird?

Signed, Wondering if it's weird that people bend down and talk to my dog

Dear Wondering . . .
It's only weird if they're expecting an answer back from your dog.
It would also be weird if somebody asked you how old your dog was and you looked down at her and said, "Say that you're two years old," in the same voice that people talk to babies with. Because no matter how long you pleaded, the dog is never going to talk (neither is the baby, unless you plead for a year or so).
Also, a dog doesn't care how old she is. Yet some people have birthday parties for their dogs. Some

people have *surprise* birthday parties for their dogs. That's just a waste, because any party would be a surprise to a dog. She has no idea when her birthday is. A dog doesn't sit around thinking, "Boy, my birthday is coming up in two weeks. I hope they throw me a party."

Dear Ellen,
How would I explain to an alien that people bet on horse races and dog races, but they don't bet on people running or car races?

Please forward your answer to the Municipal 200 on the planet Qogratz, located on the far side of the Milky Way.

Signed, Going on a trip and don't expect to be back any time soon

Dear Going . . .
I guess in order to bet on a race there has to be some sort of animal involved. We'd probably bet on the Indy 500 if there was a monkey driving around in a race car. Maybe we'd bet on the 100-yard dash if all the sprinters had to carry a pig while they ran (this might make the winning times a lot slower).

Also, have fun on your trip. I hope that you read this before you leave, because I'm not sure that I can forward this answer; you didn't leave a zip code! You know how strict they are about that.

Dear Ellen,
Hi. My name is Spoogy. What do you think about that?

Signed, Spoogy

Dear Spoogy,
I think it's great.

Dear Ellen,
Who stole the cookies from the cookie jar?

Signed, Spoogy

Dear Spoogy,
You stole the cookies from the cookie jar.

Dear Ellen,
Not me.

Signed, Spoogy

Dear Spoogy,
Yes, you.

Dear Ellen,
Couldn't be.

Signed, Spoogy

Dear Spoogy,
Then who, my dear Spoogy, then who?
    You obviously need more help than I can give. I
recommend you talk to a counselor or a clergyman or
basically anyone else besides me.

crazy

superstitions

that really

work!

....

If your palms are ringing...

1.   If your nose itches, someone wants to kiss you.

2.   If the clasp on your necklace has turned to the front, someone is thinking about you.

3.   If your ears are burning, someone is talking about you. If your ears are itchy, they are dirty.

4.   If your palms are burning, you will be coming into some money soon. If your palms are ringing, you are crazy.

5.   If you hit your funny bone, you will hear a joke within twenty-four hours. If you hit your head, you will cry.

6.   If you find a bunny in your yard, a distant relative will marry a Finnish diplomat in September.

7.   If a spider is in your pants, you will hop around and scream.

8.   If you sleep with a teabag tied around your head, I don't know why.

the benefits
of being a
celebrity

by ....

ellen degeneres, big enormous star

What does it feel like
to be a star?

Many people ask me, "Ellen, how has fame changed your life? What does it feel like to be a star?" And really, it makes me laugh—I mean I'm no different from anyone else. I guess just because I'm a "celebrity" (or, if you prefer, America's most beloved comic sweetheart) they assume my life is weird or something. My daily routine is pretty much the same as yours—or even yours.

I wake up around—oh seven, seven o' five. My houseboy, Quaw, prepares my breakfast, usually a Figurine and a glass of apple juice and maybe half of a banana. Then I'll play with my pony for a while out by the lake—that brings me up to lunchtime. Quaw will usually surprise me for lunch. Sometimes he'll be dressed up as an Indian and serve some spicy Indian dish and a Pepsi with a straw. Or, he'll be a Spanish conquistador or a Chinese emperor and I'll pretend to be a peasant girl from the village who's hungry and he invites me into the palace for a cup of soup. Then he asks me if I want to use his washroom to bathe, and I do and then at 3 P.M. I'll watch *Oprah*. After that, I'll write a letter to *People* magazine or *US* magazine to compliment or protest some story they wrote about Johnny Depp or Madonna or somebody.

Okay, that brings me to around six o'clock when I go pick up the kids from day care. Not my kids; I drive a van for the neighborhood moms who are busy. Then I'll be home in time for *Wheel of Fortune* and a hot meal: maybe lasagna or pasta with a creamy pesto sauce or some vegetarian burritos.

From 8:30–9:30 Quaw will do some exotic dancing in the disco for me and some of my close friends. Then we will talk and visit and finally head on into the den to the big-screen TV to watch either Jerry Springer, CNN, or whatever is on my outdoor security camera. Around midnight my friends mosey out of my house, I take a couple of Excedrin PMs and a glass of Diet Sprite, and call it a day.

Though my typical day is nothing out of the ordinary, I must begrudgingly admit that being a celebrity does carry with it some pretty cool perks. I'd like to list for you now some benefits of being a celebrity.

"Hey," you might now be interjecting, "I don't have to read the rest of this—I already am a celebrity." Well let's make sure you know what the term *celebrity* means. A celebrity is a well-known famous person who is easily recognized. If you are a person who has chosen not to have sex, you're not a celebrity—you're celibate. Now, I'm sure there are many benefits to being celibate, though the only two that spring to my mind are: one, you probably become better at other things, like, for instance the Jumble or remembering *Star Trek* trivia; and two, I would imagine you don't have to change your sheets quite so often. But that's not what I care to talk about right now.

Here then are some advantages of being a celebrity.

When you're a celebrity you tend to get special treatment. For instance, I was at the Sizzler yesterday and a woman who worked there came up to me and told me that I could eat all the shrimp I wanted. I heard her say it to a lot of other people, too—which goes to prove one thing: A lot of celebrities eat at the Sizzler.

At the Gap they have a special changing cubicle just for celebrities—it's just like all the others except it has a star on the door and a bowl of fruit inside. Also, you're not limited to three items, you can bring in four.

When a celebrity plays Scrabble, the letters Q and Z are worth twenty points and not ten, the celebrity is allowed to see her opponents' tiles, and whatever a celebrity says is a word is a word (e.g., ZQWXJEM). This may lead to some arguments with your noncelebrity friends, but don't let that worry you. Another benefit to being a celebrity is that you get to win every argument you're in.

In every election, whether it's local, state, or national, a celebrity's vote is counted twice.

One of the major benefits of being a celebrity is that more people know how to pronounce your name correctly. That may not sound like much, but when you have a name like DeGeneres, believe you me, that counts for plenty. An added plus is that more people know how to pronounce my brother's name as well.

The National Board of Health says that celebrities are allowed to eat five eggs a week and not four. If you win a People's Choice Award you're allowed fifteen eggs a week.

Celebrities get free HBO for a week once or twice a year. I know this happens for me; I'm guessing it happens for other celebrities, too.

Though it might be considered pretentious in others, it is never showy for a celebrity to have an entourage. I personally don't go anywhere without an entourage of fifteen to thirty-five people complimenting me incessantly and laughing loudly at all of my jokes. Though it gets kind of crowded when I go into one of those little booths to have my passport picture taken, I find that it's worth the inconvenience. Among the members of my entourage (or if you prefer retinue or gang) are: Stumpy, my personal trainer; Lupé, my sheep herder (I keep her around in case I ever decide to purchase some sheep or even just one sheep); Pantry, the woman who brushes my teeth; Todd, my food taster (I'm sorry, Todd was my first food taster—he died after eating a bad batch of Rice Krispies Treats that I must have undercooked. Dutch, my second food taster is gone, too. He didn't die; I fired him for either looking me in the eyes, using the word "and," or forgetting to start each sentence with "Madame do you wish that I . . ." A celebrity can fire anybody for whatever reason they decide and not be thought of as rude—in fact it's considered to be sort of cute and whimsical.); Bong Bong, my tennis pro; and a group of people who don't look familiar to me but claim to be my friends.

Celebrities can drive eight thousand miles without

changing their oil. Plus, they get a 5 percent discount at participating Jiffy Lubes.

If a celebrity goes to a hospital for a major operation, any plastic surgery the celebrity desires is included for free. Or if you pay to get one lip injected with collagen, you get your second lip injected for free.

The sign NO SHOES NO SHIRT NO SERVICE never applies to celebrities.

At the supermarket, celebrities are allowed to take thirteen items into the ten-items-or-less lane. They can also pay by check if the sign says CASH ONLY. When they buy milk they can add five days to the expiration date.

Celebrities can go on any ride in any amusement park no matter how short they are.

If a celebrity is on a boat that is sinking—the rule becomes celebrities first, then women and children.

So when you're walking down the street and you think you've spotted your favorite celebrity but you want to be sure, just remember this rule of thumb: A horse sweats, a man perspires, a woman glows—but only a celebrity twinkles.

your own

fantasy

conversation

with ellen

degeneres

....

But I think it's you
who are so cool.

I received the cutest letter the other day. Here it is:

Dear Ellen,
How are you? I am fine. I hope you are fine, too. I mean it. You are my most favoritest celebrity in the whole world. I like you even more than that guy in the commercial who talks with a funny voice. (He makes me laugh. Ha Ha Ha!!!)

You seem very nice. I wish that I could meet you so that we could have a nice talk. Here is a picture I've drawn of you and me having a nice talk.

The dog in the picture with me is my dog. His name is Mr. Doggy. I named him. My wife thinks that it's a stupid name. She says that a forty-two-year-old man who works as a High School Vice-Principal should be able to come up with a better name. I think it's a good name.

Yours truly,
Bobby Munchloney

Actually, upon rereading that letter, it's not all that cute. But, it does raise an interesting question: What would it be like to talk with Ellen DeGeneres?

I know that before I became a celebrity I always wondered what it would be like to talk to somebody famous like Carol Burnett, Stevie Wonder, Elizabeth Taylor, Zamfir, Punch, Judy, or Marlon Brando. Would they be nice, would they be interesting, would they lend me money?

Most of you will never get the chance to talk with me, unfortunately (or fortunately, in the case of Bobby Munchloney). So for your benefit, I've decided to provide you with a fantasy interactive conversation between yourself and myself. All you have to do is fill in your own dialogue in the space provided. My responses are 100 percent my own and exactly what I would say in reaction to whatever you would say.

For the purpose of this little fantasy, your character will be called Complete Stranger (later shortened to CS). I will be Ellen. Even if your name is Ellen, only say the lines you've written for Complete Stranger. Otherwise, we'll have anarchy on our hands. (Anarchy, by the way, is very hard to get off of your hands. Again, you'd think club soda might work, but it doesn't.)

Let the fantasy begin.

SETTING: The housewares section of a large department store.

ACTION: You are browsing, carrying a bag of clothes you just bought, when you see me looking at a selection of fry daddies and electric butter churners. You do a double take and then tentatively approach me.

Suddenly, you are lifted off the ground, your feet dangling in the air like the branches of a banana tree during a monsoon (I'm sorry—I couldn't think of a better simile). Seeing that you mean me no harm, I motion for my 250-pound bodyguard to put you down. He does so in a surprisingly gentle way.

ELLEN: Hi, I'm Ellen DeGeneres. Who are you?

COMPLETE STRANGER: _____ _____.

ELLEN: And what do your friends call you?

C.S.: _____ _____.

ELLEN: Wow! That's one of my favorite names. In fact, I have a goldfish named (your name). You're not my goldfish, are you? Because if you are, I don't think it's safe for you to be out of the bowl for very long.

C.S.: ___ _____ _____ _____.

ELLEN: Well, thank you for saying that. It makes me happy that you find me very, very funny.

C.S.: ___ _____ ____.

ELLEN: I stand corrected, very, very, *very* funny. Say, (your name), what is it that you do for a living?

C.S.: ____ _____ _____ _____ ___.

ELLEN: That is such a coincidence. If I wasn't doing what I'm doing, I'd want to be a (your job). I even thought of studying to be a (your job), but everybody said . . .

C.S.: _____ _____, " _____."

ELLEN: (Laughing) That's right! That's exactly what everybody said. I guess being a (your job) makes you really understand people.

(*Note:* While we're talking I'm looking at you and only you. You have my complete attention. I'm not staring around bored or planning some way to escape. I am genuinely interested in what you have to say.)

C.S.: _____ _____ _____.

ELLEN: Excuse me, but I think it's you who are so cool. And I can tell that you have a great sense of humor.

C.S.: _____ _____ _____?

ELLEN: Sure, I'd love to hear a joke.

C.S.: _____ _____ _____
_____. _____ _____
_____." _____," _____
_____ _____?" _____
_____, " _____ __ _____
_____!" _____ (_____) _____.

ELLEN: (Laughing hysterically) That's hilarious. I usually don't like dirty jokes, but that was very good. That was a great impersonation, too. I hate to be a bother, but do you know any other jokes?

C.S.: _____ _____ _____?

ELLEN: Who's there?

C.S.: _____.

ELLEN: Tomato, who?

C.S.: ___ _____ _____ _____
_____ _____ _____ ___.

ELLEN: (Laughing even harder than before) That is so clever. I never would have figured that one out in a million years.

C.S.: _____ _____ _____
_____ _____.

ELLEN: You are absolutely right. But, I guess I've learned to see through the pain. You are very perceptive. Say, you know about me, I'd like to know about you. What are your dreams, your goals, your philosophy of life? I'd really, really like to know.

C.S.: _____ _____
_____ _____ _____.
_____-_____! _____ _____
_____ _____ _____?
_____ _____ { _____ } _____
_____. _____ _____
_____ _____ _____.

ELLEN: Uh-huh.

C.S.: _____ _____ _____. __ _____
_____ _____ _____
_____ _____.

ELLEN: Yeah.

C.S.: _____ _____ _____?
_____ _____. _____ _____
_____ _____ _____
_____. _____ _____ _____
_____ _____ _____:
_____; _____; _____!!!!!! _____
_____ _____ _____
_____ _____ _____.

(*Note:* I'm sure that you'd have a lot more to say, and I'd have let you go on for pages, but my editor insisted that *I* have more words. In his narrow worldview, your words don't count toward the 60,000 words that I'm legally bound to provide for this book. And as much as I insisted that (your name) had some bold ideas that people ought to hear, he, obviously, felt otherwise. That's life.)

ELLEN: I agree with every word you said. Also, just to change the subject slightly, I think you've got the coolest clothes I've ever seen. I think I'm going to start dressing just like you.

Just then I take a bite out of my sandwich and start choking. By the way, we're both eating sandwiches. You're eating a fried chicken sandwich—unless you're vegetarian; then it can be a cucumber sandwich. If you haven't been eating, I'm afraid you're going to have to go to the beginning of our conversation, grab a sandwich, and start over again. Sorry, rules are rules.

You reach behind me and give me the Heimlich maneuver. A chunk of food flies out of my mouth.

ELLEN: You saved my life. For now on in I'm not going to call what you just did the Heimlich maneuver, I'm going to call it the (your name) maneuver. Honest. Is there anything I can do for you?

C.S.:   _____ _____ _____?

ELLEN: Sure, how much do you need?

C.S.: $__, ____, _____.

ELLEN: That's an awful lot of money, but . . . What the hey, you deserve it. Hey, are you thinking what I'm thinking?

C.S.: _____ _____ _____.

ELLEN: Exactly. Let's go right now. Time's a wasting, my friend.

fin

And that is the end of the fantasy conversation. I hope that you enjoyed it as much as I did. Take care and see you next time.

experiments

in human

behavior

....

You're just so vulnerable
at that time.

SOME THINGS THAT I HATE IN PEOPLE
Impatience
Intolerance
Infidelity
Insecticides

I don't like to generalize, but you can always tell people's personalities by the cars they drive . . . and the bumper stickers they put on their cars (Sometimes it's no more than pure sexual advertising: "Honk if you're horny." You never see people putting those stickers on their front door: "Knock if you're nasty.") . . . and the clothes they wear . . . and the music they listen to . . . and the way they walk . . . and what they say . . . and what they do. But, once again, that's just a generalization.

Here's what I'm really trying to say: If we don't want to define ourselves by things as superficial as our appearances, we're stuck with the revolting alternative of being judged by our actions, by what we do.

Now there are the big issues of good and evil. (Murder is evil; donating blood is good. If either of these statements is news to you, put down this book, go to the nearest police station, and turn yourself in—they'll know what to do with you there.) However, I'd like to deal with the smaller issues. I want to talk about the things that are neither good nor evil but by which we judge ourselves anyway—the little things we do and the countless situations we find ourselves in that conspire to make us feel like idiots.

Do I feel like an idiot? If I had a nickel for every time I felt like an idiot, I'd be very rich. But I'd be too embarrassed to spend any of what I'm sure I'd refer to as my "idiot money." If I were to spend it, buying an expensive item like a car with about 800,000 nickels would make me feel even more like an idiot. Though the good news is, I'd get another nickel for doing it. This might be a moot point.

We all feel like idiots at one time or another. Even if we feel we're cool 98 percent of the time, that 2 percent doofus is poised to take over our bodies without any warning. It just takes a crack in the sidewalk—one little trip. We feel like fools, turning back to look at it. "There's a pebble, somebody better put up some orange cones to warn the others. Everybody's gonna trip like I did." Then we look back that one more time to show the pebble who's boss, "Damn pebble, why-I-oughta . . ."

We do that because we think that people are staring at us, sensing our inadequacy, noting our flaws, mocking our clumsiness. But perhaps, sadly (though, for the purpose of this book, perhaps not—perhaps humorously instead), nobody is noticing. Everybody is too busy worrying that they look like idiots to care about you.

If you think that none of this applies to you, just take a look at your picture in your high school yearbook. Because closer to the surface than you think is that awkward adolescent hoping that people like her and praying that nobody notices how much she hopes that people like her and knowing that if people knew what an idiot she was, they'd never like her. Or maybe not. Maybe you'd just see how funny you looked back then and have a good laugh. Either way it's worthwhile.

One activity that can bring out feelings of idiocy is singing. Sometimes it's because you're belting out a tune to yourself (That sounds violent, doesn't it? "You've been a very bad tune. I'm a gonna give you a belting that you won't soon forget!") and you're feeling good—you're sure that you sound just like Whitney Houston. Then you look up and realize that you're not by yourself—people are watching you (if you're in a car or a house with picture windows) and perhaps even hearing you (if you're in a plane, wearing headphones, and listening to "Pop Goes the Country" or "The Now Sound").

Sometimes it's because you're singing with a group of people and you don't know the lyrics to the song. Then you have to play that little game we always play. We mumble through the words we don't know, but then to make up for it, we sing the chorus really, really loud.

We're hoping the others are thinking, "I guess she didn't wanna sing on that little mumbly part back there. Obviously she knows the song—she sang the chorus *really* loud. She is cool."

Have you ever heard somebody sing some lyrics that you've never sung before, and you realize you've never sung the right words in that song? You hear them and all of a sudden you say to yourself, " 'Life in the Fast Lane?' *That's* what they're saying right there? 'Life in the Fast Lane?' " You think, "Why have I been singing 'Wipe in the Vaseline?' How many people have heard me sing 'Wipe in the Vaseline?' I am an idiot." But it sounds like that, you know?

There are certain songs you just know have parts where there aren't any real lyrics, because nobody can figure them out even after hearing the song over and over and over again. For instance, that Aretha Franklin song "Respect." Everybody gets the part: *"R-E-S-P-E-C-T. Find out what it means to me. R-E-S-P-E-C-T."* But what follows is anybody's guess. To me it's either *"Da cha, te ee cee tee. Ho!"* or *"Something about a tee-pee. Ho!"* But then everybody is back on board with *"Sock it to me. Sock it to me. Sock it to me."*

Sometimes it's just as embarrassing to get the words to a song right. I think in the seventies we really had some songs that were just idiotic songs, and the lyrics were clear as can be. Do you remember that song by Three Dog Night, "Joy to the World"? It started off with "Jeremiah was a bullfrog." It was catchy, so you wanted to sing. And then we were hooked, and we were just singing along . . . *"Jeremiah was a bullfrog. Was a good friend of mine. I never understood a single word he said, but I helped him drink his wine."*

Of course that made perfect sense to us. Why should we question that? We've all had friends who were frogs. We didn't fully understand what they were saying, but if it seemed like they wanted you to help them drink some wine, you did it. They would always have some mighty fine wine with 'em, too. Frogs could get ahold of that stuff.

But back to feeling like an idiot. Two places that tend to bring out the "Oh my God, I'm such a nincompoop" in most of us are elevators and public bathrooms. Now, the difference between an elevator and a public bathroom is . . . Wait. If you don't already know the difference between an elevator and a public bathroom, nothing I say is going to be of much help. In the best-case scenario, you're going to be standing in a stall for a long time, wondering why you're not going anywhere. I don't even want to think about the worst-case scenario.

When we're inside an elevator we feel we have to look above us at the floor numbers changing, as if it's by the force of our will that the elevator is rising. If you want to make others in the elevator feel uncomfortable, stay facing the back wall after you enter. The downside of this little gag is that you're pretty likely to miss your floor.

We always do this: we walk up to an elevator, someone's already there, they're waiting, they've pushed the button, the button is lit. We walk up and push the button, thinking, "Obviously you didn't push it correctly. I'll have to push it myself. *Now* the elevator will come." Then someone else walks up and they push the button again. Suddenly you're offended. You want to say, "You idiot, I pushed it, he pushed it." Then, to the original pusher, "Can you believe people?"

Or, if you go to the elevator by yourself, you push the button, you wait for the elevator to come, the elevator doesn't come. You push the button six more times. Like that's helping. As if the elevator's thinking, "Oh, a half dozen people are there now. I better hurry. I thought it was just that one woman. I was resting. Oh no, I . . . , I could lose my job! I could become stairs!"

In a public bathroom you're in your own little individual private stall, actually going to the bathroom. For some reason either you forgot to lock the door, or the lock is gone. Suddenly, a perfect stranger opens the door on you. They look at you. You always look at them the same way (sort of a cross between a deer caught in the headlights and a deer caught doing something else, I'm not sure what). They close it immediately and always say, "Oh, I'm sorry." Then we say, "It's okay."

We don't mean this. I think we'd be surprised if they turned around and came back in, actually. "Oh-oh!" "You said it was all right. Hey everybody, come on in! She said it was okay! Get Julie! This is Julie. And you are? There's no need to holler. Let's go, Julie. Yeah, she said it was okay, I wouldn't have just walked in."

It's just so scary if there's no lock on that door; you're so vulnerable at that time. You're scared someone's going to push the door open on you. Imagine if someone had an aerial view of what we looked like in there, trying to keep the door shut. The positions that we have ourselves in. Then we have the *"em-em"* noise, that territory cough that we use. Somehow it scares people away. *"Eeemmmm."*

But, even if there is a lock, there are some people who will continue to try to open the door until you say, "Somebody's in here." What are they thinking? "It's just stuck, I know it. Just somebody's shoes they left in there earlier. Get the ramrod, this one is tight."

Some of the bathrooms are fancy, they have the railings on each side of the toilet, and you might assume that's for the elderly or the handicapped. It's really for people who are paranoid about catching germs—they can balance themselves above the toilet. That iron cross is hard to do, I tell you that. And the dismount! You need a spotter, you do. That's why women go in pairs—"I'm going. Spot me." And when you do an incredible job the judges (you bet there are judges in there) yell, "TEN!"

Sometimes you need those bars, don't you? Sometimes you walk in, the seats are wet. That is a horrible experience. Have you ever just not been thinking, you're in a hurry, you just walk in, you sit, "OH! Eeeesh!!" How does this happen? I mean, what are these women doing in there?

I'm sorry. I got carried away.

I think we do some idiotic things out of habit. Have you ever noticed that whenever you're with someone and you taste something that tastes bad, you always want the person with you to taste it immediately?

"That was disgusting, taste it. Taste it, it's gross. Taste how bad it is." And they always do.

Or, do you ever run out of room on the front of the letter you're writing then write "Over" on the bottom of the letter? We're not giving the person getting the letter much credit. It's not like if it wasn't there, they'd get to the bottom of the page, " '. . . and so Kathy and I went shopping and we—' Now that's the craziest thing. I don't know why she just ended that way. I hope nothing happened to her. She managed to seal the envelope. She must have gotten it to a mailbox somehow.

"Could it be this way? On the back? Never mind, don't call her, I found it. It was on the back. I followed the arrow."

....

Sometimes I feel like an idiot when I'm with people who have more power than me. I don't mean someone like Hercules (though he probably would make me feel uncomfortable; the age difference alone—a few thousand years, I'm guessing—would make it hard for us to find things in common to talk about), I mean someone who has power over me. I mean policemen. I mean policemen who pull me over when I've been speeding.

I get nervous, so I try to lighten things up by using humor. And you know what? I'm always amazed that people (and by people I mean policemen) don't have the same sense of humor that I do.

For instance, I was pulled over in Los Angeles last week. I was driving—I was speeding. It was obvious I was speeding; I was going very, very fast. So, this policeman pulls me over. He comes up to the window of the car and says, "You know why I pulled you over?" And so I said, "Because of the dead bodies in the trunk?" To make a long story short, he didn't see the comedy in my remark. Like I said, no sense of humor.

Do you ever lie to a policeman when you get pulled over for speeding? If you look real good that day, you might think you can flirt your way out of the ticket. But, unfortunately, we usually don't dress anticipating a traffic ticket. We're usually wearing some horrible outfit that we just threw on to go out and buy some Häagen-Dazs ice cream. But, we try flirting anyway, and nine times out of ten we end up feeling like idiots (the tenth time we feel even worse).

"Hi, I think Nehru jackets are sexy—don't you, officer? HA, HA, HA. Well, anyway, listen—you know what happened? And I think you'll find this funny—well, not funny, but, well . . . Anyway, okay, I was in my house and I·got a phone call from my mother. She said,

'Ellen honey.' That's what she calls me. Well, that's my name—not the honey part—Ellen. Honey's just an endearing term. You can call me Ellen Honey. Anyway, she asked me to 'rush' over—that's the word she used, 'rush.' I said are you okay? She just said, 'Hurry, *please*, hurry.' That's what she said, 'Hurry, please.' Well, you heard what she said. Well, you didn't hear her, but you heard me saying what she said. Anyway, I just hung up. I said, 'Okay, bye.' First I said okay, bye, then I hung up really fast and threw this horrible outfit on—because I was naked—doing some aerobics. I like to keep in shape. I'm single so I feel it's important to look my best for men because that's my job as a woman to look good. Because that's important, being single and a woman. I date a lot of guys; I'm not seeing anyone seriously at this particular time, not that I just go out with anyone—that would be trampy—I have to know a person fairly well first before I would go out and I don't think it should always be the man that pays for the dates. I find it's hard to meet decent people. Well, I'm shy—normally. You're easy to talk to though. I don't know what it is about you, there's something very special, unique. I can't quite put my finger on it. Anyway, woo, it's hot today, isn't it?"

Then you bat your eyelashes in what you hope is a sexy way. Then the policeman hands you the ticket and drives away. Then you feel like an idiot for the rest of the day.

Another thing that we do that can make us feel like we're not only idiots, but crazy idiots to boot (to boot is human, to forgive divine) is talk to ourselves. It's hard to walk down the street these days without hearing somebody talking to themselves. In fact, it's safe to assume that anybody you see walking down the street is talking to themselves. Sometimes people walk in groups of two or more to disguise that they're each having their own individual conversations, but they don't fool me.

"You crazy people are talking to yourselves!" I yell out at them.

But, trapped in their own tiny little worlds, they never hear me. Or maybe they don't hear me because I'm in my car with the windows rolled up. Either way, it's safe to say that something is going on.

Though most people engage in what scientists call "Talkee to Selfee," I never talk to myself.

"Oh, yes I do."
"Oh, no I don't."
"Oh, yes I do."
"Oh, no I don't."
"Oh, yes I do."
"Oh, no I don't."

Author's Note: This conversation was supposed to go on for another ninety pages, and in my mind would have gotten funnier and funnier (I swear, after fifty pages you would have just been screaming with laughter) and, at the same time, fulfilled my obligation to turn in a book of at least 60,000 words.

My editor tried to convince me that this wasn't a good idea. I said, "Is too." He said, "Is not." I said, "Is too." He then said he wasn't going to fall into that trap and that furthermore, none of those words would be counted in the 60,000 that I owe him.

"Why?" I asked. He replied something that to my ear sounded like, "Blah blah blah blah blah blah blah blah blah blah blah blah blah blah blah blah blah blah blah blah blah blah blah blah blah blah blah blah blah blah blah blah blah blah blah blah blah blah blah blah blah blah blah blah blah blah blah blah blah blah blah blah blah . . ." This would have gone on most humorously, but my cold-hearted editor said he wouldn't count any of the blahs as words either.

Finally, when my editor was unable to convince me to change what I saw as my personal vision of what this book should be, my editor's lawyers tried a different approach —something about breach of contract and wanting their money back, I think. Well, we all had a good laugh, after which I completely caved in.

So back to the story, which, in case you forgot, is about talking to yourself.

"Oh, yes I do."
"Oh, no I don't. Hey, go behind that door."
"Okay." *SLAM!!!!* "Hey, you fooled me. Let me back in."
"No, I've got a book to write. Leave me alone."
"Okay. Sorry. Good-bye."

Now where was I? Oh, right. Though most people do talk to themselves, a lot of people don't. But don't get me wrong, they would like to learn how. So, for their benefit, I thought I'd jot down a few words on how they can join the majority and learn the art of self-conversation.

The main advantage of talking to yourself is that sometimes you're the only person who wants to talk to you. Unfortunately this could be because you are extremely boring. If that's the case, then talking to yourself can be a benefit to both you and the outside world— sparing others the expense of listening to you and your mundane ramblings.

Other times, you are the only person available to talk with. Maybe you're in solitary confinement or stranded on a desert isle, or, in the worst-case scenario, mistakenly buried alive. But, luckily for you, you've been buried alive with this book—even though it may be difficult to turn the pages. Also, the lighting probably isn't that good.

Then again, when you're buried alive, eye strain is probably the least of your worries.

Some people need a crutch in learning to talk to themselves, so they talk to their television sets first. If for some reason you feel that talking to a TV is less insane than talking to yourself, then more power to you. If you're not sure how to begin talking to your TV, here are a few sample starter phrases:

"Oh boy, this is going to be fun fun funny."

"Look out behind you!"

"I think you're lying. I don't think it's going to rain tomorrow. What do you say about them apples, Mr. Weatherman?"

"Oh yeah, laugh while you got the chance, you criminal scum. Because I got the feeling that in a few minutes that laugh is gonna be wiped off your face by Barnaby Jones, P.I."

After you've gotten the hang of talking to your television you can begin the weaning process by moving on to talking to your radio. If you already sing along with your radio, this will be especially easy for you; though you may want to switch from a music station to talk radio—which, I should note, was specifically designed for people who talk to themselves. If you already sing along to talk radio, well . . . I don't know what to say. You're on your own.

From there on, the weaning process will be easier and easier for you. You've already moved from talking to your TV to talking to your radio. You follow this by talking to your toaster ("Oh yes, make it brown and crisp, just the way I like it."), then to your toast, then your pen, then your pencil, then your eraser, then you talk to a tiny piece of lint in your pocket, and finally you're ready, willing, and able to talk to yourself.

Remember, a person who talks to herself is a healthy person. There's nothing wrong with it. In fact, there was a survey done on people who talk to themselves. . . .

"No, there wasn't."

"Yes, there was. Hey, how did I get back in here?"

"I had a key to the door, ha ha ha."

"The survey said that 90 percent of all people talk to themselves."

"I'm crazy. I'm just making that up."

"Oh, no I'm not. I read it; it's healthy."

"I'm just saying that because I want to feel better about myself."

I'm sorry, but I'm going to have to stop right here. I and myself have an appointment to go to couples therapy to try to work out some of these issues. In the meantime, good luck in talking to yourselves.

ellen's sure-fire

cures for the

things that ail ye

....

For a headache...

Contrary to what you may have heard, I am not a doctor. I do not play a doctor on TV (if you think that I do, then you either have some sort of attention disorder or you've been watching the wrong show). I have not even played "Doctor" for a very long time—at least fifteen years . . . okay, ten.

I do not own a stethoscope. Your medical insurance, no matter how good, will never cover anything that I do. If you were to see me on the street and yell out, "Hey, Doc, how's it going?" I would walk away without responding (thinking to myself that you either mistook me for somebody else or were potentially dangerous). I cannot legally prescribe drugs.

I have no medical training whatsoever. Since I was raised a Christian Scientist, in high school I was excused from all science classes; I wasn't supposed to learn about the human body. On the plus side, I never had to dissect a frog. (I don't see why anybody has to dissect a frog these days; I know I'd be upset if a giant frog came to earth and decided that he wanted to dissect humans, and I bet that nine out of ten Americans would agree with me in regard to the giant frog. The tenth guy . . . well, he's the kind of person that, if you happen to see him walking down the street, it's probably best that you avoid eye contact.)

The negative side of being excused from all those science classes was that for the longest time I didn't know anything about the human body at all. When my stomach hurt, I said I had a stomach*cake*—I didn't know it was stomachache. While that sort of mistake is cute in a four-year-old, in a teenager it raises a few eyebrows. There are still parts of the human body that I'm just learning about now (internal parts—I know the outside really well; I know my hands, my legs, those ten little things at the end of my feet, and everything else).

All that being said, despite my lack of even the flimsiest credential, I have some advice on how to cure some common ailments that might bother you. I know nothing about nothing, but these are things that have either worked for me occasionally, or things that I've never tried, but feel strongly enough will work nonetheless. I think that you're going to find them extremely useful.

Hiccups

We get hiccups when our esophagus and trachea get into a fight over who is better friends with the gallbladder. When you divide the word *hiccups* into two parts, you get hic and cups. If there is any significance to that, scientists have yet to find it—though, to be fair to scientists, they're probably not looking very hard.

CURES FOR HICCUPS

While holding your breath (or the breath of the person standing next to you), swallow three thousand times. Immediately shampoo your hair, but don't use conditioner. Repeat.

Hold a kitten on your lap and pet it gently on its little head while singing any song by Air Supply (except from their first album).

With your head bent to a thirty-five-degree angle, bite on a slice of lemon with one eye open and the other closed. If you have an additional eye, do whatever you want with it (your eye, not the lemon).

Start hopping for approximately five minutes, scream as loud as you can, "Hey Mr. Tally Man, tally me bananas!" then do a backward flip. This should only be done if you have plenty of room.

Wearing nothing but a Viking helmet and snowshoes, watch reruns of *Dynasty*.

Call up Tokyo and order Moo Goo Gai Pan. When the delivery man comes, tip him generously. If you live in Tokyo, then call up Belgium and order anything except sweet potatoes.

The Common Cold

Research shows that the common cold is not as common as most people think it is—it's even more so!! It's so common you wouldn't be out of line to call it a floozy. A lot of so-called experts have a lot of so-called cures for the so-called common (so-called) cold. Mine are better. And I should know; I'll have had my current cold for three years this March.

CURES FOR THE COMMON COLD

Starve a cold, feed a fever. Punch a cold in the stomach, kick a fever in its ass. Strangle a cold, tickle a fever with an ostrich feather. Throw toilet paper at a cold's house, make a fever sit on a whoopie cushion.

In treating a cold remember the three C's: Cheese, Cheese, and Cottage Cheese (actually those are four C's).

While sitting in an icy, cold bath, smoke a carton of menthol cigarettes and eat plenty of—you guessed it—cheese.

Only eat solids, avoid all fluids (except for liquid cheese).

Steal the bedding from a hospital, wrap yourself in it, and pretend to be The Mummy.

Drive your car while sitting in the passenger seat. Oh, did I tell you, I put a bomb in your car, and it will go off if you drive under fifty miles an hour. What do you do? What do you do?

With unwashed hands, touch your eyes, nose, ears, tongue, and throat as many times as you can in one minute.

Tease your neighbor's hamster. If your neighbor doesn't have a hamster, then tease your neighbor's ferret.

Walking Pneumonia

I don't know who had the bright idea of teaching pneumonia how to walk, but I'd like to find that dunderhead before he decides he wants to teach it how to drive. Some people don't know how to leave well enough alone. I'm not trying to imply that regular pneumonia is "well enough," I'm just saying . . . Well, I'm sure you know what I mean.

CURES FOR WALKING PNEUMONIA
Sit down!

Headaches

A lot of people will tell you that if you have a headache, you should take an aspirin or some other type of pain reliever. What they don't tell you is that aspirin and its pals cost money. You have to invest something like two dollars. Sure, my book is $19.95, but look what else you're getting . . . Okay, let's get past the money and change the subject.

A lot of people will tell you that if you have a headache you should pinch that little flap of skin between your thumb and forefinger. What they don't tell you is maybe you don't feel like pinching that flap, or maybe you've been dieting so you don't even have a flap anymore. I'll tell you one thing. I wish I had never written this paragraph, because now I'm starting to get a headache.

CURES FOR A HEADACHE
Pummel a bag of chattering teeth, rubber chickens, and other joke items with a shillelagh. If you don't own a shillelagh, then either borrow one from a policeman or rent one.

Set your clothes dryer for an hour, sit on top, and "ride 'em cowboy!"

Pinch the flap between your neck and your waist.

When your neighbors aren't home, sneak into their house, fix yourself a drink, then see if they have anything weird in their closets. If they're gone long, take a nap on their new couch.

Eat pancakes and keep eating them until your headache goes away.

Go to the nearest high school and take the SATs again.

Pretend to be Swedish for a whole day. This might not cure your headache, but it's bound to be a lot of fun, by yimminy.

Sit as close to your television as you possibly can and watch any Ernest movie. Either that or go to an ABBA concert. It's your choice.

I think that I have proved conclusively that I am not in any way, shape, or form in the medical profession. If you persist in thinking otherwise, then there is a good chance that you are, if not completely insane, more than halfway there. And don't go giving me any of that "Laughter is the best medicine" business. If I get strep throat, I'd much rather take penicillin than watch a lot of Benny Hill reruns.

the last

chapter

....

The lawyers have reminded
me that the book must be
at least 60,000 words.

I really feel that this is a complete, well-rounded, fleshed-out piece of work—an eclectic book. A little something for everyone in the family to enjoy. And if it were up to me, I'd say "The End," but it seems that contractually I have not fulfilled my duty—the lawyers have reminded me that the book must be at least 60,000—that's *sixty thousand*—words.

"Wow," you say. Or maybe not—maybe some of you said "wow" or simply thought it in your head. Those of you who did not react at all surely have no concept of the pressure to write that many words, for that is a *whole* lot of words.

In conclusion (and, just between you and me, in order to get the law off my back), I'd like to say a few things that perhaps I neglected or merely didn't expand on or go into detail about. For instance, I have enjoyed writing this book over the past year. It's been a learning experience that I shall never forget. My one regret is that I don't know how to type so I did not use a computer. I have written the entire book in longhand, and I'm not positive, but I believe my right arm is now considerably larger than the left—because I am right-handed.

Sometimes I think much faster than I write, therefore . . . Hey, is *therefore* one word or two? I think it should be two even if it's one word because it is actually two words joined together—it's certainly long enough to be counted as two words. Anyway, sometimes I've misspelled words because I can't write as fast as I think, and I have worried that my publisher will think I am stupid—although spelling should not represent the level of intelligence of a human being.

I prefer to use the term *human being* not because it is two words, but because I like it better than person—that is just my personal taste. I do use the word *person* as well, but I just sometimes prefer *human being*. What does that mean, anyway? I understand saying he is a human—but a *human being*? I also enjoy using the words *homo sapiens*, from time to time. It's funny how many words there are for people (see, there's another one right there). *People* is a term or word used for more than one person. But still we say, "There were a whole bunch of people." Why? You know what I'm saying: if people is already plural, why do we need to say a whole bunch? I'm not saying you, the reader, do that. But surely some people do. I know I have used the phrase before many times.

I just glanced out the window—what a beautiful day it is today. It's so clear I can see the mountains. I live in the Hollywood Hills, and sometimes Los Angeles is so smoggy that I can't see the mountains. But today it's so clear I can see them.

I'm sitting at my desk with my computer next to me—almost mocking me. I do have a computer to store all of my writing on disk. I just type so slowly that I can't write this book on it. I rarely sit at my desk and write. I have written most of this book on airplanes, in hotel rooms, in coffeehouses, in bed, in the kitchen—everywhere but at my desk. Sitting at a desk reminds me too much of school. I hated school. I'm so glad to be out. But when I look back on it, I wish I had paid attention more, studied, learned a lot more. So if you're reading this and you're still in school, don't do what I did. You go ahead and enjoy this time in your life; it only happens once. Knowledge is power and you need power in this world. You need as many advantages as you can get.

There are two little birds outside my window—I'm not sure what kind they are—and to be perfectly honest (and I have been all throughout my book, so why stop now), I don't really care. I believe them to be blue jays—they are "talking" to each other. One will skwawk or squawk or however you spell it, then his pal will respond. It's quite obnoxious and makes it hard for me to concentrate on my poignant writing.

I do wonder what the commotion is all about. What on earth could they be arguing about? Is it possible that they are lovers and in a lovers' quarrel? Did one bird flirt with another bird and the other bird found out? I'm sure that must happen—don't you think so? If you care to respond send all letters to Bantam. Because if it weren't for this 60,000-word clause, I would have been finished and I would not have gone this far and I wouldn't have been sitting here being disturbed by these loud birds. So, it's all their fault, really.

Well, I think I am just about to reach my quota, so thank you for hanging in there with me. (If some of you stopped on the last chapter, it's okay because that is really where my book ended—this is just for the lawyers.) But if people stopped reading it—then who am I writing to? No one will ever know that I am telling them it's okay to have stopped there.

I am sitting here writing to myself and to the lawyers. Maybe I should say something to them because I know they are reading. "Hello, lawyers. How are you?" Hey, maybe they aren't reading, they're just counting the words. In that case, I don't even have to form sentences. I can make up total nonsense. Nothing has to mean anything; I can just look around and write down everything I'm looking at or thinking about and no one will ever know. Fireplace, firewood, candles, pictures, lamp, vase, tulips, clock, television, rug, bed, computer, printer, dog, telephone, monitor, books, globe, chair, hats, shoes.

THE END

Phew!

100% of your daily requirement.

the new album

Ellen DeGeneres
an hour of stand-up comedy

IN STORES
OCTOBER '96

*Look what people are saying about
Leslie Kelly's Santori stories...*

"Kelly's sweet, made-for-one-another couple and her warmhearted Italian family are impossible to resist."
—*Romantic Times BOOKreviews* on
That's Amore ("There Goes the Groom")

"*Don't Open Till Christmas* by Leslie Kelly is a present in itself where the humor and the sizzling sex never stop. Top Pick!"
—*Romantic Times BOOKreviews*

"Leslie Kelly's Christmas-themed Harlequin Blaze [novel] has plenty of good things to be cheerful about: an adorable look at romantic Stooges dealing with over-the-top Christmas festivities, a hero that is simply too adorable for words, and plenty of nicely written sexual tension to keep the worst chill at bay."
—*Mrs. Giggles* on *Don't Open Till Christmas*

"Well-written and fast-paced, *Asking for Trouble* is a page-turning delight and a delicious contemporary nod to the Gothic novel."
—*The Romance Reader's Connection*

"Leslie Kelly's entry ably combines the traditional spooky elements of a gothic with the modern sensibilities of a more contemporary tale. The result is a highly enjoyable read I ate up like a starving person."
—*All About Romance* on *Asking for Trouble*

Blaze™

Dear Reader,

Well, this is it. I've finally come to the end of my journey with the Santoris of Chicago.

I've had such a fantastic time creating this family, revisiting them now and again and getting to know them a little more with each book. Honestly, when I wrote the first story—"Sheer Delights" in the *Behind the Red Doors* collection—I had no idea that I was stepping into the lives of a whole Chicago Italian clan for the next five years. And I'm so very grateful to my editor and my readers for supporting me as I snuck back for visits now and then, both in novellas and in Harlequin Blaze novels.

This particular book allowed me to close the overall story and also to really stretch myself as a writer. Being asked to launch the new Blaze ENCOUNTERS miniseries was an honor. Actually sitting down to write five individual-but-connected stories in one book was an incredible challenge. I wanted them to stand alone, I wanted them to be different from each other, with different types of plots, characters and conflicts. And, of course, I wanted them to be hot.

I think I accomplished all of that in this book. I sincerely hope you agree.

Happy reading!

Leslie Kelly

LESLIE KELLY
One Wild
Wedding Night

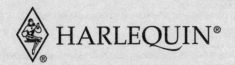

HARLEQUIN®

TORONTO • NEW YORK • LONDON
AMSTERDAM • PARIS • SYDNEY • HAMBURG
STOCKHOLM • ATHENS • TOKYO • MILAN • MADRID
PRAGUE • WARSAW • BUDAPEST • AUCKLAND

ISBN-13: 978-0-373-79373-0
ISBN-10:   0-373-79373-1

ONE WILD WEDDING NIGHT

ABOUT THE AUTHOR

A two-time RWA RITA® Award nominee, eight-time *Romantic Times BOOKreviews* Award nominee and 2006 *Romantic Times BOOKreviews* Award winner, Leslie Kelly has become known for her delightful characters, sparkling dialogue and outrageous humor. Since the publication of her first book in 1999, Leslie has gone on to pen more than two dozen sassy, sexy romances. Honored with numerous other awards including the National Readers' Choice Award, Leslie writes sexy novels for Harlequin Blaze, and single-title contemporaries for HQN Books. Keep up with her latest releases by visiting her Web site, www.lesliekelly.com, or her blog site www.plotmonkeys.com.

Books by Leslie Kelly

To the Santori family. I know you're fictional...
but thank you for becoming so real in my heart
and in my mind.

And to my editor Brenda Chin. Thanks so much
for letting me take this family all the way to the
end. You are the best!

Prologue

SCHEDULING A JANUARY wedding in Chicago probably hadn't been among the world's best ideas. Especially since the Windy City had been humped all week by a meteorological snow monster that seemed to want to stick around for the entire winter.

Somehow, though, despite the thick, white flakes that had swirled down around the church, everything had gone as planned. And now a winter wonderland surrounded the hotel where the afternoon reception had been held.

In Izzie Santori's opinion, the day had been perfect.

"Happy, Cookie?" her new husband, Nick, asked as he kicked the door to their room shut. His hands were too full to do the job. Full of Izzie, still clad in her long-trained wedding gown.

"Deliriously."

He pressed a kiss on her throat as he lowered her onto her own feet. "Only you could make a white wedding gown look sinful."

"I'm a natural at sin."

"Don't I know it. I work with you, remember?"

Arching toward him, she twined her fingers in his black hair, which had grown out from its military cut since he'd left the marines. The length suited him, especially when he pulled the silky strands back into a ponytail at Leather and Lace, the upscale strip club where they both worked. "I'm so glad we had an early wedding so everyone from work could come."

"Me, too. I doubt that church has held so many strippers, cocktail waitresses and bouncers at one time before." He kissed his way to her earlobe. "You were so beautiful today, Iz. Like always, you made every other woman fade into insignificance."

"I did have some very pretty bridesmaids," she pointed out.

He nodded, lifting her hand to start unbuttoning the long row of tiny buttons at her wrist. "You did, not that they looked anything alike. Talk about variety."

That was true. Izzie's bridesmaids had certainly run the gamut. Her maid of honor—and cousin—Bridget, was a quiet, sweet-faced brunette who never had a harsh word for anyone. She'd been Izzie's best friend since childhood.

Bridget was nothing like Leah, a feisty stripper who worked with Izzie at the club. The girl was young and sweeter than anyone would suspect, given her rough background. Blond and bouncy Leah was definitely the antithesis of Izzie's sister Mia, with her short, jet-black hair and hard edge.

Mia's years as an attorney, prosecuting some pretty awful crimes, had made her even tougher than she'd been growing up. A fighter and a tomboy, Mia had eschewed big sister Gloria's good-girl desire to be a housewife and little sister Izzie's bad-girl desire to be a dancer. Frankly, Izzie had held her breath after asking Mia to be in the wedding, knowing it was *not* her sister's thing. But family was family. She'd come through.

Then there was Vanessa. While, like Mia, she had some serious attitude, Vanessa also oozed sex appeal and warmth. The stunning African American was a good friend of Izzie's from her Radio City days.

Finally came Gloria, the oldest Natale girl. Married, thirtysomething. Pretty in an Italian housewifey way. Gloria was bossy and old-school, which was why Izzie had both a maid *and* a matron of honor. Gloria would have been mortally offended if Izzie hadn't asked her.

Definitely a varied menu of bridesmaids. All of whom had looked stunningly beautiful in their dark red velvet gowns. All of whom were women she adored, for their strengths and their kindness, their intelligence and their loyalty. "They were so wonderful and supportive," she murmured.

"Well, hopefully some of my single cousins are keeping them company downstairs in the hotel lounge this evening."

"Sorry to disappoint your cousins, but Leah just led a group of them to a bar up the street."

Nick frowned for the first time in days. "In this weather?"

"It's stopped snowing and I'm sure the roads are slowly being cleared." Nibbling her lip Izzie added, "It's only a couple of blocks away and I paid the limo driver to make sure they got safely back here to their rooms tonight."

"Look out, Chicago, horny bridesmaids are on the prowl."

"I don't imagine *too* much can happen since Gloria's with them." Gloria was happily married to Nick's oldest brother. The mother of three had seemed relieved when her husband had offered to take their boys home so she could enjoy the night on the town with the rest of the bridesmaids. "She'll play chaperone."

"Oh, right. Chaperone to a lawyer, a bookkeeper, a stripper and a Rockette."

"You got something against strippers and Rockettes?" she asked, cocking a challenging brow.

He had finished working her sleeves open and slid around behind her to start on the long row of tiny buttons up the back of the dress. As he slid each one free, he kissed the tiny bit of skin revealed, sliding his lips over each of her vertebrae with heart-pounding restraint and sensuality.

"Uh-uh, Cookie. Some of my favorite people are strippers and Rockettes."

She dropped her head forward, sighing as he continued to undress her. Conversation was the last thing she wanted. Thoughts of her bridesmaids began to fade.

But before thrusting the whole subject out of her head altogether, she reassured them *both*. "They'll be fine. They're grown women, they're not driving, and they're in a group. What could possibly happen?"

* * * * *

Getaway

1

THROUGHOUT THE EXCITEMENT of the past week, Bridget Donahue had managed to keep a happy expression on her face. It hadn't been easy. Because while she *was* genuinely happy that her cousin Izzie had landed the guy she'd loved for years, Bridget had two big worries on her mind almost constantly.

First, she had to testify in a criminal trial against her former boss in two days. And second, her own experience with love had left her a little sour.

Not love, she reminded herself. She hadn't been in love with the guy who'd broken her heart. Damn it, she *hadn't*. She hadn't even gone on a real date with him.

But they'd kissed. Oh, that one day last August, they'd kissed wildly, passionately, right in her own office. And his kisses had left her weak in the knees. So, she supposed she *had* cared about him, maybe even more than she wanted to acknowledge. Dean Willis had snuck into her heart back when she'd thought him a simple used car salesman. That he'd done it intentionally was what made it so hard now.

Done it as part of his job. The bastard.

"Whatcha thinkin' about?" asked her cousin Gloria, Izzie's oldest sister. Though they sat at a table with the other bridesmaids, surrounded by the loud patrons of a trendy Chicago bar, Gloria had obviously noticed Bridget's pensive mood. "Sweating the trial?"

"A little. I've been dreading it. It looks like the defense has run out of motions and I have to testify this week."

The petite brunette, a mother of three who managed to pull off sexy *and* maternal, waved an airy hand. "They've got this guy cold. He was slime, laundering drug money through the car lot while pretending to be so nice." She frowned. "To think I liked his 'Come down to the most honest guy in town' commercials."

"Which just proves you have questionable taste," said the black-haired woman to Gloria's right, a slight grin on her lips.

Gloria smirked at her sister, Mia, who was the middle Natale sister. Wagging her left hand in the younger woman's face, she quipped, "A *married* woman with bad taste." Mia's single status was apparently especially rankling now that both her sisters had tied the knot.

"It's a good thing you're doing," Gloria said to Bridget. "More people need to get involved, step up and do what's right."

Mia jumped in. "I wish there were more people like you. Would sure have made my last job easier." Mia had, until recently, been a prosecutor in Pittsburgh. Now she was back in Chicago, though honestly, Bridget didn't see her cousin much more than she had before. Mia was a private one.

Bridget didn't doubt she was doing the right thing in testifying against Marty, her former boss at Honest Marty's Used Cars. But the trial, which started Monday, could also bring her face-to-face with *him*. Dean Willis. The FBI agent who'd used Bridget to get the evidence he needed against her boss.

"That doesn't look like an 'I'm nervous,' expression. Looks more like a 'who was that guy who knocked me on my ass' one." This came from Vanessa McKee, a friend of Izzie's from her days with the Rockettes. The striking woman wagged her eyebrows. "Come on, we've been sharing man tales."

"Not Mia," said Gloria, her tone saccharine sweet.

Her sister made a rude gesture, which Gloria ignored.

The last of their group, Leah, a sweet-faced young woman who worked with Izzie at a local strip club, tapped her fingers on the table and frowned. She was so cute, trying to look fierce when she resembled, more than anything, a Kewpie doll, with her blond curls, pink cheeks and full lips. "Ignore them. You don't have to tell us anything you don't want to, Bridget."

The others appeared to follow her lead and fell silent. Good. Bridget truly didn't want to talk about it. Only Izzie knew the full details—the way Dean Willis had feigned interest in her, then backed off the minute he'd realized she was not involved in her boss's illegal activities.

He'd made a fool of her. And there was no way Bridget was going to talk about that. Especially not to a bunch of tipsy bridesmaids who'd just come from a gloriously romantic wedding.

Fortunately, the subject quickly changed, everyone distracted from Bridget's problems by the sight of a tall, rock-solid hottie walking by their table. The distraction was a good time for her to take her leave. "I really am tired. I think I'll head out now. I'll send the car right back for the rest of you."

A chorus of nos followed, but she didn't relent. She'd had a long few weeks. As Izzie's maid of honor, she'd been planning showers and bachelorette parties. All while worrying herself to almost physical sickness over the trial.

Besides, she'd never been into the bar scene. She preferred quiet evenings with someone special. Not that there'd been anyone special in a long time. And considering how hard it had been to get over Dean, she didn't see that changing soon.

To her surprise, Leah rose, as well. "I have to nap off those mai tais in case I decide to go in to work tonight," she said with a yawn.

After hugs good-night, Bridget led the way to the exit. The place was packed and she and Leah got a lot of looks. It was probably due to their lovely red gowns…though, Leah, at least, was sexy in a girlish way, with a body to die for.

Bridget, on the other hand, was no inspiration for lust. She was a bookkeeper, with boring, straight brown hair and an average figure. Still, the looks she got said the men in this place were too far gone on twenty-dollar martinis to notice.

Once outside, Bridget spied their stretch limousine. Then she saw another one, very similar, parked just beyond it. "Which one is ours?" she mumbled with a frown.

Hoping Gloria would know, she decided to give her cousin a call rather than go back through the club. But when she opened her tiny purse, she realized she couldn't. "Oh, no. I lost my cell phone." While in the ladies' room earlier, she'd dropped her bag, spilling its contents. She must have lost the phone then.

Leah, a few steps ahead, swung around. Bridget waved her on. "Go on. No sense in both of us going back."

Without waiting to see if Leah obeyed, she hurried inside. The bouncer offered her a smile. "Back so soon?"

"I think I lost my cell phone in the ladies' room."

The guy took pity on her, obviously seeing her distress. "There's a back way, if you don't want to go through the club." He opened a door marked Employees Only. "Go to the end of this hallway. The last door on the right comes out by the bathrooms."

Smiling her thanks, she followed his directions. The long, narrow passageway seemed far removed from the bright neon beer signs and loud patrons next door. Her own footsteps echoed loudly, reiterating with every tap that she was entirely alone.

Following the directions, she found the ladies' room easily. "Oh, please be here," she whispered as she went inside.

As far as public restrooms went, this one wasn't *too* nasty. Still, she hid a grimace as she bent down and felt around on the dingy, tiled floor where she'd dropped the purse. Her fingers touched moisture. *Ick.* Then…

"Yes!" Pay dirt. Tucking the phone into her purse, she hurried out, heading back into the dark, private hallway.

It was *so* dark that Bridget didn't even see the man until she almost ran right into him. He stood in the shadows, silent and still, tall and broad. Maybe even dangerous. Why she should think that, she didn't know. He could very well be hanging around outside the ladies' room waiting for his date.

The Employees Only side of the *empty* ladies' room.

Uh-huh. Bridget's breath sped up. Her entire body went on instant fight-or-flight alert.

Don't be ridiculous, you're in a public place.

Right. There were a hundred people in the next room. So why was her heart racing just because she'd almost walked right into a very tall, very broad, black-clothed man who emanated heat and hinted of danger? One who seemed to be intentionally clinging to the shadows. One who smelled like…

"Oh, God," she whispered, instinctively reacting to that warm aftershave she'd only ever smelled on one other man before.

The heart that had been racing before stopped for a full second before bursting into a rapid thud hard enough to be heard in the next room. Her thoughts racing, she strove for calm…but could find none. Anger, fear, regret, they all fought for control of her emotions.

She tried to spin around, to hurry back the way she'd come. But his firm hand on her arm stopped her, squeezing and keeping her still. "Stay here."

"Let go of me."

"You have to come with me. Now."

"I'm not going anywhere with you," she snapped. "Get your hands off me."

"We don't have time for this." He pulled her tightly against him, though, judging by the way he kept his attention fixed on the distant end of the hallway, where Bridget had come past the bouncer, that was where his true interest lay.

Good. Because toward the big, burly bouncer was exactly where Bridget intended to go. *He* could deal with this overbearing man whose distraction had caused him to finally loosen his grip. She took advantage of it, trying to spin away. Seeing a sliver of light emerge as the door at that end of the hallway opened, she prepared to shout for help.

But she couldn't. Because before she could make a

sound, she was hauled up against a big, rock-hard body. And a firm, hot mouth was descending onto hers. Gasping, she inadvertently parted her lips and he took full advantage, plunging his tongue against hers, stealing her breath and every bit of her brainpower. Bridget just hung there like a rag doll, too shocked to pull away and punch his face off.

To be honest, she also didn't pull away because she was starting to like it. But as she began to mentally admit that—and to contemplate fully participating in the kiss—he let her go.

"They're gone."

He was cold, determined, not at all breathless or shaky the way Bridget felt. Which infuriated her further. She opened her mouth to tell him that, but before she could, his strong hand came up to cover it. "Don't make a sound."

Her intelligence had returned, along with her anger and she was done taking orders or being distracted. She tried to scream, biting at his fingers.

"Damn it," he muttered, lifting her off the floor as if she weighed nothing. He reached for a fire alarm on the wall. "I'll explain later. Right now, we just have to get out of here."

Without another word, he yanked the handle down. A piercing siren wailed overhead. And before Bridget had even had time to acknowledge the fact that he really had set off the fire alarm in this crowded club, she found herself tossed completely over his shoulder. She emitted an *oomph* as her stomach hit those flexing muscles. Scorching heat enveloped her, every inch of her body curled against the man, touching him—though *not* in a typical man-woman position.

With his hand cupping her bottom and her palms pressed flat against his back, she could hardly process everything that had happened in the last few minutes. It didn't help that the achingly sensual scent of his skin filled her head and rattled her thoughts. Or that she could feel his warm breath against her hip, through her coat and dress.

From the sound of it, loud patrons of the club were heading for the front door. But she couldn't focus on that. Couldn't focus on anything except the feel of him. And without saying another word, he pushed through a rear emergency door and carried her out into the cold night.

It was really happening. Bridget was being kidnapped, right out of a public place.

By Dean Willis. The FBI agent she'd spent the past several months loathing.

SPECIAL AGENT DEAN WILLIS had been following Bridget Donahue for three days. Long, painful days during which he'd mentally kicked himself a hundred times for ever letting this happen. Any of it.

He regretted getting involved with her. Taking advantage of her. Using her.

Falling for her. Hard.

Oh, she'd never believe it, especially because of the way she'd found out that he was working undercover. She'd known him as nice, solid, boring car salesman Dean Willis, with the ill-fitting suits, the shaggy hair and the crooked glasses.

He'd wanted her to know him like that. To like him, to trust him. And he'd played on that like and trust, needing to know—to be sure—that Bridget had not been involved with her employer's financial games. Her boss had been cleaning up some filthy money for a couple of local drug-dealing thugs.

Bridget Donahue had been his bookkeeper.

Everyone—including Dean, at first—had assumed she

was an accomplice. It was only after he'd met her that he'd begun to suspect everyone was wrong. He'd become determined to prove it, and he had—but only after he'd gotten close to her. Close enough to make her trust him. Close enough to make her care about him.

Close enough to care too much himself.

She had been—still was—the loveliest woman he'd ever met. Sweet and funny. Good-natured and intelligent. Everything he'd always wanted in a woman…but he'd had to use her.

So she had a right to hate him when the truth came out, when she'd walked into the dealership one morning and found him there, with his team, tearing the place apart and taking *Honest* Marty into custody. She hadn't wanted to hear a thing he had to say. She'd brushed him off, not sparing him a second thought,

She wouldn't have trusted him now if he'd come to her to tell her she was in danger.

So he hadn't come to her. He'd stayed out of sight, certain she hadn't spotted him. But oh, he'd definitely kept his eyes glued to her. Sometimes walking close enough behind her to breathe in the remnants of her soft, flowery perfume lingering in the air after she'd passed through it. He'd kept his hawkish gaze on her slim, vulnerable back, the long, light brown hair falling in a curtain over her shoulders. He'd caught tantalizing glimpses of her creamy cheek and her full lips when she smiled and heard the echo of her laughter more than once as she'd participated in her cousin's wedding.

All the while knowing someone wanted to kill her.

"Damn it, put me down," she snapped.

He complied, lowering her to stand on her own feet, though he kept one arm around her waist to prevent her from making a run for it. With the other, he unlocked the door of his SUV. It was parked out back, behind a Dumpster, near a few cars in private employee spaces. Unimpeded by the crowd probably gathering out front…with easy access to a rear alley. He'd left it here when he'd followed Bridget's limo earlier this evening, anticipating the possible need for a fast getaway.

"Let me go!"

"Shut up, Bridget, we're getting out of here. I'll explain everything later."

She wriggled and kicked, seeming to suddenly have eight arms and legs, all of which were battering at him, demanding her freedom. "I swear I'll scream."

"Nobody'll hear you over the emergency alarm," he replied, not a bit fazed by her threat. "Now get in and stay down… This is serious." He pushed her into the backseat. Knowing he couldn't trust her not to make a break for it the moment he moved to the driver's seat, he took her chin in his hands. Staring into her blazing eyes, he said, "Someone's been following you."

"You," she spat.

"No," he replied, crouching down behind the open door. "Someone doesn't want you to testify next week and they're going to try to make sure that you don't."

Her mouth opened, then quickly snapped closed. Bridget's eyes narrowed and her brow scrunched as she tried to make sense of his words. To process the idea that someone might actually want to hurt her.

He still hadn't quite processed it. Because since the moment he'd found out—after being called in by the Bureau chief three days ago—he'd been operating on pure anger and adrenaline.

God help the bastard sent to harm her. When Dean found him, the guy was going to wish he hadn't been born.

"Trust me, Bridget," he asked, his voice low and resolute. He needed her to cooperate. Now. "I know you hate me, and that's understandable. But I swear to you, I'm trying to protect you."

She glared and he knew she was planning a sarcastic response. That sarcasm and strength were two of the things he liked about her, especially because they were so unexpected given her quiet demeanor and beauty.

Whatever she'd been about to say was cut off by the sound of sirens approaching. She glanced toward the building and the driveway leading to the front lot as if contemplating taking refuge among the crowd with the rescue workers. Then she looked back at Dean. The frown faded. And though the anger remained, the distrust disappeared from her expression.

The woman was furious, all right. But she was not stupid. She might hate him, but she knew he could protect her.

"All right. What is it you want me to do?"

2

DEAN HAD PROVED HIMSELF a liar several months ago when they'd met. But now, tonight, Bridget knew he was telling the truth. His tension and barely controlled fury spoke volumes about his genuine worry. For her. *The star witness.*

That was the only reason he was here, she knew enough about him to realize that much. It certainly wasn't out of any personal regard. The kiss he'd just laid on her had rocked her world as much as the ones they'd shared in her office last August. But they hadn't so much as caused *him* a tremor. She meant nothing to him—he'd made it clear that day when he'd let her be interrogated for hours by his other FBI buddies, who thought she had something to do with Marty's not-so-honest dealings.

Letting her be interrogated had been the least of his crimes. Letting her care about him…that was the one she couldn't forgive.

"Stay down," he barked as he started the vehicle, gunning the engine hard.

She did as he ordered, crouched in a ball on the backseat.

The SUV jerked and swayed, angling sharply to the right, almost knocking her to the floor. Dean's big hand appeared out of nowhere, blocking her fall with a firm grip on her shoulder.

God, she hated her own weakness for immediately sucking in a breath of pure excitement at the rough touch of his hand. "I'm fine," she managed to say between clenched teeth.

"Don't move."

As if she could.

"And don't pop your head up."

"I'm not a jackrabbit. Just pay attention to the road."

He didn't respond, but he removed his hand, putting it back on the wheel. He obviously needed it because he intentionally maneuvered in jerks and swerves as he tore off down the street, as if physically trying to shake off pursuit. He drove like it was a sunny, warm day with miles of dry blacktop in front of them. Not as though there'd been a blizzard up until this afternoon and patches of slick ice were lurking beneath snowdrifts, anxious to send a car into a deadly spin.

He drove that way for a good five minutes. Bridget watched him from between the front seats, seeing the way he leaned forward, his chest almost against the steering wheel. He stared out, his gaze constantly moving from side to side. But even that rapt attention couldn't keep him from almost fishtailing into the path of a long, black stretch limo.

"Watch out!" she yelled.

"You're supposed to be staying down."

"You're supposed to be *preventing* me from getting killed."

"I'm the one driving."

"Seems to me like you're the one almost wrecking," she muttered under her breath, even as he brought the SUV back under control and the limo driver honked his horn wildly.

Oh, did she wish she was in one just like it, preparing to go back to her hotel and her nice, plush bed. Rather than here. With him. The guy who messed with her head and filled her senses up with the musky smell of him and the big, strong sight of him and oh, Lord, his heat.

The Dean she'd known had been cute and endearing. Good-looking but usually appearing self-deprecating. Boyish.

There was nothing boyish about the man whose whole body was tense with adrenaline as they tried to outrun danger.

Danger. To *her.*

"Does someone really want to kill me?" she whispered.

Even in the low lighting from the dashboard, she saw the way his jaw jutted out and his eyes narrowed. "Yes."

It was almost too much to believe. Bridget was a big fan of crime shows and mystery novels, but the idea that *she* could be a target was so crazy she had trouble grasping it. "Is it Marty?"

He appeared to hear the note of hurt in her voice, which she just couldn't hide. She'd known Honest Marty since she was a kid growing up in the neighborhood. He'd been a nice, paternal, if slightly overbearing, boss. And he wanted her to *die?*

"Not Marty," Dean finally replied, sounding loathe to admit it. "His...former colleagues."

She didn't know why it relieved her that a bunch of drug dealers wanted her dead but one pudgy, blustery car dealer did not. But it was true. A little, anyway. "You're sure?"

He nodded. "He was the one who came forward with the information about the hit."

"The hit?" she yelped. "As in *hit man?*"

He reached back, seeming to want to calm her down with

a hand on her shoulder. But he didn't touch her shoulder. Instead, those strong, rough fingertips of his brushed her cheek. Lightly, carefully.

Bridget felt the touch clear down to the bottoms of her aching-in-spiked-heels feet.

He'd touched her only a few times in the past. And, like the passionate encounter they'd shared in her office, his touch had imprinted itself on her memory. The thoughts sometimes eased out of her subconscious to torment her during long, sleepless nights when she wondered why she couldn't get over him. Why the fully clothed kisses they'd shared had seemed much more intimate and erotic than the sex she'd had with other men.

Dean's fingers traced a delicate path on her cheek, but when his thumb dropped to her bottom lip, scraping across it in a sensual caress, he obviously realized what he was doing. He pulled his hand away quickly.

He cleared his throat. "You'll be fine."

Swallowing hard, Bridget rubbed the back of her hand against her cheek, which felt so cold again now. Trying to keep her thoughts strictly on the crisis that had made him haul her into his car, she asked, "What exactly did Marty say?"

"He had been keeping his mouth shut about his accomplices, until he got word that they were going to try to remove some of the evidence against him. Starting with *you*."

"I don't know anything!" she insisted, as she'd tried to explain to the other FBI agents and the prosecutor. "I never saw any drugs, never handled anything suspicious."

"It's not what you know, it's the context you can provide about his business. How much money *should* have been coming in versus how much did. Accounts you saw open and close." He lowered his voice, as if not liking what he had to say. "You are important to the case and Marty's former associates know it."

Yes. That's what the prosecutor had said.

The full implication of Dean's words finally washed over her and she sucked in a quick, hopeful breath. "So Marty's cooperating now?" Meaning maybe she wouldn't have to testify!

"Not exactly."

She sighed.

"He's not naming names, he's trying to score points by being cooperative *only* as it pertains to you. I think he's hoping whoever is after you will get caught and turn on his bosses so Marty doesn't have to."

"What a guy."

"Yeah, I'd really like to *thank* him one of these days."

Dean's tone suggested his "thank yous" would be punctuated with his fists.

She shivered a little, not only because of his audible rage, but because she still couldn't get over the strength and power of the man. She hadn't seen this side of him, not ever. He'd been the cute guy she worked with, then the cold investigator. She had never seen the powerful, enraged man.

"I think it's safe for you to sit up now."

Bridget did so, slowly rising, keeping her hands on the backs of the two front seats. She remained forward on the seat, her butt perched on the edge, her face leaning close to his shoulder. Close enough to smell him. To see the tiny hairs at the nape of his neck, with the hint of curl she'd loved in his much-less formal, used-car-salesman look. Her fingers almost throbbed with the need to slide against that thick, blond hair and mess it up, push away the conservative agent and bring back the nice guy she'd once laughed with.

Why did her body not remember that she hated him?

But it didn't. She was obviously still very susceptible to the man, at least physically. Despite being scared out of her mind that someone could have blown her away in front of her family and friends at the bar just now; despite being furious at having been kidnapped for her own good the overwhelming feeling flooding through Bridget was awareness. Physical awareness. Her thighs were clenched, her fingers shaking. Her heart was racing out of control; her breaths were ragged and irregular.

And her most feminine parts were running a foot race trying to be the first to remind Bridget that it had been a *long* time since she'd had sex. As if she could forget. Between her nipples scraping hard against the soft fabric of her dress and the warmth gathering between her thighs, there was no mistaking her physical response to Special Agent Willis.

If he pulled over and invited her to climb into the front seat and get on his lap, her legs would be scrambling forward even as her brain told them to stay put. She knew it just as she knew she'd hate herself for it afterward, when she got her hopes up about Dean again, only to watch him cruise back out of her life once his job was done.

Which meant one thing. She had to get away from him at the very first possible moment.

DEAN DROVE. He wasn't entirely conscious of where. Not where he was going or of his final destination. He just drove away from any danger to the slim young woman in the backseat. The one who'd probably been glaring fireballs at the back of his head from the minute he'd shoved her inside.

"Where are we going?" she eventually asked. "Are you taking me to your office?"

He shook his head. "Somewhere else."

No point telling her that the local field office was the *last* place he could take her. Considering Dean hadn't exactly been authorized to snatch her off the streets, he didn't imagine his boss would be happy if they showed up there.

He might end up unemployed after this. But damned if he could bring himself to regret it. The rest of the Bureau might not care about putting a young woman's life on the line in an effort to nab a bigger suspect, but Dean wasn't about to go along. Definitely not when the woman in question had not given her permission to be used as bait.

And especially not when the woman was Bridget Donahue.

"Where else is there?" she insisted, leaning closer between the front seats. So close her long, smooth hair brushed his arm. He wore not only a jacket but also a long-sleeved shirt, yet something in him swore he'd felt the contact. Maybe because he'd imagined it. Imagined sinking his hands into her hair, wrapping it around his fingers, holding her still as he explored the depths of her mouth…then every inch of the rest of her.

"*Hello?* Are you taking me home now?"

"Absolutely not. We're going someplace safe and you're staying there until we eliminate this threat." And he suddenly thought of the perfect place. It might be difficult to reach in this weather, but the SUV had four-wheel drive. They should be able to make it. Or at least get close enough to hike in.

Not with her in that dress, an internal voice reminded him. He ignored it. He'd deal with that issue when he had to.

"Is it a safe house?"

"No."

She met his stare in the rearview mirror, her eyes narrowing in suspicion. "Please don't tell me you're taking me back to your place *for my own good.* Because I might have been Miss Naive a few months ago when I fell for your routine, but I'm not that girl anymore. And if you kidnapped me for any personal reasons, I'll have you thrown into jail."

Dean couldn't help barking a laugh at her fierce expression and threatening tone. The woman was not the quiet bookkeeper he'd first met last summer, which wasn't a bad thing. In fact, the fiery, feisty Bridget was the one he'd most missed after he'd had to cut ties with her because of the case.

"We're going to a place right outside the city." He watched her expression as she absorbed that news, not missing the way her lips parted on a quick, inhaled breath, or the slight widening of her glittering eyes.

He'd bet money it wasn't fear he saw in her face. It was excitement. Because though Bridget might want to deny it, they'd had intense chemistry. That had been proven one afternoon in her office. Dean had found one of the other salesman making an aggressive move on her and had tossed the other guy out on his ass. Pure anger and the sexual awareness that had been sizzling between them for weeks had come to a head and he'd ended up with his tongue down her throat and her legs wrapped around his hips. He could have had her right there, on top of her desk, and he'd wanted that more than he'd wanted to see another morning.

He hadn't done it. Both because of the job…and because she'd have hated him even more once she found out who he was.

Not that it mattered. She hated him enough already. Except…that little flare in her eyes and the way her tongue now flicked across her lips to moisten them said her hatred hadn't stopped the *other* feeling she'd had for him.

Desire.

"I can't go stay in some hotel with you. I don't have so much as a toothbrush with me, much less any…" Her words trailed off, her eyes dropping, no longer meeting his in the mirror. And he knew her mind had instantly gone to other, more personal items she might be missing.

Like spare panties.

His teeth almost breaking as he clenched them together, Dean cleared his throat. "We'll make do."

"I am not going to wear this bridesmaid dress until I testify Monday."

She had a point.

Apparently getting over her embarrassment, she tossed her head back in visual challenge, she added, "And you can absolutely forget about me wearing nothing but what's *under* this bridesmaid dress until then, either."

Damn, there she went reminding him of the panties. And not only that, her words had sounded almost like a challenge. The thought of accepting it—of seeing how long he could hold out if he saw her wearing nothing but silk and lace, maybe in the same sexy shade of red as her dress—made Dean shift in the driver's seat. A litany of images flashed in his brain as he pictured her in her strappy high heels…with nothing else on her but *him.*

"Stop somewhere so I can get some clothes."

"It's ten o'clock on a Saturday night after a blizzard." His voice sounded gruff, even to his own ears. The tone was caused not by irritation with her for the demands, but rather at himself…for being unprofessional enough to get a hard-on for a woman he was supposed to be protecting.

"Then take me back to my hotel so I can grab my suitcase."

"Your hotel room was compromised."

Bridget's mouth fell open and she sagged back into her seat. *"What?"*

He began to explain, assuming she'd have questions. But when he caught sight of her reflection, the words disappeared. Bridget's eyes were closed, her lips sucked into her mouth. She was shaking her head back and forth in silent denial. And she was trembling, long shudders racking her body.

But not, he suspected, from the cold.

She'd been strong, holding it together, not asking *too* many unnecessary questions and trusting him enough to come with him. Now everything was obviously sinking in. Reality was washing over her, cold and unrelenting. And terrifying.

"I won't let anything happen to you," he whispered harshly, talking as much to himself as to her.

She opened her eyes and met his stare for a long, pregnant moment. Then, finally, she nodded once. The shudders finally ceased and she drew in a few deep breaths. "I'm sorry. That just hit me hard. Made it all real, you know?"

He knew.

"I'm okay now." Pure strength…she was the picture of it.

Dean wanted to pull over, tug her out of the backseat and into his arms to offer comfort. Just that. To let her know she didn't have to be strong *alone*.

But they needed to push on to make sure nobody could locate them—not the man following her. Not even his own coworkers. Then, when he knew they wouldn't be found, he'd get her out of the car and keep her secure. Warm. *Safe*.

Or die trying.

3

THOUGH SHE BADGERED HIM, it was another hour before Bridget could get Dean to even consider stopping for supplies. God, how she wanted a toothbrush, at least. But he refused, saying he wouldn't risk it until they were clear of the city.

Clear of the city…as in, he was removing her from Chicago, far from her home and her family and her friends. She had not a stitch of extra clothes, no one knew where she was and he'd essentially kidnapped her.

Why am I not terrified?

Maybe it was because of the calmness of his tone, his certainty that she would be fine. Or the way he'd said those seven words: *I won't let anything happen to you.*

He'd meant it… It had been more than a promise, it had been a vow. Physically, he would not let her be harmed.

Emotionally, however, was another story. It had taken months for her to get over what he'd done to her…and if she were to be truly honest, she *still* wasn't over it. So she had to get away from him. As soon as possible.

In the meantime, though, she figured she ought to find out what she could. She listened in silence as Dean told her what he knew, then finally said, "So if Marty hadn't come forward with the information, I could have walked into my hotel room tonight or my apartment tomorrow and found a gun pointed at me."

"It won't happen, Bridge."

"How can you be so sure?"

"Because you won't be there," he replied, his tone even and unhesitating. "And after you testify, it all becomes moot. There's no gain in removing you from the equation."

"So whoever's been following me just gets away with it because he doesn't *have* to kill me anymore?" she asked, her anger rising. It had been growing with every word Dean had said. Especially when those words included *contract killer* and *gunning you down*.

"He won't get away with it." Dean didn't so much speak the words as growl them. She instinctively knew he meant it—whatever he felt about her personally, Dean had sounded almost vengeful.

"So if you don't know who is after me, how did you know he'd followed me to the club?"

Dean glanced at her in the near darkness of the car. From the glow of the dashboard, she could see the way his brow was furrowed into a deep frown. "We've been running plates on cars that have been near your home and office in the past forty-eight hours. One turned up at your hotel—right before a guest reported a man acting suspiciously outside your door."

Her stomach rolled. "He broke into my room?"

Dean nodded once.

"My cousins…"

"They're no threat and wouldn't be on this guy's radar."

Dean's voice grew deeper—slow and tense. "He's only after you."

Great.

"I got the call about your room just as I saw you heading for the exit. The surveillance team had lost the car. Then the local PD called in a sighting of it…in the area of the club."

"Oh, my God," she whispered.

"I followed you outside, but stayed out of sight when you came back in. Not knowing for sure who was after you, I couldn't just let you stay there—*or* go back to the hotel—when you had no idea what was going on."

Still trying to find a way to comprehend it all, she whispered, "So you grabbed me."

"I grabbed you."

Before she could continue, he surprised her by flipping on his turn signal and heading for an exit. Fortunately, the plows had done a good job of clearing the main roads and exits…but the side one they ended up on was still dusted with white.

"We'll be okay, it's a four-wheel drive."

It was as if he'd read her mind.

"Are we going to stop now?"

"Yes. We'll need some food. We're going to be roughing it."

Roughing it. In a velvet bridesmaid gown and skimpy lingerie. Wonderful.

Then Bridget thought about it and realized she wouldn't have to. Because he was stopping in a public place, where she could get help from someone else. Someone who wasn't *Dean,* who didn't arouse her even as he infuriated her.

She owed him for getting her out of danger this evening. That didn't mean he was the one who had to *keep* her out of danger from now on. She had friends, she had family.

Heck, her cousin Mia knew the law inside and out. She was as tough as any criminal and had prosecuted dozens of them.

Bridget made her decision quickly. She was going to ditch Dean at the first opportunity.

He headed for the only well-lit area near the exit, a small gas station with a convenience store. Parking out front, he said, "Wait a second. It's too snowy."

She didn't have any idea what he meant to do about that until he opened the back door, reached in and picked her up off the seat. "You'd break your neck on this ice, even if you *weren't* wearing those ridiculous things on your feet."

Those ridiculous things had cost her half a week's paycheck. But she couldn't even open her mouth to argue it because all the air had been sucked from her lungs when he'd swung her into his arms. He held her close, tight against his warm, powerful body, picking his way across the ice and snow.

The contact was electrifying. His arms cradled her, his breath falling on her cheek and her hair. Bridget lost all sense of time and place, not even noticing the cold until he carefully set her down on the cleared sidewalk.

Finally, with the gift of distance, she could breathe again, *think* again. Calling herself a fool, she yanked the door open and strode inside.

He was right behind her. "Where are you going?"

"Where does it look like I'm going?" She nodded toward the ladies' room door in the back corner of the dusty old store, empty but for a dozing man behind the counter.

He frowned, offering a brief nod. "Be quick."

Oh, she'd be quick all right. Quick to make a phone call to Mia—*anybody*—to get her out of this mess. Because while she appreciated Dean getting her to safety, there was no way she was spending the next day and a half alone with him.

A tiny voice of doubt told her she'd be smart to go along. Smart and *safe*. But she knew that little voice meant safety in the physical sense. Emotionally, she would not be safe being closed up with Dean for thirty-six seconds, let alone hours.

As soon as she'd shut the ladies' room door behind her, she grabbed her cell phone out of her purse and dialed Mia's number. Mia was not only a lawyer, she was a serious, no-nonsense woman. She wouldn't go nuts like Gloria might and she wouldn't worry herself into a heart attack like Bridget's parents would.

But after three rings, Mia's cell phone was answered by a voice that was much deeper than her beautiful cousin's. "Hello?"

"I'm sorry…I think I might have dialed the wrong number," Bridget admitted, knowing her cousin hadn't been seeing anyone since she'd moved back to Chicago just before Christmas. "I was trying to reach my cousin, Mia Natale?"

"You've got the right number," the smooth, deep voice said.

Whoa. Mia had picked up a man for the night. A sexy man, judging by the deep, slow voice. "Can I speak with her, please?"

"Sorry," he replied, "Mia's in the…*middle* of something."

Oh, great. She was having sex with a stranger when Bridget needed her to come bail her out of her predicament. Though she hated to do it, she was going to have to play the it's-an-emergency card. But before she could do it, before she could say another word, in fact, the connection ended.

The jerk had hung up on her.

A knocking on the ladies' room door told her Dean was growing impatient. "Come on, we need to hit the road."

Damn. She hit redial and got Mia's voice mail. "It's Bridget. I'm in trouble. Call me the minute you get this."

"Who are you talking to?"

"Nobody," she called, turning on the faucet and letting the water run loudly. That was the first time she caught sight of herself in the mirror. Bridget was shocked to see the wide-eyed, pale-faced, wild-haired woman staring back at her.

She was a mess. The hair nightmare had probably been caused by being dangled upside down over Dean's big shoulder. Her makeup was smeary, her eye shadow gone and her mascara runny because of the few tears she'd allowed herself to shed over the thought that somebody wanted to kill her.

And her lipstick…had been kissed off.

Well kissed off.

She kept staring at her lips, her moist, parted lips. Then she focused on her eyes, which sparkled in the dim lighting cast by the bare overhead bulb. There was something in them, even she could see it. It wasn't exactly fear—though she was, in fact, afraid. Rather, she realized, it was excitement.

"Not at being chased," she murmured, knowing it was true, "but at being rescued." By a man she'd once wanted desperately.

That excitement—anticipation—made her stop and really think for the first time since Dean had grabbed her at the club. She had the chance to spend the rest of the weekend alone with a guy who was like sex in a jar. Far from home, with no possible future between them after he made sure she got safely to the courthouse on Monday. Which meant she couldn't get her schoolgirl hopes raised as she had last August. She *knew* this was a one weekend event and would go nowhere else.

Hmm. How would *they spend their time?*

As always, when faced with a dilemma, Bridget played the What Would Izzie Do? game. And without a doubt she knew what her gutsy cousin would do. She'd seduce Dean and get the most fabulous sex she could. Further, she'd keep her heart out of the equation so there'd be no false expectations. Then walk away next week with some incredible memories and absolutely no ties.

"I can take him and get him out of my system once and for all," she whispered, wanting so much to do it. To stop hurting, to stop wondering. To stop fantasizing in her bed late at night when she thought she'd die from the hollow emptiness between her legs, knowing he was the only one who could fill it.

He'd wanted her once. He might have kissed her only to shut her up tonight, but there had been no denying his physical response when he'd kissed her at work that day. If someone hadn't come into the dealership, he might very well have taken her right on her desk. Being honest, she'd pushed him to that point, wearing provocative clothes, flaunting herself, letting him know what she wanted.

What would happen if she did so again?

She didn't know…she only knew she wanted to find out. And luck seemed to be smiling on her, because beside the sink was one of those bathroom vending machines. And it carried condoms.

She bought six. That seemed like a good number, one for every six hours they'd be together. Optimistic, but not slutty.

"Open the door," he growled with another hard knock, "or I'm breaking the lock. And if I find you climbing out a window I'll tie you up for the rest of the ride."

Well, that did it. Because instead of feeling threatened by

Dean's words, a sharp stab of excitement shot through her. With one last look at the almost unfamiliar, hungry-looking woman reflected in the mirror, Bridget grabbed for the knob. Flicking the lock, she swung the door open. She met Dean's surprised stare, quirking a brow. "Kinky," she forced herself to say.

He gaped. "*What* did you call me?"

Channel Izzie, she reminded herself, squashing her instinct to pretend she'd been asking for a Twinkie. "I wasn't calling you that." Bridget cleared her throat, plunging forward. "Just saying bondage is pretty kinky. Especially for you FBI types." Tapping her fingertip against her cheek and ignoring his shocked expression, she continued. "Though, I suppose you guys are probably good at using handcuffs."

Dean's jaw clenched into something that resembled granite and Bridget could see the pulse raging in the side of his throat. It was just below a tiny, errant curl of blond hair…one small reminder of the friendly, laid-back guy she'd fallen so hard for.

She didn't want those reminders *or* that guy who'd hurt her so badly. She wanted the one she could have for the next thirty-six hours, then walk away from and completely *forget.* So she tore her attention from the curl and onto the jutting jaw, the blazing blue eyes, the slashing line of his full lips.

Better. Much better.

"I think you'd better stop talking now." He shifted closer, until his foot brushed the bottom hem of her gown.

"Or what?" she asked with a sweet smile. "Going to get out the chains and whips to go along with the cuffs and rope?"

Towering over her, he opened his mouth as if to retort, but quickly snapped it shut. His eyes flashed, his breath audible between his lips. Awareness and heat erupted off him.

He was angry. He was worried. And he was interested.

No matter what his silence said, his body language made it clear.

Yes, this was *definitely* better. This angry, wildly sexy man would take what he wanted and not plan to give anything more than a few hours pleasure. Which was all she'd expect.

Now she could forget all about the nice, smiling guy she'd fallen for. And focus on the sexy, dangerous man she was going to be getting to know *much* better before the night was out.

HE MIGHT HAVE MADE a very serious mistake.

Dean hadn't planned on physically hauling Bridget out of danger tonight, he'd acted on instinct. He'd seen red when she'd come sauntering back into the club, heading down a dark, silent hallway where *anything* could have happened. And when the surveillance team had radioed that her room at the hotel had been broken into and the suspect's car was in the vicinity, he hadn't given a moment's thought to what he was doing.

He'd taken her and run

Still high on adrenaline, as well as fury that she might have walked into her hotel room and into the arms of a killer, he'd headed out of Chicago, aiming for *anywhere* that took her out of the line of fire. Eventually, he realized that *anywhere* was a small, old fishing cabin a buddy of his owned. It was off the main road and had little in the way of amenities. Though he remembered there being adequate plumbing, he wasn't even sure it had heat. But it had a woodstove and firewood. And they had the food he'd just picked up at the convenience store. Most importantly, nobody could connect either of them with the cabin so there was no way anybody could track them—*her*—down.

They could rough it until Monday. At that time he'd deliver Bridget to the courthouse, then go back to the office to lay his head on the chopping block.

Sounded like a plan. A bad one, maybe, but better than leaving Bridget in the city and giving some armed scumbag an extra thirty-six hours to get to her. So he'd stick with it.

But he'd known by the glint in Bridget's eyes when she'd exited the ladies' room that she was going to do something to screw with that plan. And to screw with his head.

When she climbed into the front seat of his SUV and took off her coat, he knew he was in trouble. She claimed it was too warm—as if their breath wasn't fogging up the interior, which had grown frigid in the brief time they'd been in the store. Dean, however, knew what she was really doing.

The woman was tormenting him. Laying herself out like a rich, delectable dessert in front of a diabetic, just daring him to take a bite. And she'd be just as dangerous to him as a deadly overdose of something sweet.

He couldn't be sure about her motives. She was almost certainly *trying* to drive him crazy with lust as she crossed her legs, the red fabric of her dress parting at the slit to reveal her long, slim thighs. She didn't relent, leaning over to adjust the radio, coming close enough for him to feel her body's warmth and see the soft line of cleavage revealed by her low-cut gown. Yeah, it was definitely intentional.

But *why* she was doing it was another matter. It could be that she already knew he couldn't act on that lust and she wanted him to sit with an uncomfortably full lap. Or she hoped he *would* act on it so she could shoot him down as some kind of revenge for what had happened between them four months ago.

Either way spelled trouble for Dean.

"Are we almost there?" she asked.

"Mmm-hmm."

"Where exactly *is* 'there'?"

"A friend of mine owns a fishing cabin near here and I know where he keeps a spare key." The place wasn't far at all, if he remembered correctly. He kept his eyes front, watching for the small side road. Not just because he was afraid he'd miss it, but also for pure self-preservation.

"Does your friend stock warm women's clothing?"

He couldn't help casting a quick, corner-of-the-eye glance at her. Bridget smoothed her hand over her gown, trailing her fingers across the deep V-neck then lower, over her midriff and down to her hips. Dean glanced at her, as she'd obviously wanted him to. She caught him looking and smiled.

Yeah. He was definitely in trouble.

"I remember there being some old clothes there."

"Size eight?" she asked sweetly.

A throbbing started in his temple.

"And 34 C?"

It turned into a pounding.

"I can't very well go around in this tiny little red bra I have on. It was meant to push up, not really *cover* anything."

Give me strength.

"And the thigh-high stockings I'm wearing won't do a thing to keep my legs warm."

The woman intended to torture him. She knew he wanted her—had wanted her for a long time. Playing sexual games she had no intention of following through on would make him uncomfortable physically and would test the limits of his control.

Because if she pushed him too far, he might just push back. As he had that day in her office when he'd almost banged her brains out right on top of her desk.

"And it's not like I can just wear my wool coat. It'd be much too rough against my bare skin."

"Knock it off," he muttered.

She ignored him. "I certainly can't be expected to walk around naked for the next day and a half, now can I?"

"Enough, Bridget," he snapped.

"Enough what?"

"Enough of the sexy come-ons."

"I don't know what you mean." The glittering eyes and self-satisfied expression made a lie of that statement.

"Yeah, you do. Look, I know you're angry because I used you to get information on Marty…."

"Don't forget the kidnapping part."

He sighed heavily. "I know. But you can get even with me another time, after this is all over, okay?" Swallowing, he added in a low voice, "Don't do it like this." *Don't.*

"Like what?" she asked softly, her smile fading, like she really wanted him to answer.

So he did. "Don't throw yourself out as sexual bait with no intention of being caught."

She said nothing for a long moment, but she didn't look away. Then, finally, she licked her lips and slowly smiled. "But Dean…I *do* intend to be caught."

4

DEAN HAD REMEMBERED correctly—there *were* some clothes in a trunk in the small, remote cabin, which they reached about thirty minutes after leaving the store. But Bridget didn't grab the neatly stacked sweatshirts or pants when they arrived. Nor did she go for any socks, though her feet were freezing. Dean had carried her through the snow from the SUV to the door, but her toes still felt numb.

Being in his arms had warmed at least the rest of her up, especially since steam had practically been rolling off the man ever since she'd flat-out said she planned to let him catch her. He'd barely said a word since and Bridget had been too busy wondering how to get caught to force him into any more conversation.

Now, however, they were alone, inside, with nothing between them but some cold stale air that smelled of pine and earth…and Dean's own stubborn, protective nature.

Not for long. He would *not* be resisting her for long.

The cabin might be a half hour from the nearest telephone and lacking electricity, but it was no shack in the woods.

Clean and comfortable, this was a wealthy man's idea of roughing it. The pine floors sparkled, the butcher-block table gleamed, and the leather furniture looked like it'd stepped off the pages of an Ethan Allen catalog. She'd bet there was a generator and probably a portable heater. But she didn't mention that to Dean.

She wanted low lighting and an excuse to demand body heat.

"I'll get a fire going." Dean lifted some logs from a pile by the hearth and put them in the woodstove. "You hanging in?"

"Yes."

And she was. Remarkably, she really *was*. If anybody had told her twenty-four hours ago that she'd be spending the night in a rustic cabin in the middle of nowhere with Dean Willis, she'd have asked what they'd been smoking. But it was true, she was here…for the next thirty-six hours, at least.

The question returned: *what shall we do to fill our time?*

Those condoms were singing a siren's song from her purse.

"Why don't you just go to bed?" Dean asked, not looking up at her. "There's a futon in the loft. I can take the sofa."

Bridget shook her head. "I'm not leaving this wood-stove."

"Heat rises, it'll be fine up there in a half hour."

Lowering herself to the edge of the plush, dark leather sofa, she smiled sweetly. "Then I'll wait a half hour."

He mumbled something under his breath but she ignored him. Bridget watched his every move, knowing he had to feel her hot stare on him but not really giving a damn. The man was so powerful, the thick muscles in his arms and chest flexing and rippling beneath his long-sleeved black shirt as he worked. He was also so obviously uncomfortable around her. All because she'd made her intentions clear.

In Bridget's opinion, it was about time *someone* did. Because Dean certainly hadn't. Not when he'd been pretending to be Mr. Nice. And not tonight, when he'd grabbed her and bolted.

"So what is it you plan to do with me?" she asked, both because she wanted to know and because she liked the way the tips of his ears turned red when she said something outrageous. Asking him what he planned to do with her—with the emphasis on the word *do*—probably sounded outrageous to his strict FBI ears.

"I'm going to sit on you here until Monday morning, deliver you to the courthouse, watch you testify, then let you go."

She knew what he meant but played dumb. Smiling as she leaned over from the couch, knowing her red gown gapped away from her chest, she murmured, "Sit on me? Sounds uncomfortable."

Dean, who'd been squatting as he stuck bits of kindling into the woodstove, jerked his head up and stared at her. His eyes blazed with more intensity than the struggling flames and his mouth pulled taut. "Just what is it you're trying to do here, Bridget?" he asked, sounding not only angry but intensely curious. As if he truly didn't know.

How could he not know? Was he really ignorant to the fact that she was absolutely *dying* for him? Would give anything to *have* him, if only for a few hours?

Maybe. And if so, she really ought not to keep him in the dark any longer. So without another word, Bridget rose to her feet. She reached around to the back of her dress, slowly drawing the zipper down, letting the sleeves loosen and slip off her shoulders until the tops of her breasts were gradually revealed.

With a gulp of air for courage, she let the gown go, until it dropped to the floor at her feet.

"I'm trying," she finally replied, "to finish what you started that day last August."

THOUGH THE AIR hadn't changed and he hadn't moved a muscle, Dean began to sink down under an almost tangible weight on his entire body. He couldn't speak, couldn't think, could only sit in shocked silence while Bridget let her wicked red dress fall away. Beneath it she wore even more wicked lingerie. Skimpy, tiny panties, wickedly seductive stockings and a red demibra that, as she'd threatened in the car, plumped her luscious breasts up rather than making any effort to cover them.

His hands clenched into fists and his mouth went dry. The heat blasting every inch of him had nothing to do with the fire he'd just started in the woodstove. And everything to do with *her*. How she looked. How she smelled. How she stared down at him with pure hunger in her eyes.

How he'd felt around her since the day he'd met her. Off balance, breathless, confused.

Captivated.

"I know you're doing your job," she whispered, "and I know there's nothing personal about it and after Monday, we go our separate ways again. But we're adults, we're alone. We're here for the next day and a half…and you wanted me once."

He shook his head, denying that last part. "I have *always* wanted you, Bridget."

He could have said more. Could have told her that he'd been attracted to her since the first time he'd gone into the dealership last summer. Or that he'd become addicted to her smile, intoxicated by her laugh as every day had passed. That on the day he'd kissed her, he'd been so out of his mind with desire for her that he'd walked around with a hard-on for two days.

And more…that it had infuriated him when his colleagues had badgered her for hours after Marty's arrest. That it had killed him to stay away from her since.

But none of that needed to be said now. Not while Bridget was watching him with glittering wide eyes and moist, parted lips. Offering herself. "You are the most beautiful thing I have ever seen," he murmured, watching her from below, sitting on the faux bearskin rug in front of the stove. He devoured her with his gaze, coveting the delicate curves of her breasts, dying for a taste of the dark nipples peeking through her bra.

She shook her head. "I'm not beautiful."

He rose to his knees. Lowering his hands to her ankles, he fingered the straps of her high-heeled sandals, then moved his palms up her stocking-clad legs. "No, you're *stunning*."

She didn't deny it this time, merely hissed in a breath as he reached the top hem of her sultry, thigh-high stockings. The breath was released with a tiny whimper when his fingertips transitioned from silky nylon to the silkier skin of her thighs.

"So soft," he murmured. The skin was creamy and delicate, the limb slender and supple. He couldn't wait to feel those legs wrapped around his hips as he finally plunged inside her the way he'd wanted to for so long. "I love the way you feel."

She swayed on her feet. The movement brought her hip close to his mouth and Dean leaned forward to brush his lips against the lacy edge of her panties. "I'll love the way you taste."

"Oh, my," she whispered, dropping her hands onto his shoulders, as if needing his support to stay up.

"I've got you," he muttered, spreading his fingers around to grip her hips. Then he rocked her close to his mouth again until he was breathing directly onto the silky triangle of fabric covering that intoxicating spot between her legs.

"Dean…"

"Shh. Let me experience you. I've waited a long time and I want you in every way I can get you."

She said nothing else, but sighed and lifted her fingers to tangle in his hair. Dean leaned into her again, brushing his lips over the elastic edge of her panties, then tugging at it with his teeth. Pushing them down to fall at her feet with the dress, he stared for a long moment, admiring her femininity, his mouth watering for more.

When he grazed his lips across her soft curls, he felt her quake in response. "I've still got you," he whispered, seeing the way her skin quivered and flushed beneath the heat of his breath, the contrast from the cold air of the cabin.

"Good. I won't be able to stay on my feet if you—"

He cut her off by opening his mouth on her, covering her mound and licking deep into her sweet, wet crevice. Fortunately, he had a good grip on the delectable curves of her ass because Bridget's legs did give out. She cried out in stunned delight, collapsing back toward the sofa, Dean helping her down.

He remained on the floor. Kneeling between her spread legs.

"If this is how you start, I can't imagine how you finish."

He laughed softly. Staring at her soft body, cast in pools

of light and shadow from the flames in the woodstove, he murmured, "Oh, Bridge, we started *months* ago."

She glanced down at him and nodded. "I know." Tangling her hands in his hair, she tugged him. "Come up here and kiss me."

"I *was* kissing you," he teased, dropping his mouth to the V of her thighs again. He flicked his tongue out to sample her pert clit, rewarded with her delighted gasp and the thrust of her hips toward his hungry mouth.

Dean devoured her, knowing there was so much more to be done but not ready to give up this particularly intimate pleasure until, hearing her frenzied cries and seeing the tensing of her muscles, he realized she was close to climaxing. "Come on, beautiful," he murmured, wanting to take her there.

And suddenly he did. She arched hard, crying out in delight as tremors ran throughout her body.

Dean gradually worked his way up her body. Every taste whetted his appetite. Every brush of his lips sent fresh quivers through her. She was slender—not too curvaceous but so feminine she could illustrate the word. Soft everywhere. With smooth lines of creamy skin and delicate curves, every one of which he simply had to taste and stroke and adore.

Finally, when he thought Bridget was going to sob if he didn't finish his leisurely journey northward, he moved over her and stared into her eyes. "I'm glad you let me catch you."

"I think *I* caught *you*," she murmured.

"You're absolutely sure?" he asked, already past the point of no return but figuring he ought to pretend to be a gentleman.

She nodded. "Very sure."

"Thank God. Because there's no way I'm stopping."

"I'd never forgive you if you did." Tugging him close, she

brushed her lips against his, then parted them and slid her tongue out to play with his.

Dean groaned, turned his head so he could get even closer, and explored her warm mouth. Their tongues danced wildly, as she began to push his clothes off him. He lifted himself away long enough to lose the shirt, but when she reached for his belt, he pushed her hand aside. "Better let me do that. I have about as much control as a horny kid where you're concerned."

Her eyes glittered, as if she liked that she drove him crazy. Hell, he liked that she drove him crazy. He went especially crazy when Bridget reached for the front clasp of her skimpy bra and flicked it open with her thumb. The lacy fabric fell away, revealing perfectly proportioned breasts.

She nibbled her bottom lip, as if uncertain of his reaction. "Not quite centerfold material…" she whispered. "I might have been, uh, exaggerating about the 34 C."

"You are perfect, Bridget Donahue," he said, his voice throaty as he studied the perfection of her, the soft skin, the dark puckered nipples that begged to be tasted.

He tasted.

"Dean!" she groaned when he covered one nipple and sucked it hard, while tweaking the other between his fingers.

"So sensitive," he mumbled as he played with her breasts, moving back and forth to nibble and suck. As he did so, her silky, stocking-covered thighs lifted and encircled his hips. She arched against him, rubbing that hot, wet center against the rock-hard erection straining against his pants.

"I need to touch you." She was reaching for his belt again, not to be denied this time. When her slender hands brushed against the front of his trousers, his cock lurched toward it. Dean waited for more of that touch, needing it desperately.

She rapidly unfastened his belt, tugging at his zipper, almost shaking in her want. She pushed them down just far enough to reach inside, then encircled as much of him as she could take with her cool hand. "Oh, heavens," she whispered, sounding the tiniest bit intimidated for the first time all night. Clearing her throat, she added, "I want that. I want it *now.*"

Her demand for *that* suddenly made his whole body stiffen as much as his dick. "Oh, God, please tell me you're on the pill."

She shook her head and Dean's stomach fell out of his body.

"But check my purse. I, uh, made a purchase from the vending machine at the service station."

"So you *were* planning to seduce me."

She licked her lips. "It didn't take much."

No, it hadn't. But Dean simply didn't care. He reached for her red bag, opened it and saw a half-dozen condom packets resting inside. "Ambitious."

"But not slutty."

As if. The woman had *lady* written all over her and had since the day they'd met, which was why he'd suspected from the beginning that she wasn't involved in her boss's dirty dealings.

He thrust that thought away, not wanting anything to interfere with what they were doing. Grabbing one of the square packets, he studied it doubtfully. "I wonder if these things have an expiration date." The plastic was dry and crinkly, the label smeared.

She writhed up against him. "Just *put it on!*"

Dean almost chuckled at her desperation. But when he opened the condom and tried rolling it on, he stopped laughing. "Shit."

She glanced down, then groaned. "No."

"Yeah. It broke." When he reached for the next the packet didn't look to be in much better shape and his attempt to sheathe himself ended with the same result.

"Just shoot me now," she mumbled when she saw yet another one break just as he began to unroll it over himself.

"Remind me to stop at that gas station Monday and throttle that guy. He's a damned sadist."

When he reached for the fourth and fifth and got the same dried up, useless condoms, he felt like throwing himself in front of a train. Anything to put himself out of the misery of having everything he wanted in his grasp…and being unable to reach out and *take* it.

Bridget looked on the verge of tears. "Can you put two of them on? Just double up? They can't be torn in the same places."

He choked out a laugh, almost desperate enough to do it. "I don't think they'd hold up, even if I put all six on over top of each other and cut my circulation off completely." Though, to be honest, at this moment, he believed the temporary release would be worth it, even if his dick fell off afterward.

She grabbed the remaining packet. "This one doesn't look too bad." The hopefulness in her voice was so damned adorable he had to bend down and kiss her again, slow and sweet.

But she wasn't satisfied with that for long. She arched up again, spreading her legs wider, looking utterly wanton and irresistible. "Don't you dare give up on me now."

"I'm sure the last one is just as—"

"I *need* it, Dean. I have to feel you inside me or I'll explode." She arched toward him, rubbing her hot core against the length of his erection, wetting him with her body's luscious juices. Inviting him to utter insanity.

"Bridget…"

"I'm healthy and I know you wouldn't have gone even this far if you weren't."

That was true and, despite the gravity of the moment, he appreciated her faith in him.

She rubbed harder, wrapping her legs around him. The silkiness against his back drove him crazy and he knew it would be matched by the silky smoothness inside her. It would be amazing to dive into her with no impediment, skin to skin.

She seemed desperate for him to do it, arching her back so she could tease the tip of his cock, the creamy lips of her sex offering the ultimate pleasure. "Give me a taste," she begged. "You can come all over me when it gets to be too much, but please, take me just a little."

The *please*—and the tremble in her voice when she begged him to take her *just a little*—shattered the last remnants of his control. He didn't want to take her just a little, he wanted to drive her into oblivion. So with one last curse at his own weakness, he thrust hard, driving home inside her.

She sobbed in relief. "Oh, yes."

It was amazing, feeling her wrapped around him, her muscles tugging at him, gobbling him up with sensual greed.

"This is insane," he muttered as his body wrested control from his mind. "Reckless." *But so incredibly good.*

She clenched her arms around him, digging her nails into his back, thrusting up against him. "I don't care."

And honestly, at that moment, neither did he. Pregnancy wasn't on his radar…but a future with Bridget most definitely was. The idea of having her and a child to come home to didn't make him shrivel up and pull away, it only drove him to thrust harder into her, imprinting himself on her, deep inside.

She probably wouldn't believe it, but he'd fallen in love with her long before this night. And there was nothing he'd like more than to *claim* her. Claim *them*. A future. All of it.

But it might not be what she wanted. So while they were being reckless, going *all* the way to the shattering climax he knew was waiting for him would be out of the question. While he wanted more than anything to explode inside her, he couldn't force Bridget into something she wasn't ready for.

The pressure grew exponentially, being unsheathed ratcheted up the intensity and he knew he wasn't going to last for long. And while on one level it sounded sexy as hell, he didn't want their first time to end with him coming all over her stomach like they were starring in some porn movie.

With almost frenzied desperation, he pulled out of her and grabbed for the final condom. As he tore it open, he made mental deals with whatever entity was listening to do all the nice-guy crap he knew he should do, if only the thing stayed intact.

It did.

"Please, Dean," she begged, reaching for him the very second he'd unrolled the rubber to the base of his shaft.

He was back inside her a second later, mournful of the loss of that blissful skin-to-skin sensation, but quickly losing himself in the renewed pleasure of their connection.

Kissing her frantically, he gave himself over to it, to physical bliss and emotional satisfaction. Within moments, he allowed himself to reach his explosive climax. Her loud cries told him she was right there with him. Again.

The very second it was over, he scooped her in his arms and rolled her onto his chest, lying on the thick rug. And surrounded by a sea of broken condoms and all their clothes, they quickly fell asleep in front of the fire.

5

THEY ATE DOUGHNUTS for breakfast the next morning. Naked. On the bearskin rug. And it was the best meal Bridget had ever had. There was one problem with eating sticky-sweet doughnuts naked: the crumbs and smears of sugar left on their bodies invited tasting.

"You taste so sweet," Dean murmured as he kissed a bit of powdered sugar off her nipple. It hadn't landed there by accident—he'd scraped his doughnut across it. About a dozen times.

Bridget's doughnut had been coated with cinnamon sugar. Now Dean's chest...and his lap...were covered with tiny bits of the spice, all of which she intended to lick off him. "So do you."

"You know we can't do this again, right?" he mumbled as he kissed his way across her chest. He pushed her onto her back on the rug, looking down at her with rueful sorrow. In the morning light, with his shaggy hair and the lazy, well-satisfied expression in his eyes, he looked every bit like the guy she'd cared so much for a few months ago.

As well as the lover she'd fallen head over heels for the previous night.

"Maybe not *that*. But I think we already did *this*," she mumbled, moving her mouth down his body in search of cinnamon.

And they definitely had. During the night, when they'd awakened, warm and relaxed in front of the fire, they'd both instinctively wanted more. Without protection, they'd found other ways to pleasure each other. Amazing ways.

But she wanted him inside her again. "Don't you think…"

"No." He pulled away and rose to his feet, as if not trusting himself. "Once was reckless, twice is stupid."

Bridget couldn't help sucking in a breath at the sight of him, big and male, fully erect. *Yum.*

"I'm going to get dressed, drive back to that store and buy a fresh box of condoms off the shelves." Anticipating her next comment, he added, "And I've gotten over my urge to punch the clerk." He smiled wickedly. "I have to admit I liked what we were forced to do last night."

Oh, yes, so had she. But she still frowned. "That'll take an hour. And they might be as stale as the ones in the machine."

He smiled as he pulled his trousers over his naked form, zipping them carefully over his engorged sex. "Then I'll drive to the next town." Reaching down to cup her cheek, he added, "Just be waiting right here, *like that,* when I get back."

And she was. She didn't remain in that exact spot during the ninety minutes he was gone. Taking advantage of the privacy, she washed up and brushed her teeth, then laid herself back down like some virgin being offered up to a ravenous sex God.

But the ravenous sex God wasn't the one who walked

through the door a short time later. As soon as she saw the tightness of his shoulders and the frown on his handsome face, Bridget knew who'd returned. Not the nice salesman. Not the erotic lover.

She was once again in the company of Special Agent Willis.

"What happened?" she asked, sitting up. She grabbed the blanket they'd used during the night and covered herself, feeling awkward when before she'd felt completely free and uninhibited.

"I got within cell phone range of my partner."

Bridget closed her eyes and began to shake her head.

"It looks like everything's fine."

That wasn't what she'd expected to hear. "What?"

"When they realized you weren't going to be that easy a target, Marty's former drug buddies made a move on Marty's wife, figuring that would shut him up for good."

Bridget gasped. Marty's wife was a nice lady. Stupid to stick with an icky criminal with a bad toupée, but nice.

"She's okay. They caught the guy. He's talking, as is Marty. He was so angry they went after his family, he offered to cooperate fully."

Meaning… "I don't have to testify."

He met her eye and shook his head slowly. "I don't think so." Walking across the room, he squatted down beside her and lifted a hand to her cheek. "Thank God."

He looked truly relieved about that—yet his mood remained somber. When he spoke again, she understood why. "So there's no need to remain here. You can go back to your life." Cocking a brow and sighing, he added, "And I should get to the office."

"Why?" Then understanding washed over her. "You weren't supposed to grab me, were you." It wasn't a question.

"No."

"And you're in trouble?"

"As I told my boss when I called in, I don't care."

She nibbled her bottom lip. "How did he respond?"

Another shrug. "We had words."

"Serious ones?"

"I told him to go screw himself."

"Oh, boy," Bridget mumbled, lifting a hand to her brow.

"I did say *with all due respect* first," he added, as if that made everything better. "It'll be fine," he said. "He didn't handle this thing by the book, either, using you for bait. And if my head rolls, so does his." As if he'd said as much as he was going to say on the matter, he reached for her dress and handed it to her. "Now, we should get ready. I'm sure your family's worried."

"You mean you *want* to leave? *Now?*" she asked, so startled she didn't dwell on the using-you-for-bait comment.

He thrust a hand through his hair. "It's time to leave. You said yourself this was a one-shot thing, a physical escape from reality by two people stuck together for a few days."

Bridget blinked rapidly, shocked that he was so ready to end their incredible interlude. Then again, that interlude had only happened because he'd been protecting her—even against his own self-interests. Now that the danger was apparently finished, he was ready to return her to her real world and go back to his. With no looking back at the few hours they'd shared here.

"I kidnapped you. You had no choice."

Oh, she'd had a choice, at least as far as their lovemaking went. How could he not see that? Because she certainly did.

And she wanted more. Was it possible he didn't feel the same way, even after the incredible things they'd shared?

She wanted to ask him, but the words wouldn't come. Dean was already loading up their few things and carrying them out to his SUV, as if not trusting himself to continue the conversation. The quieter he got, the heavier her heart grew. He meant it. He was taking her home, whether she liked it or not.

Finally, when he handed her her coat and said it was time to leave—again, so aloof, so impersonal—it felt like her heart cracked completely. Like one of the icicles falling off the roof of the cabin to the ground below.

It was the sudden, unexpected crash of one of those icicles that snapped her out of her self-pity. She'd been in a fog since he got back, now she burst out of it. Not because it was what Izzie would do. But because it was what Bridget had to do if she wanted Dean to remain a part of her life.

And she did. Oh, she truly did.

So as Dean came out of the cabin for the last time, his keys in his hand, Bridget didn't think. She acted. Plucking the keys away, she threw them as far as she could, shocking even herself with the spontaneous action. *He's going to kill me.*

He gaped, looking stunned. "What the hell are you doing?"

"I want the rest of our weekend," she said. Lifting her hand, she thrust an index finger into his chest. "I have until tomorrow morning, damn it, and I want it."

His mouth fell open, as if he didn't know what to say.

"And if you think you're going to drive me back to Chicago, dump me on my doorstep, then disappear out of my life again, you'd better think twice, Dean Willis. We started something last night and we're going to finish it."

She was prepared for a frown, even a yell that she'd

tossed his keys into the snow, possibly stranding them here. The one thing she absolutely did not expect was what she got.

"What if it takes a lifetime to finish it?"

His voice was soft, his tone so unexpectedly tender, that at first the words didn't sink in. Once they did, her heart started beating again, the world started turning again. This was the lover speaking…quiet, introspective. And very, very serious. "If *we* take a lifetime, you mean?"

He slid his hands around her waist, beneath her coat, so she felt the warm possession of the touch. Tugging her close against him, he stared down at her, his eyes sparkling beneath the brilliant rays of morning sun. "Yes. Us, together. Bridget, I am in love with you and I have been for a long time."

She sucked in a shocked breath. "You *love* me?"

He nodded, then, with a regretful frown, released her from his embrace. "Enough to take you back to the city, let you get back to your real life and decide if you want me to be a part of it." Clearing his throat, he added, "With no forced proximity—no kidnappings—to mess with your head."

His words *finally* helped her figure things out. Why he'd come back looking so dejected, why he'd been so determined to take her home. Back to reality.

He wanted her to choose him…not be stuck with him.

Funny. She'd chosen him months ago, even before she knew who he really was. "I love you, Dean. I've loved you for a long time, too." His smile dazzled and Bridget reached up to cup a tender hand around his rough cheek. "If you hadn't kidnapped me last night, I would have eventually pounded down your door to see if there really was something between us."

"But you were so mad after Marty's arrest…."

"I was. Mainly because I was heartbroken. I thought you'd used me, that you'd felt nothing."

"You were wrong. I felt everything." He turned his face to kiss her palm. "I'm so sorry."

Bridget rose on tiptoe, twining her arms around his neck. Pulling him down, she gave him a sweet, tender kiss, offering forgiveness. And a lot more. "Can we please stay?"

His eyes twinkled. "I think we're going to have to, at least until the snow melts."

Chuckling, Bridget tugged him back toward the door. But suddenly remembering why he'd gone out, she gasped. "Please tell me you finished your shopping before your cell phone rang."

He knew exactly what she meant. Because with a smile that was pure sin, he reached into his coat pocket and pulled out a shiny, new-looking box of condoms. Two dozen.

Laughing in sheer happiness, she said, "Ambitious."

"But not slutty," he replied, a twinkle in his eye.

As he put an arm across her shoulders and led her back inside their secluded hideaway, Bridget considered how different the world looked on this bright winter morning. Was it really possible that a life could change completely in one short night?

Watching as Dean closed the door behind them, then pushed her coat off her shoulders to draw her into his arms, she knew it was most definitely possible.

Anything was.

* * * * *

Runaway

1

LEAH MULDOON HADN'T known the other members of the wedding party until a few days ago, but she knew she liked them. Which wasn't too much of a surprise—Leah liked everybody.

That was a rarity in her business, considering every pretty woman was a potential rival on the stage, but she didn't care. Stripping was merely a way to pay the bills while she went to school to get her nursing degree. Just an easy way to sock away the cash by exploiting the only asset she had: her body.

It sure as hell beat using that body for the kinds of games her stepfather had asked her to play when she was sixteen. Well, he'd asked her *once*. Then she'd stabbed him and taken off, becoming a teenage runaway…another statistic.

That probably sounded worse than it was. She'd only stabbed him in the wrist. And it had been with a fork. But the pig had definitely deserved it, if only for destroying her few remaining decent feelings about the home she'd grown up in.

"You're all lucky to be part of such a great family," she said, offering a loopy smile to Izzie's sister Gloria, a petite brunette with a big mouth and a lot of hair. The woman sat on the other side of the table at the crowded Chicago pub.

Vanessa, one of Izzie's friends from New York—a tall, gorgeous black woman with the longest legs Leah had ever seen—cleared her throat and lowered her rum and Coke. "Hello?"

"Okay, we're both outsiders. Want to be my sister?"

"Sisters can be a pain in the ass. Let's stick to friends."

Friends. Sounded great. Exactly what she needed most.

Well, *almost.* Lovers would be a big plus, too. It had been a long time since she'd had a man in her bed.

Gloria took offense. "Hey, not all sisters are pains in the ass." She glanced at her own sister, Mia, the attorney.

Mia stared at her glass, a grin tickling her full lips. "I'll plead the fifth."

When the laughter died down, Bridget rose, saying she was ready to leave. Leah glanced at her watch and decided to leave, too. "I have to nap off those mai tais in case I decide to go in to work tonight." She yawned, having worked until two last night.

"I dance better when I've had a drink or two," said Gloria.

"You *think* you do," muttered her sister.

"Watch it or I'll pluck the little hair ya have left."

Smiling, Mia shook her head. Her short black hair gleamed. "Uh-huh, sure. I'd like to see you try, *old lady.*"

Gloria had been getting ribbed all week about being the only married bridesmaid and had endured lots of mother-of-three-never-gets-laid comments.

Leah wished she could stay and enjoy more of the friendly bickering, as well as the typical men-suck griping among single women, but she figured she ought to at least *think* about going to work. She wasn't on the schedule, but even a short Saturday night beat any other night of the week at the club. And her bank account was singing the blues this month after paying for her spring tuition, plus buying wedding and shower gifts.

So saying goodbye, she followed Bridget to the door. They wove through the crowd of people cruising between tipsy and tanked. Leah hadn't gone that far…but two drinks on top of no food or sleep had affected her. She ignored the come-ons…Leah was used to those. She usually had a bouncer watching her back, however, and was *not* used to dealing with actual gropes. So when a third guy *accidentally* bumped into her, she just as *accidentally* impaled his foot with the spiked heel of her shoe.

Reaching the door, she slipped into her ratty coat, regretting having to cover the stunning gown. Unlike most bridesmaid dresses, this one wasn't painfully ugly. The soft, red velvet sheath was something Leah could use again.

"Button up." Bridget sounded motherly, which was funny since she was probably only a couple of years older than Leah.

The command was easier said than done since half of Leah's buttons were missing. Leah pulled the coat around her body, crossing her arms. Hopefully the position would prevent Bridget from seeing the frayed sleeves or uneven hem. She'd love to replace it. But the money she'd spend on a new one was better spent on trivial things like food and rent.

Her gloves were even worse, with holes in the tips of two fingers. Those she *could* afford to replace…she just hadn't had the time. But they were better than nothing.

Stepping outside, she burrowed her face into her collar, her skin prickling under the assault of the wind. Spying the stretch limo parked across the lot, she put her head down and headed for it. She hadn't gone far when she heard Bridget.

"Oh, no, I left my cell phone inside." Bridget waved her on. "Go on. No sense in both of us going back."

Bridget didn't even wait. She spun around and hurried inside, leaving Leah to either go after her and brave the crowd of fast-fingered guys or crawl into the warm, private car.

No contest. Yanking the back door open, she slid inside, hearing the driver talking on the phone up front. She was immediately enfolded in warmth and comfort. Luxury, even.

Sinking back against the cushiony seat, she let her body absorb the heat and her nostrils inhale the unfamiliar odors of fine leather, good whiskey and a spicy, masculine scent reminiscent of the sea. She closed her eyes to enjoy it, idly wondering why the car seemed so much more luxurious— not to mention masculine smelling—than it had earlier in the evening.

Mai tais. That explained it. Everything seemed better looking after a few drinks, which was one reason Leah rarely drank. She'd hate to be tipsy enough to look out in the audience one night, think she saw Prince Charming and wake up in the arms of a fat, hairy guy named Rocco the next day.

Rocco definitely wouldn't have a car like this. The Prince Charming of her dreams would, though. She'd been fanta-sizing about him since she was a kid, waiting for him to whisk her away from her lousy life. Only, he'd never come. She'd whisked herself and done a damn fine job of it, if she did say so herself. With or without her clothes.

Smiling and letting just a tiny bit of princely fantasy slip into her brain, Leah yawned, curled deeper in the seat.

And fell asleep.

"Let me get this straight. You have no idea who this woman sleeping in my car is or how she got here?"

Slone Kincaid kept his voice low as he talked to his driver through the open partition between the front and passenger areas of the limo. He didn't know why. He *should* be shaking the irresistible blonde awake and kicking her out of his car, which she'd either mistaken as her own or stumbled into drunk. But something made him whisper as he kept his eyes on his unexpected guest.

Curled up in the corner of the backseat, she was a petite package with bright blond curls and pouty lips. He'd stared at the lips and the creamy cheeks for a minute when he'd gotten in, unable to tear his gaze away. She looked young—vulnerable—and while pretty, she wasn't stop-your-heart gorgeous, as some women he'd dated were. So why she'd stopped *his,* he had no idea.

Unexpected, that was all. He just hadn't pictured his evening going like this—with him forced to leave a bar he'd stopped at on a whim due to a fire alarm, then stumbling over a sexy, unconscious girl in his own car.

He'd pointed her out to his oblivious driver. Richie—who'd been fighting with his girlfriend every other hour since Slone had hired him—wasn't the most observant sort when not driving. As proven by the blonde in the torn coat.

The coat. It looked old, like something out of a rag bag. So did the gloves covering her small hands. He couldn't see what else she had on as she was curled into a ball in the corner, her legs tucked under her on the seat. And suddenly Slone thought of a third reason for her presence: she could be homeless. Cold. Desperate.

He understood the feeling. At least, the desperate part. And some people would probably describe him as cold.

Homeless, however, he was not. In fact, avoiding his home, where he would have to play host to his pushy family

tomorrow, was why he'd had Richie cruise around Chicago
for a while tonight, rather than heading right to his penthouse. And the resulting pit stop at a downtown bar to kill
some more time—and wait for the snowplows to get ahead
of them—had left him with this unexpected stowaway.

"I swear, boss, I didn't hear her get in, didn't even see her
back there. She musta been real silent. Sneaky-like."

Slone doubted that. More likely Richie had been trying
to out shout his girlfriend.

"You want I should roust her outta there?"

Glancing at his watch, Slone gave it some thought. It was
only nine-thirty, he had nowhere to go and nothing special
to do until the Bossy Women's Brigade, in the form of his
family, descended tomorrow afternoon for lunch. The bar
was closed and fire trucks with sirens blaring—not that his
guest noticed—were now pulling into the parking lot.

This woman could provide a nice diversion. "Let's drive
around for a little while."

His driver gaped. "You mean…with her?"

Slone nodded. "Yes. With her."

"Are you going to wake her up?"

"That isn't my intention."

His employee slowly shook his head but didn't say a
word. Instead, he turned around in his seat. Slone watched
the woman, wondering if the car's shift from a slow idling
rumble into Drive would awaken her. But it didn't.

Not thinking about it, he reached for the switch and
closed the privacy panel. It wasn't as if he was planning
anything private. He'd never had sex back here—though
there had been one occasion when a singer he'd dated had
been determined to give him a so long blow job before she
moved out of state. Now, though, nothing could happen

with an unconscious stranger. But he wanted to watch her…
without Richie watching *him.*

He slid down the long side seat until he sat across from
the blonde. Close enough to feel her warmth and to smell
the subtly exotic perfume rising from her skin.

Who are you?

Shrugging out of his coat and jacket, he loosened his tie,
which he'd had on for a dinner meeting, then unbuttoned the
top few buttons of his shirt. He sprawled back in his seat,
pouring himself a drink from a glittering decanter in the limo's
bar. Bringing the crystal glass to his lips, he slowly sipped
from it, never taking his eyes off his slumbering companion.

The car was warm, yet her arms were wrapped tightly
around her waist. It was as if in her dreams she was still
outside and needed more protection than her ragged coat
could provide against the bitter winter air. The way she hugged
her body pushed the curves of her full breasts high—high
enough to put the taste buds in Slone's mouth on high alert.

She was much more voluptuous than he'd first realized.

With her chin tucked into her collar, her golden hair had
fallen across her face. Long, curly strands hung well down
the front of her, draping the curves of her breasts. An image
swept through his brain of her wearing nothing but that hair,
with her rosy, hard nipples thrusting through in invitation.

He sipped before continuing his visual survey.

Slone obviously couldn't determine what color her closed
eyes were. But he had a perfect view of that full lower lip
pushed out in a tiny pout. Not to mention the high curve of
her cheek and the delicate length of her neck.

Shifting as a hot flow of sensual interest washed through
him, he took back his earlier determination. She *was* beautiful. And perfectly made-up, wearing women's armor de-

signed to bring a man to his knees. From the thick mass of
curls surrounding her face to the gleam of glittering shadow
on her eyelids and the trace of pink on her cheeks, she
looked ready for a night out at someplace much more ex-
clusive than the bar they'd just left.

None of which matched his homeless theory.

But Slone wasn't a stupid man. It didn't take long for him
to put it all together. The ragged coat and gloves told one
story…the face, hair and dramatic makeup another. Even her
presence in the car now made much more sense.

She'd seen him inside. Recognized him from one of the
articles the local papers and even some national tabloids had
done on him. He was, after all, the bachelor heir to a multi-
million-dollar real-estate empire right here in Chicago. So the
blonde had seen her chance with him and had climbed into
his car to make him an offer she hoped he wouldn't refuse.

The stranger didn't live on the streets. She *worked* them.

He was still mulling on that realization—what he felt
about it…what he would *do* about it—when he saw the
woman begin to move. Still slumbering, she stretched
slowly, sighing deep in her throat and tilting her head side
to side.

The hair fell back from her face, the arms released the tight
clench on the coat. It fell open even further, exposing not only
the long line of her neck, the hollow of her throat, the creamy
skin of her chest and that mouthwatering cleavage, but
more…the shapely midriff, small waist and the long line of
upraised thigh pressed hard against her bloodred dress.

Slone's body reacted. Every ounce of blood not required to
move oxygen from here to there roared to his groin. His cock
sprang from lazy interest to full, raging want. And there was
no longer any question of what he was going to do about it.

Though they'd been riding in steady silence for several long minutes, Slone was forcibly reminded of the condition of the roads when the limo swerved sharply to the left. He flattened one hand on the leather seat next to him, feeling the car go into a slide, but it quickly straightened out. Richie's voice came over the intercom. "Sorry, boss, some jackass in a black SUV is coming up way too fast behind me."

Before Slone could respond, the car slid again, harder now, with a long screech of brakes and a strident beep of the horn. This time, his hand wasn't enough to stop him from sliding to the edge of his seat…or to keep the sweet package in the red dress safely in hers.

She bounced and tumbled, falling from her curled-up position in the corner…and landing right on his lap.

"Well, hello," he murmured, hardly noticing as the driver righted the car and things got back to normal. Because now that this sexy, sweet-smelling, incredibly soft female was in his arms, he didn't know if anything would be normal again.

Her lids didn't rise immediately. It seems as if even the jostling of the car wasn't enough to rouse her out of her pleasurable dreams…but the warmth of his embrace was. Because she suddenly went from sleep to full consciousness, taking everything in on a quick, quiet inhalation.

Confronted with the bluest set of eyes he'd ever seen, he couldn't help smiling down at her and sweeping a long strand of blond hair off her face. Nor could he prevent himself from saying what had most been on his mind since he'd figured out who she was. And what she most likely did for a living.

"So…how much?"

2

LEAH WAS DREAMING. She had to be. She'd dozed off thinking of her Prince Charming. Her subconscious brain had conjured him up and gifted her with the fantasy that he was sprawled right beneath her, warm and solid against her hip and thighs. Asking her...*how much?*

"What?" she murmured, shaking her head to clear it even as she blinked once, then again, trying to figure out if she was awake or not. Because if this wasn't a dream, then she really was half lying across the lap of an incredibly sexy man eyeing her with speculation and visible hunger.

He appeared tall, broad in the shoulders, with thick arms that flexed beneath the rolled-up sleeves of his pristine white dress shirt. His light brown hair had streaks of gold that caught the low amber light in the car, reflecting it back in a series of dazzling glints. Those intense eyes, locked solidly on her, were a vivid green, widely spaced and heavily lashed. Seeing everything. Revealing nothing.

Sporting a light five o'clock shadow, his square jaw was slightly swarthy, but perfectly matched his tousled hair, loosened tie and open collar. And the cords of muscle in his neck hinted at the power of the rest of his body, made so obvious by the firm thighs beneath her.

He was utter male perfection. A man right off a movie screen or a magazine page…masculine, devastatingly handsome, overpoweringly male.

And she had absolutely no idea who he was.

A dream. Just a dream. But I don't really want to wake up.

"Well? Are you going to name a price?"

Those words convinced Leah she was not dreaming. Jerking straight up and scrambling off his lap to her own seat, she stared at him. Her jaw hung open, her heart pounding so loud he could probably hear it.

"I never do this, but your ploy worked. I'm hooked." The man straightened in his seat. Dropping his elbows onto his knees, he leaned forward—close enough that she could feel the warmth of his breath on her cheek and inhale the most deliciously masculine scent she'd ever experienced.

"I want you," he said, his voice soft but unwavering.

Leah continued to stare, too shocked to even think right. Her pulse beat wildly in her throat, she could feel it, and her audible breath provided the only sound in the otherwise silent car. *The car.* Whose car? "Where are we? Whose car is this?"

Where was Bridget?

"Come on, you don't have to pretend. Your plan worked—you climbed in here and waited for me, laying yourself out like an irresistible appetizer on a banquet table." He almost growled as he added, "And it worked. You've aroused my…appetite."

Leah gulped. The man was devouring her with his eyes. As if knowing he was looking at her like a wolf eyeing a sheep, he glanced away. "You looked so peaceful in your sleep that I told my driver to cruise around for a while." He smiled, his teeth glittering in the semidarkness. "While I figured out what to *do* with you."

Do with her? His tone said he wanted to do everything with her. While she should have immediately panicked, wondered if he was a serial killer who wanted to do crazy, psycho things to her, she knew what he *really* meant.

He wanted to have sex with her. Wild, uncontrolled, body-rocking sex. And he thought that was what she was offering by stowing away in his car.

Everything suddenly made sense. She'd been so focused on getting out of the cold that she'd assumed this limo was the correct one. What were the chances of two black stretches being parked outside a raucous club on a dark, snowy night? Though she'd sensed something was wrong at first, her fatigue and the drinks hadn't let her think too much about it.

"Uh, listen…" she began to explain, not even sure what she was going to say. Then, suddenly, his original question returned to mind, bringing with it new implications as she reevaluated the situation. *"How much?"*

He thought she was a prostitute?

"How much do you want for the night?" he murmured. He reached for her, lifting a hand to her hair and pushing it back, the tips of his fingers brushing against the pulse in her temple. Leah shivered a little, though not from cold. She was suddenly hot…absolutely on fire. Though she got naked in front of men every night of the week, it had been months since one had touched her intimately. Seductively. Wickedly.

"The night," she repeated, probably sounding brainless. That was appropriate. She *was* brainless, weak, devoid of thought or will. At this moment, she was capable only of sensation.

He frowned forbiddingly. "I want the *whole* night." He continued to touch her, as if he liked the feel of her hair against his skin. She liked it, too. And she did not want it to end. Though she had turned down dozens of men ever since she started taking off her clothes for a living, *this* one, she wanted to take. To savor. To indulge.

She had one last moment of hesitation. "Are you single?"

He laughed softly, as if amused to have met a hooker with a conscience. Then he nodded and Leah didn't care what he thought of her. She only thought of the many long nights she'd spent alone since moving to this big, cold, impersonal city. And of the pleasure he could give her.

He was obviously wealthy—this was no rented limo and the thing practically wrapped around him like a cloak around its owner. A guy so far out of her league she'd probably never have laid eyes on him if not for this strange series of events tonight. One who wanted her on his terms: professional ones only. "Well, uh…"

His eyes narrowed. She suspected this man wasn't used to bogged-down negotiations. "Name your price."

He was a high-powered businessman, making a deal. Wanting a service and willing to pay for it.

Would he refuse that service if it were offered for free? If he felt there were strings attached because she was not what he thought she was?

"Do you want my driver to let you off somewhere?" he asked, his tone growing cool, as if he'd read a rejection in her pause.

Leah shook her head hard, making her decision fast. There was really no other decision to be made. She didn't *have* to go to work and she was being presented with a once-in-a-lifetime opportunity: to spend an erotic night with the kind of man she'd only ever *dreamed* about meeting. One who already had her heart in hyperdrive and her panties damp.

The situation was a definite no-brainer.

"No. I don't want to get out." Clearing her throat, she added, "You can have the whole night."

His eyes glimmered in satisfaction and a tiny smile widened those sensuous lips. "Your price?"

She might be allowing him to think she was a professional, at least for a little while—long enough to get what they were both, she suspected, dying for. But she couldn't outright lie. So she didn't. "Nothing. I don't want your money."

His brow furrowed and he opened his mouth as if to argue. Leah didn't give him a chance. Putting her fingers against his lips, and gasping as he nipped at them with his teeth, she used her free hand to unfasten the few buttons on her coat. The man's green eyes widened as he watched her push the thing to the edge of her shoulders to display the entire glittery bodice of the low-cut velvet gown beneath. The neckline revealed a large amount of her more-than-ample cleavage and his attention zoned in there and there it stayed.

"My God, you're incredible," he muttered.

Liking the pure avarice in his voice, she leaned over, letting the gown gape further, knowing exactly how to give a man a few glimpses to whet his appetite. This particular man looked like he was starving.

Leah found herself getting caught up in the fantasy. It was like being part of a sultry game played by two lovers—hooker and rich john. But she was the only one who realized it was just an act.

"Lose the coat," he ordered, sounding demanding and

powerful. The intensity made her shiver, because it illustrated his pure, unadulterated desire for her.

Letting the coat fall away, she slid her dress up, revealing her legs an inch at a time. His gaze shifted to them, his body stiffening when the red fabric reached the top of her thighs to reveal the hem of her silky stockings. "I don't know what I want to do with you first," he muttered as he stared at her legs.

"You have the whole night to find out," she whispered. Climbing onto him, she spread her thighs to straddle his lap, shivering at the feel of his heat and the massive erection that brushed against her moist panties. She didn't settle in for a hot ride through their clothes, though, instead pulling herself slightly off him…to heighten the anticipation.

She'd waited a long time for a night like this with a *man* like this. No way did she want it to end too soon.

"The whole night?" he confirmed, back to bargaining.

"Uh-huh." Twining her fingers in his hair, she pushed his head back and murmured, "And all you'll have to pay me is pleasure."

THE INCREDIBLY SENSUAL young woman was playing some kind of game with him, but right now, with her long hair brushing his face and her delicious body right above him, Slone didn't really care. She was no street-corner hooker, he realized. The blonde was, judging by her sensual-yet-elegant dress, a highly paid professional. Despite the coat.

So this game she played was obviously part of her routine. She was holding out to ask for more later—a sort of money-back guarantee based on how much she pleased him.

Slone was a businessman, he could understand and

respect that. But she was taking a risk that he'd not be satisfied. So she must be very confident of her...abilities.

Staring down into his face, she began to smile, sweet and sensual. She was kneeling a heartbeat above him, her body held a scant inch above his. Slone reflexively jerked up, needing to feel her heat, to lose himself in that feminine moisture that raised his appetite every time he breathed it in. But she remained just out of reach. Teasing, tantalizing, arousing him until he was holding his breath in pure expectation of something very good to come.

Snagging her bottom lip between her teeth and closing her eyes, she swayed—slowly, gracefully—then leaned closer. Her upper body brushed against his, her puckered nipples scraping him through her gown and his shirt. "You're so warm."

And *she* was so incredibly *hot*. "Let me taste you."

Unable to stand it, Slone lifted his hands to her hair and tangled his fingers in her long curls. He needed more. He needed to experience every bit of her.

He'd never been with a professional, but he remembered from the movies that they didn't want to be kissed on the mouth.

Tough. He had to kiss her or die.

Tugging her closer, he held her tight, not letting her refuse him as his lips met hers and parted. She didn't even try to resist, welcoming him into her mouth, tilting her head to the side so their tongues could play and mate more deeply.

Lowering one hand to her zipper, he slowly tugged it down, traipsing his fingers across her spine, savoring each tiny bump and curve as it was revealed. She was so soft, her skin as pliant and smooth as the velvet of her dress.

Releasing her hair, he reached for the top of the loosened

dress, slowly pushing it to the edges of her shoulders. His senses reeling, he finally drew his mouth away from hers, hauling in a deep ragged breath as he reminded himself to slow down. Savor. Enjoy.

Kissing his way down her cheek and jaw, he nuzzled into her sweet-smelling throat, then tasted a path along the shoulder he'd just uncovered. "What's your name?" he murmured.

Quivering—arching toward his mouth every time he moved it—she replied, "Leah Muldoon. Yours?"

He suspected she knew but played her game anyway. "Slone Kincaid."

"Slone," she repeated, her voice throaty, almost a purr. "I like the way that tastes."

"My name?"

She nodded. "Some words taste good when you say them. Like…*serendipitous.*"

He got that. Especially on a night like this one.

"*You* taste good," he replied, tugging on both sleeves now, watching the dress drift down her arms. It didn't fall away completely, however, hanging on the tops of the full breasts he'd been coveting since he'd spotted her.

"Use your mouth on me," she ordered, as if knowing he was dying to do just that.

He lowered his face to the generous cleavage, breathing her in, rubbing his cheeks against the plump curves. Nudging the dress out of the way, he groaned at the sight of her strapless pink bra, which pushed her up invitingly. He did as she asked—tasting her—running the tip of his tongue across the seam of the fabric, feeling her jerk in reaction.

She arched back, wanting more, and he gave it to her. Tugging the lacy bra away, he swiped his tongue across her puckered nipple. She jerked in response, grinding against him, finally removing that last inch of space between them.

The heat of her eliminated any remaining patience Slone had. Thrusting against her, he mimicked the way he'd soon be pounding into her tight, wet channel. She gasped and rode him, gliding up and down his rock-hard erection, making mewling little sounds of pleasure as she took what she needed.

"Get out of this," he ordered, pushing the bra down. He barely noticed her complying as she reached around to unfasten the bra. He was much too busy catching the lush curves in his hands, squeezing them and bringing them to his lips. Sucking hard on one nipple, he was rewarded by one more spasmodic jerk and then an audible cry.

Slone looked up, shocked to see the blonde's head thrown back, her face flushed, her mouth opening on several tiny gasps. If he didn't know better, he'd think she'd just…

"Oh, how I *needed* that," she muttered, finally opening her eyes and staring down at him. Her breathing remained ragged, her pulse fluttering visibly in her throat. Finally, she smiled. "A few more of those and you will absolutely have paid in full."

God. She *had* just…. Either that, or she was good at faking it. Of course, she would be, given her profession. Slone thrust that thought away. He knew how to pleasure a woman. Just because she had sex a lot didn't mean she couldn't enjoy it.

Leah would enjoy it. He'd make damn sure of it.

Knowing now that she was capable of gaining real pleasure and feeling almost challenged to ensure she continued to, Slone forced himself to slow down. His frantic caresses and strokes became slow ones. He teased her nipples, kissing his way around them but not giving her the hard suction he knew she wanted. And all the while she squirmed on his lap, trying to push her dress—now gathered at her waist—off her body.

Finally, as if knowing he wouldn't relent, she went to work on him. "You don't look very comfortable," she murmured. She tugged his tie free, then undid the remaining buttons of his shirt. When she pushed it off his shoulders, she leaned back and stared at him. "Good Lord, you are amazing."

He almost smiled at her candor, unused to such openness. She seemed to genuinely delight in touching him, kissing his neck, wrapping her hands in his hair. Finally, when she reached for his belt and worked it open, then unbuttoned his trousers, Slone knew they were both ready for a much deeper connection. If she kept her hands down there, he'd lose precious minutes of having his cock where he most wanted it to be.

"Undress." He scooted her back to help her.

"About time. I was beginning to wonder if you were going to just slide into me through the velvet."

"That sounds…interesting," he murmured, watching her intently as she moved off his lap and pushed the dress down over her curvy hips, then past a set of pale, slender thighs encased in those silky, thigh-high stockings, until she wore just a tiny pair of lacy pink panties.

The car rocked. Or at least his insides did.

"But I think latex would probably be more appropriate," she said, reaching for her handbag. She plucked a condom from it.

Obviously, the professional came prepared.

The sight of it in her hands—and the knowledge that

soon it would be the only thing separating his sex from hers—made him even harder, his cock swelling out of his unbuttoned pants.

She noticed. Hell, a blind nun would have noticed. Widening her eyes, she licked her lips. "Oh, my goodness," she murmured, sounding adorably innocent. And suddenly looking very young.

That gave him pause. "How old are you?"

Her eyes glued to his crotch, she replied, "Twenty-two."

Old enough. Not quite his twenty-seven, but old enough.

Leah slid off him completely, moving to the other seat. With the skill of a temptress, she caressed her body in a slow stroke until her fingertips rested on the hem of one stocking.

"Leave them on," he ordered.

Nodding, she reached for the lacy edge of her panties.

"Leave those on, too."

Quirking a brow in confusion, Slone made his intentions clear. He reached for her, tracing the elastic of her panties, from hip down to the juncture of her thighs. The fabric was moist there. Leah moaned as he slipped his finger around the barrier, tangling it in her soft curls, then sliding it into her slick crevice. She was sweet and hot and incredibly wet. There was no mistaking pure, genuine arousal. Whatever the reason she'd wound up in his car, she wanted him now, that was certain.

Using his thumb, he found her taut little clit and played it like a tiny, beautiful instrument while continuing to make love to her with one finger, then two. But her cries of pleasure soon turned into pleas for more. And Slone gave up any effort to draw this out. He needed her…needed to be in her. Now.

Pushing his clothes out of the way and sheathing himself,

he tore her panties off and tugged her back onto his lap. This time, there was no teasing, no holding herself away. Leah wrapped her hands in his hair, pressing her mouth to his in a hot kiss, then impaled herself on him in one deep, hard stroke.

Bliss. It was pure, physical perfection. She was so damn hot, wrapped around him like a glove, bathing him in sensation. Slone pushed up harder and Leah groaned as she took everything he had to give her, gasping at the intensity of it.

"Beautiful," he muttered hoarsely as they began to rock and sway. She met every upward movement and answered it with a hard plunge down, and they found a perfect syncopation.

They thrust hard, kissing and stroking in almost violent need. "You're so damn tight," he muttered. He caught her hips to hold her still so he could pound into her so deep she'd never be able to forget he'd been inside her.

"It's been a long time," she replied, her words choppy. Her head was back, her eyes closed as she silently urged him onward.

Hot sensation roared through him, every nerve ending coming alive to join in the final race to the finish. Heat sluiced through his veins, gathering in his groin with a demanding throb that wouldn't wait any longer.

He couldn't stop, not for anything. Not even when the strange words she'd said sunk into his head, bouncing around but not making any sense to his lust-drenched brain. Until finally, with his hands twined in her hair as he ravenously kissed her willing mouth, he let his climax come and emptied himself inside her.

3

THERE WERE WORSE PLACES to fall asleep than in the arms of a supersexy, naked rich guy. Leah could think of a lot of them. A whole lot.

But she couldn't think of many better ones.

So when she did wake up from the brief, satiated sleep she'd tumbled into after their wild lovemaking, she wasn't too quick to move away. He'd shifted her around, so they were both lying on the long bench seat, and tucked her in front of him with a possessive arm around her waist. Settled in against him, as comfortable as if they'd known each other for months rather than an hour, Leah yawned.

Though she thought he might have dozed off, too, his voice told her otherwise. "You're not a prostitute, are you?"

Not even turning in his arms to look at him, Leah chuckled and shook her head. "Uh, that'd be a no."

"Hell."

"You're disappointed that I'm not a prostitute?"

She wondered why his answer mattered so much to her. What difference did it make? She'd gotten what she wanted:

some great sex. Who cared what someone she'd never see again after tonight thought?

He ran the tips of his fingers up and down her bare arm, the contact sending little trills of delight through her. "Not disappointed, just feeling like shit for assuming it."

His answer pleased her, which was when she realized she definitely did care what someone she'd never see again after tonight thought.

"Has it really been…a long time?"

Men. So territorial. She answered truthfully. "Yes. Quite a while."

She'd swear she could feel his chest puff out. Again. Men. So territorial. "It's not like I prefer celibacy," she retorted.

"So why do you carry condoms in your purse if you're not having sex?"

She snorted. "Who better to carry condoms than someone who isn't getting it…but really *wants* it?" Blowing out a harsh breath, she added, "Imagine if I hadn't had any on me tonight, now wouldn't I be frustrated?"

"No, you'd be in the parking lot of the nearest twenty-four hour convenience store that sells them."

Chuckling at his vehemence, she replied, "That would have been an interesting stop to explain to your driver."

"He's not paid to think about what I'm doing." A trace of arrogance appeared in his voice. The man was used to getting what he wanted and was probably a little spoiled. But he was so darned sexy, she just couldn't bring herself to care.

"My turn to ask a question. Why did you think I was a prostitute?"

"Well, you did just have sex with a complete stranger in the back of a limo."

Pot meet kettle. She shot back without thinking. "So did you." She held her breath for a second, wondering how he'd react, then heard him chuckle.

"True."

Wanting to see the laugh lines beside his eyes, Leah shifted in his arms until she was lying flat on her back. Looking up at him as he continued to recline on his side next to her, she couldn't help but notice again just how handsome the man was. Shockingly handsome—much too suave and sexy for a small-town runaway, a high-school dropout who'd just taken her GED a year ago and wasn't likely to finish college until she was thirty at the rate she was going.

But maybe not too out of reach for the siren she played when she danced at Leather and Lace. Men of all classes wanted that woman. And she—Leah's alter ego—*was* worthy of a night in the arms of a man like this one.

Damned if Leah wasn't going to take it.

"I'm very glad we were both so easy," he murmured.

Aside from giving her a perfect view of his strong jaw and lean cheeks, Leah's new position tugged Slone's attention in other directions, too. His gaze shifted down, his lips parting on an audible breath as he studied her full breasts. Her nipples hardened under his stare, practically begging for more of the thorough attention he'd given them a little while ago. Beside her hip she felt his sex stirring again and she arched as warm awareness surged through her again.

The man certainly seemed able to fill a "whole night."

She could hardly wait to continue it, but was curious enough to continue their conversation. "Okay, so we *were* both pretty easy. But why did you assume what you did about me even before I woke up?"

"Jaded, I guess. I figured you recognized me and saw the chance to make a buck by stowing away in my car…."

"I got in the wrong limo," she explained. "I rode down to the bar with a group of women in a rental limo, which looked a lot like this one in the dark." Shaking her head, she added, "Do you assume every woman you bump into is a hooker?"

He glanced toward her pretty velvet gown, now lying in a rumpled heap on the other seat. "The dress was a little…provocative and not exactly neighborhood-bar appropriate."

Leah couldn't help snorting a laugh. "Wait till I tell Izzie somebody mistook her bridesmaid gowns for hooker getups."

He sighed. "Bridesmaid?"

She nodded.

"Sorry. I just thought the rich-looking gown and the, uh, worn coat didn't quite fit together."

"You're right. They don't. I need to replace the coat, just haven't had the bucks." Before he even asked for an explanation, she added, "I'm working nights to put myself through school to become a nurse."

She didn't mention *what* she did on those nights…admitting she was a stripper might have him rethinking his initial suppositions about her. Some people couldn't separate exotic dancer from paid whore, as she knew from the occasional nasty client at the club.

Not that this guy was nasty, not in the least. He was sexy and hot and gentlemanly. Especially now when he was looking at her with tenderness and even a hint of sheepishness. "A nursing student. Well, I couldn't have fouled that up much more, could I?" Lifting a hand to her hair, he tenderly smoothed a long, blond strand away from her face. "Forgive me?"

"Don't sweat it. I'm not the type of woman to go all crazy, whacked-out, vengeful virgin because some guy made an incorrect assumption."

That smile widened. "Crazy, whacked-out, vengeful virgin, huh? Guess I should count myself lucky."

"Guess you should."

He slid his hand down her arm again, this time not stopping there, but continuing on so he could brush his fingertips over her hip. Then closer to the junction of her thighs. Leah quivered, arching toward his touch. "You're ready to count yourself lucky again, hmm?"

He nodded, bending down to cover her mouth with his, kissing her deeply, slowly, so thoroughly she felt as if he was memorizing the inside of her mouth for all eternity. No breath reached her lungs that hadn't crossed his lips first and by the time he lifted away from her, she was absolutely on fire for him again.

"You know, I'd like to slow things down. Why don't we take this someplace a little more comfortable," he whispered.

Leah opened her mouth to protest—she was fine right where she was—but before she could, Slone had reached for a small button on the wall and depressed it. "Time to head home now, Richie."

Leah immediately scanned the car, looking for a camera or something, praying the driver couldn't see back here. Why she should care about yet another man seeing her naked, she didn't know. But it probably had something to do with the fact that she was not standing on a stage in a darkened room, writhing to music, removed from the men watching her. Instead she was lying sated in the arms of a naked man, her whole body flushed with pleasure, her legs casually parted, her sex still swollen from his possession and slick with her renewed arousal.

Yeah, that'd be quite an eyeful.

"He can't see us," Slone murmured, reading her thoughts. Gently sliding her off his lap he reached for his shirt.

"We making any stops first, boss?" the voice from the intercom said.

The driver obviously wanted to know if they were taking Leah home. Considering she'd intended to go in to work tonight, she supposed she should be responsible about it. But she had promised this amazingly sexy man a whole night.

And she was selfish enough to want to give it to him.

He obviously wasn't even considering anything else. "No. Straight home." He flicked the switch off and smiled at Leah as he handed her her gown. "You're going to like my place. And you're *really* going to like my bed."

Though Slone wished the ride home would take its usual few minutes, the roads were still not in the best shape. So they picked their way through Chicago, Richie going easy on the curves and following the plows where possible.

They could have spent the time making love again, but something about the anticipation of having her in a bed made him wait. They'd jumped right into wild, backseat sex when they'd met. Now they were going back for a slow buildup before the next time.

He liked slow buildups…anticipating things. From a fine meal to a long-planned journey to the successful culmination of a hard-fought business venture, the trip itself was one of Slone's genuine pleasures.

Which made it pretty unusual that his hands were itching to stroke every inch of that luscious body now covered again in red velvet. To plunge into her and lose himself inside her and do her fast and furious until neither one of them were even capable of moving.

If she hadn't just put that dress back on and were still lying naked in his arms, he'd have said to hell with it. There'd be lots of buildup in his big, comfortable bed later tonight. After all, she had promised him the whole night.

Of course, she had promised it when he'd thought he was *paying* for it. But it didn't matter…he still intended to pay her, in exactly the currency she'd requested. Pleasure.

"So, you're rich, huh?" the adorable blonde asked as she moved to the seat opposite him. He wondered if she, too, was feeling some of the desperation in the air, and was also trying to prove—to both of them—that she could wait.

"I suppose."

She rolled her eyes. "It's not a question you can hedge on like that. If I'd asked you if you knew you were a total stud-muffin and you wanted to pretend to be modest you could say 'I suppose' or 'others might say so,' which would be total bullshit but at least understandable if you had a single modest bone in your body, which you don't."

Slone shook his head, not sure whether to laugh or be offended. "That was a mouthful."

She ignored him. "But rich is rich, it's not in the eye of the beholder."

"Unless you're some decently paid TV personality be-holding Oprah Winfrey's bank account."

Frowning, she grudgingly admitted, "Okay, there's wealthy, rich and filthy rich. Where do you fall in there?"

If he sensed she had a greedy, selfish bone in her body, he might have been concerned about the questions. But she didn't. He knew it, for some reason. Slone was a damn fine judge of character and he'd already pegged hers: ruthlessly honest, blunt and a whole lot more vulnerable than she'd ever want anyone to realize.

Her mouth confirmed the honest part. Her fingerless gloves the vulnerable part.

He'd put her in cashmere, if he had his way.

"Well?" she prompted.

"Put me closer to the I-won-the-lottery-in-a-small-state than the Bill Gates side of the scale, okay?"

"Gotcha." She shot him a thumbs-up. "And just to be fair so I don't seem rude for asking, I'll share, too. I am *so* not rich. Put me somewhere between the I-won-ten-bucks-on-a-scratch-off-ticket and the at-least-I'm-not-on-unemployment side of the scale."

Slone threw his head back and laughed, so damned charmed by her. She made him feel…young. Carefree.

In years, he was, indeed, pretty young. But carefree? Well, that he was not. Not nearly as much as some of his detractors might think.

Some would suspect that since he'd taken over a successful real-estate empire from his late father at the young age of twenty-two, he could be lazy and carefree, living off someone else's money. But Slone had been fighting for five years to keep that empire solvent. And to keep the world—and his own mother and sisters—from finding out just how far his father had let that business go in his final years.

It had taken Slone every ounce of energy and determination he had to get the Kincaid fortune back to where it had once been. There had been no time to be young and carefree. Or even to be involved in any kind of serious relationship with a woman.

Frankly, that had always seemed okay to Slone—especially given the determination of his mother and sisters to see him settled. He didn't mind dating *many* women and getting close to absolutely none, didn't mind bedding a woman, then going home alone. That was what he preferred.

Until tonight. He couldn't even be sure what had prompted him to demand a full night from Leah, nor what had caused him to suggest that they retreat to his place. He never brought a woman there if he could avoid it. But with Leah, he'd actually sought out that invasion of his personal life.

Bad move, Kincaid.

Perhaps. But at this moment, watching her, feeling smile after smile break out on his normally stern face, he couldn't bring himself to regret it.

One thing was sure, now that he'd met Leah he knew he'd been missing out on *one* thing: absolutely the best sex of his life. He'd had his fair share of women…but he'd never been as out of his mind insane with desire as he'd been with this stranger an hour ago.

"This is so much better than the L," Leah said, interrupting his musings.

She wiggled around in the seat, as if testing the cushiness against her bottom. Opening the minifridge, she helped herself to a bottle of spring water. Not content to sit still long enough to drink it, she got on her knees and turned around to peer out the window as they passed through the city.

Lord have mercy, he thought as he stared at her, kneeling, her curvy, gorgeous ass tilted right at him.

Slone reached for his nearly forgotten drink and took a deep sip from it, determined to remain strong and in control for at least the brief length of time it took them to get home.

She hardly seemed to notice. She kept fidgeting, pushing buttons—though, thankfully, not the one that operated the privacy screen. She flicked her nail against a crystal wineglass to listen to the ping and turned the radio on so loud his eardrums yelped.

She was, in every respect, delightful. And she most definitely delighted him. So much so that he wondered whether one night with her could *possibly* be enough.

4

SLONE KINCAID HAD predicted she'd like his place, but it wasn't until they reached his building, a glass-and-steel high-rise overlooking Lake Michigan, that she fully appreciated his prediction. She was awed when she walked—openmouthed—into the penthouse apartment. Not only because it was loaded with artwork that looked like it should be in a museum and furniture so warm and rich that she was afraid to sit on it, but also because the place was about as big as a football field.

But that wasn't all. He'd predicted she'd like his bed. When she saw the enormous plush monstrosity dominating the master bedroom and realized the man slept on something that could double as an aircraft carrier, she announced, "Like it? I freakin' *love* it!"

"I thought you might."

"And you own it?"

He nodded, crossing to the other side of the room to close the drapes overlooking the sparkling lake—christened with dollops of white ice—in the distance. "Yes."

Suddenly struck by something, Leah threw her arms akimbo and said, "This is *so Pretty Woman*."

"But she *was* a prostitute."

"Yeah, yeah. Come on, did you ever *really* buy her as a working girl?"

"Let's not use me as the gauge, considering how our evening started."

Laughing, Leah spun around, kicking off her shoes so her feet could sink into the plush carpeting. She'd seen places like this in movies, but couldn't believe people actually lived in them. "You live here all by yourself?"

"Some of the help comes by, but for the most part, yes."

"Then why on earth were you in that crummy bar? If I lived in a place like this, I'd never leave."

"That might get lonely," he murmured.

She snapped her fingers. "I'd just summon people here if I needed them."

Beginning to unbutton the dress shirt he'd just put back on in the car, he chuckled. "Summon? That sounds a little…arrogant." Leah offered him a wry stare. He immediately got the point and tilted his chin up, in mock offense. "What makes you think I'm arrogant?"

"You *did* accuse me of being a hooker who was trying to trap you by stowing away in your car."

He shrugged…a mere trifle, obviously. "Other than that."

"You take whatever you want." *Including her.*

"And?"

"You certainly aren't used to being told no."

"Funny, I don't recall that word coming out of your mouth tonight," he said with a tiny, wicked smile. He stepped closer, shirtless, his lean, muscled body absolutely amazing in the full light of the room.

The man obviously didn't sit behind a desk all day.

Unable to contain a shaky sigh, she murmured, "Wow, you have got it going on."

He quirked a brow. "Is that a good thing or a bad one?"

"Good. Definitely good."

"Then thank you. Now, are you going to take that dress off or are we going to try it…through the fabric?"

Leah gasped, remembering the way she'd taunted him earlier. It was very wicked. And very tempting. But also very out of the question. "Uh-uh. This dress cost me a whole week's pay."

He reached for her sleeve, trailing his fingers along it. "I'll buy you another one."

The playful, teasing tone said she should take no offense, but Leah stiffened, anyway. "Do we need to go back over that whole 'I'm not a prostitute' thing?"

His hand fell away and he stared at her in shock. *"What?"*

She may have overreacted. Guys like Kincaid were probably used to buying stuff for their spoiled girlfriends. But she wasn't one of them—she was a one-night diversion. "I'm sorry, I didn't mean to be so touchy. Just want to make sure we're clear: I'm here because I want to be here." She stepped closer, lifting a hand to his bare chest, stroking her fingertips across one flat nipple, then lightly raking her nails down his side. "Because I want you. For the rest of the night."

"And in the morning?"

"We say goodbye."

He frowned, as if not liking that, but didn't argue. Even as wildly attracted to one another as they were, he had to realize—as Leah did—that they were, in every other way, completely incompatible.

WRAPPED IN THE NAKED embrace of the lush-bodied woman with whom he'd spent so many incredible hours during the night, Slone slowly awoke the next morning to the sound of voices. Women's voices. Women's voices *inside* his apartment.

Glancing at the clock, he realized it was nearly noon. They had stayed up until late in the night, making love, raiding the kitchen, making love, taking a bath in his two-person tub. It was no wonder they'd slept so late. Late enough that it was almost time for the arrival of his mother and two sisters, doing their monthly let's-remind-Slone-he-is-a-member-of-a-family thing.

God how he hoped his housekeeper had forgotten something and come back in. But since it was Sunday morning and she was about as Catholic as one could be without actually being called Father, he doubted it.

"Hell-ooo?"

Shit. He recognized that laughing, lilting tone. His little sister, Jess, had tormented him with it throughout their childhood. And because the woman had absolutely no respect for anybody else's privacy, he felt sure she was the one who'd used an emergencies-only key to let the gaggle in when he hadn't answered the door.

"Where are you?"

He had time to do one thing—yank a sheet across his lap and Leah's naked body—before the door flew open.

"Don't tell me you're still in…" Jess's jaw dropped and her eyes widened as she saw the bright blond hair strewn across Slone's pillow. "Whoops!"

"Would you shut the damn door," he bit out from between clenched teeth.

Leah shifted and sighed heavily in her sleep. Putting a possessive hand on her shoulder, he glared at his sister. "I'll be out in a minute. Keep the others from coming—"

"Morning sleepyhead!" said another woman's voice.

Oh, brilliant. His other sister. Fortunately, Jess reacted in a cooperative way for once—rather than a mischievous one. She kept their older sister Katherine from coming in, saying, "He's not quite decent."

"I'll be out in five minutes. Shut the door before Mother walks in, would you please?"

Jess did, without another word, though her shoulders shook with laughter.

Running a frustrated hand through his hair, he gently shook Leah's shoulder. The woman was a sound sleeper—she didn't even budge. He couldn't resist bending down to nibble on her earlobe and her throat, whispering, "We've got company."

"Delivery man from Dunkin' Donuts?" she mumbled.

"Not quite. It's my family."

She remained still for a second, then, going from zonked-out sleep to wakefulness, she shot up in the bed. The covers fell off her, puddling in her lap, revealing those beautiful breasts, still slightly reddened from his kisses and the brush of his grizzled jaw against them. "Your *family?* Now?" As he nodded, she leapt out of the bed, grabbing her dress and underclothes and raced into the bathroom. "Oh, my God, do you have a back door? A fire escape?"

Laughing softly, Slone followed her. "It's fine. I'm a grown man and my mother and sisters know that. I'll introduce you to them, you can stay for lunch." The words had left his mouth without him giving them a thought, but once they were out there, Slone didn't regret them.

He'd asked her for a night. Now he knew he wanted more. How much more he couldn't say. All he knew was that he couldn't—simply could not—give up the feeling of pure delight she'd inspired in him from the moment he'd first seen her.

She stared at him, those wide blue eyes sparkling and sapphirelike in the bright light of morning. "I'm not the type of girl you introduce to the rich mama."

He took her chin in his hand, leaned down and pressed a hard, possessive kiss on her mouth. "Don't sell yourself short. You're a lovely, innocent young woman."

She rolled her eyes and blew out a disbelieving breath. "No, I'm—"

"Leah, I could tell you didn't have a lot of experience before last night…and hadn't had sex in a long time." She nibbled her bottom lip, as if wondering if he were being critical.

He wasn't. Not at all. In fact, he'd found her relative inexperience absolutely heady. Because it had left her very…very curious. And willing to try absolutely anything. "It was still so good I'm not sure how long my legs will hold me up today," he told her, wanting that concern out of her head.

That got a smile out of her. Before she could say anything, he continued. "I'm a very good judge of character. And they're going to love you." Knowing he needed to go deal with his family. "Now, take your time, I'm going to pull on some clothes and go out there to lay the groundwork."

She opened her mouth to protest, but Slone didn't listen. Instead, he went back into the bedroom, pulled on clothes, then went into his living room, where the three women in his life sat whispering. He had absolutely no doubt about what.

Not the least bit embarrassed, since, after all, they hadn't even bothered to knock, he greeted his mother, smiled at his pregnant older sister and glared at his smirking younger one. Since they were all "civilized" no one so much as blinked when he mentioned that a friend would be joining them. But just to ensure nobody got the wrong idea, he added, "She's a lovely young woman. A hardworking nursing student." He didn't really have a way to explain the gown, so he left it at that.

"Psst."

Hearing something, he glanced toward the hallway leading to his bedroom, seeing Leah there, twisting her hands. She looked about as ready to walk in and join them as Marie Antoinette must have felt when she'd walked up the steps to the guillotine.

Smiling, he murmured, "Excuse me," and strode to her side. "Come on, they're dying to meet you."

"No."

He took her arm. "It'll be fine. It's just lunch, Leah, not a big deal."

"It is a big deal to me," she snapped, trying to pull her arm away. "I don't belong here."

"Don't be ridiculous. I'm not a snob and neither is anyone in my family. There's no shame in being a struggling student."

"No, Slone…"

He slid an arm around her waist, wondering if he was going to have to pick up the amusingly stubborn young woman. Which was when she wriggled out of his embrace. "Will you *listen* to me?" Her voice grew louder, now she wasn't just embarrassed, she was getting annoyed. At *him,* for not paying attention.

Slone immediately shut up and didn't try to touch her again. But she was already on a tangent and barely noticed. Her voice continued to rise as she said, "It was one night, okay? That's it. You will *not* be introducing me to your rich, high-class family because I'm just not the girl you bring around the folks. Especially not the Magnificent Mile type folks."

"You're wrong, Leah. You're adorable and honest and—"

"And a stripper!" she snapped.

Slone froze, just watching her. Looking miserably toward the trio in the living room—who had to have heard—then back at him, she added, "I strip at a club called Leather and Lace. So you see, I'm not exactly one of the ladies-who-lunch crowd."

Stepping back, his body rigid, he stared at her, hard. "The nursing school business…"

"That's true. I *am* going to school. But I pay for it by taking off my clothes in front of strange men."

And on that note, with her words echoing in the penthouse, Leah tugged her ragged coat over her shoulders and hurried to the front door, slamming it as she left.

LEAH USUALLY HAD A SMILE on her face when she danced. But as she got off the train and walked toward the club on Sunday evening, she was *not* smiling. In fact, anyone who looked at her closely would see her red-rimmed eyes and realize the truth: she'd been crying much of the day. Crying over a guy she'd known less than twenty-four hours.

She didn't cry because she was heartbroken—hell, it wasn't like they'd had a *real Pretty Woman* romance and fallen in love or anything. But she'd liked him. Oh, had she liked him. And she'd sensed she could fall for him very easily, even if he'd been just a blue-collar guy she'd met in a bar, rather than a business magnate who lived in a penthouse.

They'd had amazing chemistry and they'd laughed and

she'd seen a lightness in his smile when they were together that hadn't been there at first. Despite having what most people would consider everything, she knew from some of the things he'd shared with her during the night that his life was not an easy one. And was, in fact, lonely.

Somehow, deep inside, she almost felt that he needed her.

"Forget it," she mumbled. "He needs you like he needs one of those ten-dollar scratch-off tickets."

Bringing her curled hands close to her face, she blew on them, trying to stay warm. Another lovely day in Chi-Town. Man, she might *have* to break down and get that coat.

Keeping her head down as she walked, she almost didn't see the big, dark car pulled directly in front of the crosswalk until she almost walked right into it. "Hey, loser, ever heard of stopping for pedestrians?" she yelled before thinking better of it. That was when she noticed the length of the car. It was a limo. "Oh, perfect." Yet another reminder of the crazy night before and the way it had ended.

About to stride around behind it, she shifted to the left, but was stopped when the back door opened. And that was when her heart just stopped.

"Kincaid?" she whispered.

"Hello, Leah."

She sucked her bottom lip into her mouth, not sure what this meant. Coincidences this big just didn't happen. Not outside of fiction. "What a surprise."

"No surprise. I was on my way to try to find you at your club when I spotted you."

He'd been seeking her out…and had been prepared to do it at Leather and Lace? "Why?"

Slone stepped out from behind the door, pushing it shut behind him. "I wanted to see you, to apologize."

"For what?"

"For being such an ass about you staying for lunch. Honestly, I dread those things and was really hoping you'd liven it up." With a sheepish shrug he added, "*And* get the women in my family to realize I can choose my own women."

She snorted. "Oh, right. I'm sure they're feeling real good right about now, you choosing to bring a stripper home and all."

"Not that I would give a damn, but the truth is, they're not snobs. My mother was a waitress, we weren't raised to feel entitled to anything. Working your way through school is damned hard and you're doing the best you can. Nobody can think worse of you for that."

He sounded like he meant it. And the look in his eyes underscored the sentiment. "Okay…apology accepted." Knowing she owed him one, too, she added, "And I'm sorry I didn't tell you right up front what my job was."

"Considering I'd already mistaken you for a hooker, I think I can understand why you didn't." Reaching for her hands, which were still clasped in front of her face, he wrapped them in his own. "You need some new gloves."

She shrugged.

He pulled her closer. "And a new coat."

"I know." She stiffened, wondering if he was going to offer to replace them, as he had last night with her gown.

"But until you can afford them," he added, his tone quiet and gentle, "feel free to use me to keep you warm."

Leah tilted her head back, looking into his handsome face. The man wasn't just flirting—making a come-on about getting naked to stay warm. He was doing so much more. Accepting who she was, conceding her right to be independent.

And actually blocking the cold Chicago wind with his back to protect her in the warm shelter of his embrace.

Nobody had ever protected her. Not her father who'd bailed when she was ten. Certainly not her drunk mother or her scumbag stepfather. Nobody.

Tears rose to her eyes again. "I appreciate that offer."

"Good."

Lifting a leather-gloved hand to her cheek, he cupped it, then leaned down to brush a sweet, soft kiss across her lips. "Leah?"

"Yes?"

"Does that mean you'll go out with me sometime?"

Go out…on a date. Pretty hilarious given the wild sensual games they'd played in his bed last night. Yet absolutely right for this new phase they were entering.

She sensed this phase could be very important indeed. One that could lead to much more laughter and happiness. And perhaps even the kind of love she'd only ever dreamed about.

And it would start with a date.

"Yes, Slone," she replied, twining her arms around his neck and smiling up at him. "I will most definitely go out with you."

He covered her mouth with his, kissing her with the passion he'd displayed the night before. Yet there was something more—something achingly sweet and patient, so tender it brought tears to her eyes.

When the kiss ended, he wiped them away with the tip of one gloved finger. "Will you let me give you a lift to work?"

She glanced at the limo, so similar to the one she was supposed to get in the night before. How different might her life be right now if Bridget hadn't forgotten her phone, if Leah had paid more attention to where she was going.

There was only one word to describe all the tiny events that could have gone another way, but hadn't…leaving her here, in the arms of a glorious man.

"Serendipitous," she whispered.

Obviously hearing her, Slone nodded. "More. I think last night might have been the luckiest one of my life."

Wrapped against him, Leah couldn't help thinking it might well have been the luckiest of hers, too.

* * * * *

Three-Way

1

"OH, GOD, is that the fire alarm? We've got to get out of here.
Is that smoke? I think I smell smoke!"

There was no smoke, Mia Natale instantly realized. Not
unless you counted the steam rising off the skid marks the
customers near the door had made when the fire alarm
started wailing. The club was emptying rapidly.

"We have to get out of here…we'll be crushed, stampeded!"

Leave it to Gloria to go nuts in a crisis. Mia sighed, not
sure whether to argue that there was no smoke, or just push
her sister's melodramatic, *married* butt toward the door.

Vanessa saved her from having to make the decision.
"Follow me," she announced. The woman was tall—Ama-
zonian—almost six feet *without* the bridesmaid heels. So
when she moved toward the exit, the crowd parted. It was
like watching a queen on parade.

"How does she do that?" Gloria whispered as they followed.

Mia shrugged. "No idea. But I'm glad she's with us."
She'd just met Vanessa this week, but she already understood why her younger sister, Izzie, counted her among her
closest friends and had asked her to be a bridesmaid.

The other bridesmaids made just as much sense. Gloria, of course, would have been mortally insulted had she not been asked. And Leah was a good friend from work. Bridget and Izzie had been inseparable as kids, more like twins than cousins.

Yes. All perfect bridesmaid material.

Except Mia. She *didn't* fit. Frankly, she was pretty sure that if Izzie hadn't felt obligated because they were sisters, she would not have asked Mia to be in the wedding.

And that would have been okay.

It wasn't that she didn't love her sister—sisters—but she wasn't *like* them. Even when growing up, she'd known she was different. Not homey and traditional like her older sister. Not flamboyant and talented like her younger one.

She'd been the tough kid. The scrapper, her father had called her the son he'd never had. She'd spent her childhood pitching baseballs and playing street hockey with the boys, rather than taking ballet lessons like Izzie or playing with an Easy-Bake oven like Gloria.

Her adult life hadn't changed matters much. She still played with the boys—rough games like, I'll Put You in Jail for Life, You Scumbag, and Don't You *Dare* Underestimate Me Because I'm a Woman. Her job with the Pittsburgh D.A.'s office had been a full-contact sport, and she'd been damn good at it. At least, until she'd decided to try playing for the other team, accepting an offer with a Chicago firm specializing in criminal defense.

"There's the car," Gloria said as they burst outside, pushed along by the crowd. "Bridget and Leah must have had the driver come straight back."

Vanessa suggested leaving immediately and Mia couldn't agree more. She wanted to go back to her room and go to bed. Actually, she wanted to go to her apartment and go to bed, but each member of the wedding party had been given a minisuite at the hotel. It would have been rude to refuse.

A few months ago, when Mia was busting the chops of every pimp, druggie and pusher in Pittsburgh, she wouldn't have cared about something like rudeness. But she was back home now. All the niceties she'd let slide in her drive to succeed were oozing their way back into her life, whether she wanted them to or not.

Along with them had come regrets. There'd been moments when she'd wondered if she'd done the right thing in coming back. Maybe more than a few moments…especially this week. Reaching the date on which she'd pinned a lot of hopes and built a lot of sensual fantasies—and spending it *alone*—had been more painful than she'd anticipated.

She still couldn't believe she'd stood Brandon Young up on the night they were supposed to become intimate in every way.

Don't think about him.

Fortunately, Gloria jabbered throughout the ride, so Mia couldn't think about *anything* but how badly she wished she'd brought her drink from the bar. Ten bucks a shot or not, Mia was breaking into the minibar in her room the minute she got there.

Inside the hotel, Vanessa asked, "Want to hit the lounge?"

"I can't," Gloria said. "Tony and the brats are waiting."

Mia made a snarky comment and got a snarky comeback. Typical sister stuff, part of their MO after all these years. Despite that, she knew her sister didn't mean the word *brats*. Gloria's adoration was plain; she was a born mother.

Mia couldn't even imagine that. It was hard enough to do something as girlie as a girls' night out. Though, she had to admit, tonight had been fun. But it hadn't come naturally. She was exhausted from the effort to keep up with the conversations about sex, relationships and the three *M*'s: men, makeup and marriage. None of which she currently had in her life.

So, exhausted, she refused Vanessa's offer. "But let's meet for breakfast in the morning," she said before heading for the other tower of the high-rise hotel. She just couldn't socialize anymore. Weddings might bring out the jolly side of most women.

But Mia wasn't most women.

She *could* have been. Could maybe even have had those things the other women had been talking about all evening. She'd come close to having them.

Six weeks ago she'd been involved with a great guy who'd made her totally happy. They'd planned to take their relationship to the next level this week, after he'd returned from a long overseas trip. Then, on their last day together, he'd told her he was falling in love with her.

Maybe that's why she'd left.

Because Brandon Young had been *too* nice, too boy next door, too laid-back and thoughtful and wonderful. An easygoing software designer, he was liked by everybody.

And Mia was a cold, brass-balled bitch. Hadn't everyone—her boss, defense attorneys, even the Pittsburgh media—said it?

As had her one serious lover. The only man she'd ever lived with, a colleague from the D.A.'s office, had accused her of having a heart of ice as he'd walked out the door.

Mia hadn't opened herself up to another man again... not until Brandon had caught her off guard with his warmth and his self-deprecating charm. "You did the right thing ending things with him," she reminded herself as she got on the elevator.

Maybe if she hadn't been falling in love with him, too, she could have been ruthless enough to take what she could get. But she *had* been falling and falling hard. So she'd done the right thing—for *him*—and ended it before he got hurt.

The good intentions didn't make her feel any less a witch for leaving town with nothing but a message on his machine while Brandon was out of the country. She could have at least called to make sure he got back okay and to wish him well.

She *did* wish him well. With someone…nice. Someone unassuming, gentle and kind. Someone with a big heart. Someone loving and maternal. Someone who was everything Mia was not.

That she already *hated* that unknown someone for having him when she, herself, couldn't, just proved what everyone had always said about her. She was a first-class bitch.

By the time the elevator reached her floor, Mia had unbuckled her high-heeled shoes and slipped them off her aching feet. They dangled by the straps from her hand. To her annoyance, however, as she stepped out, one fell from her grip. The sparkly torture tool landed *inside* the elevator…and the doors closed before she could retrieve it.

"Wonderful," she muttered, picturing having to chase an errant shoe in this huge hotel. From her experience with high-rises, she knew that particular elevator wouldn't be near her floor again for several minutes. Damned if she was going to wait or leap into another one and chase it down. "Screw it."

She strode barefoot down the empty corridor. Reaching her room, she slid the electronic key card into place, turned the handle and walked inside.

It wasn't until she tried to push the door closed behind her—and *couldn't,* because it was being blocked by a large, strong hand—that she realized she'd been followed.

HE'D BEEN WAITING for Mia Natale all evening. Having kept an eye on her sister's wedding festivities earlier in the day, knowing the reception had ended around seven, he'd expected her to come back to her room much earlier than now. He'd figured she'd come up to change or take a nap or even pack up her stuff for her return to her apartment… which he'd also swung by after his arrival in Chicago yesterday.

Oh, yes, he'd been watching her. Waiting to make his move. Planning on how best to gain his revenge…and make his point. Judging by the instant of fear, followed by shocked recognition on her face, his point wouldn't be that difficult to make.

She was intimidated by him…by his presence here. For the first time since the night they met, he had the upper hand.

And he intended to use it.

"Brandon!"

"Hello, Mia," he murmured, pushing the door back open and following her into her suite. He wasn't waiting for any invitation. Waiting for Mia to invite him into her bedroom certainly hadn't done him any good during the weeks they'd dated. Because, though they'd planned to move their relationship to the next level as soon as he returned from an overseas business trip this month, she'd skipped town before ever following through.

Now he was going to make sure she followed through. Not by force, of course. He planned to make her *beg* for it. He'd played the gentleman before but that wasn't what she'd wanted. Now he'd see if she *really* liked the kind of man she thought she did.

"What are you doing here?"

"Nice to see you, too," he murmured as he took stock of her suite. It was the same as his, which was just across the hall. This first room had a writing desk, love seat and broad windows with a view of the city. And the next—also just like his, as he saw through the open doorway—contained a huge king-size bed.

His gaze fell on the bed. The covers were turned down, the pillow replete with a mint. A silky pink nightgown rested there, obviously laid out by a member of the attentive hotel staff.

The nightgown caught his attention. And kept it. It was silky smooth, about the color of Mia's full, lush curved lips. It would be striking against her pale skin, and her short, jet-black hair. Mia was more sexy than beautiful and would have to be called dramatic, not pretty. Yet she'd stopped his heart the first time he'd seen her when he'd been testifying against a former embezzling client.

She'd ripped it out when she'd run away like a cowardly little girl rather than let something real and meaningful develop between them, as Brandon *knew* it could have.

"I see you made it back safely from Japan."

As if she cared, considering she'd packed up her apartment and left the state in the six weeks he'd been gone. Calling her and receiving a "this number has been disconnected" message had been shocking. Calling his own answering machine from Japan and hearing her cryptic, "I've taken a job and am moving back home to Chicago," message had made things worse, not better.

She owed him more than that. She owed him, at the very least, an explanation.

He'd get to that. Eventually.

"Got back a few days ago. Have a good holiday?"

She nodded slowly. "Very nice."

"How's the new job?" he asked, knowing she was disconcerted, waiting for some kind of emotional reaction that she had to know was coming. She'd be waiting a long time if she thought she'd see regret or loss or worse, pleading. And she'd probably never suspect what she was very soon going to get.

Not anger. Not sadness. Just pure, sensual determination.

"It's fine." Clearing her throat, she added, "You remember my father had a stroke last spring. It's done him a lot of good having me back in the area."

Justifications. He nearly tsked in disappointment. He'd expected defiance from her, not nervousness. At least, until she found out what he'd *really* come for.

Then, what he most wanted was excitement.

"When, exactly, did you apply for this job?" he asked as he opened her minibar and scanned its contents. Without asking, he reached in, helped himself to a small bottle of whiskey and poured it, neat, into a hotel-provided glass.

"I interviewed for it last fall. Before we met."

"Ahh." He sipped. "And you never thought to mention it."

"I didn't think I'd got the job. I hadn't heard anything at all, not until early December. After you'd gone."

Right. And she didn't know how to pick up a phone and make an overseas call. Considering he'd called her three times after leaving the states, he knew she was aware they had such things as telephones in the Pacific Rim.

Looking back, he knew she'd had to have already made her decision by his third call. She *must* have, in order to have given her notice and moved by the twentieth when he got the disconnect message, followed by the Dear John one on his machine. Yet she'd never said a word.

"You got my message, I hope?"

Brandon's hand tightened around the glass. If it had been of more fragile stuff, it might have crushed beneath his fingers. How could she act so casual about it…as if her damned ninety-second voice message could possibly be enough to explain, to put an end to what they'd shared?

No, they hadn't had sex yet. But they'd been intimate in many other ways. In the month they'd dated—before his trip—they'd seen each other four or five times a week. She'd sought him out with frequent phone calls and e-mails. She'd brightened his winter days and he'd warmed her winter nights in every way but one. And when it had come to that one thing—*he* had been the one who'd offered to wait until he got back.

He had not wanted to take her to bed then fly away a day or two later. Because he had the feeling that once he did get inside Mia's beautiful body, he wouldn't want to leave it for a very long time.

The anticipation of their first time would, she'd assured him, be the highlight of her holidays and she had promised to greet him on January 8 in the sexiest lingerie Santa Claus could buy. But on January 8, she'd been living in another state, her apartment rented to someone else, her office now being used by another lawyer.

He'd checked. Even after getting her message, he'd had to go make sure it was true—that she'd bailed with no real motivation or explanation.

"Brandon?"

It took a great deal of self-control to loosen his grip on the glass, but he did it, maintaining an even expression.

"Enough of this. What is it you're really doing here?" she asked, tilting her head back and staring straight into his eyes. Her surprise and nervousness had kept her off guard for the first few moments of his visit. Now the Mia he knew—the strong, powerful woman—was returning.

"Can't an old friend stop in for a drink?"

She glanced at the minibar, looking so longingly at it, that he raised a brow and held up a tiny bottle. When she nodded, he cracked the seal on it and poured a shot into the other clean tumbler. As he handed it to her, their fingers brushed—just a soft, quick connection—yet Mia's hand shook and the amber liquor sloshed in the glass.

He nearly smiled at the lapse of control.

She gave a good try at disguising it, sipping once, then tossing out a casual query. "So, what, did you follow me?"

"Don't flatter yourself," he mumbled, his tone uninterested—though he was very interested, indeed. "I'm here on business, heard your sister was getting married in this hotel and figured you'd be here."

Mia nodded slowly. "And you…just happened to be walking by my door just now?"

Slowly smiling, Brandon shook his head and turned to give her his full attention. "No, I've been watching your door. My room's directly across the hall."

Her mouth rounded into a surprised O. "Coincidence…"

He shook his head again, slowly, stepping closer to her. His eyes narrowed, his steps measured, he watched the way her face flushed and her pulse fluttered in her throat. *Not controlled at all.* No, she was still intimidated. Still unsure what he was doing here. *Good.*

"It wasn't a coincidence, Mia. As soon as I found out you were staying here I had my room changed."

Reaching up, he smoothed his thumb across her bottom lip. When in the courtroom, Mia kept her full, sensual lips unadorned with makeup and tightly compressed. But she had a mouth designed for pleasure and he'd quite enjoyed the pleasures that mouth had provided. During their very last sensual encounter—the night before he'd gone away—he'd briefly met the wild, wanton woman she kept under tight rein during her day-to-day life.

Tonight, he'd get to know that woman *thoroughly* if it was the last thing he did.

"You see, you owe me something," he finally continued. "And I'm here to collect."

She didn't move, just watched him with those wide, brown-black eyes, usually so unreadable but now holding both curiosity and excitement. She didn't recognize him, he knew that much. She didn't see the nice programmer in the threatening man who'd accosted her at her door tonight. And the woman was wildly excited by that fact, as he'd known she would be.

"What exactly do you think I owe you?" Visibly swallowing, she added, "I suppose you want an explanation for my leaving the way I did, without talking to you about it?"

"I know why you left. That's not what I'm referring to."

And he did know why she'd left. He'd known she wasn't happy in Pittsburgh and she missed her family, especially since her father had had a stroke. Though they drove her nuts, she obviously loved them.

He'd also known by her final message that *he*—nice, dependable Brandon—would *never* be enough to entice her to stay.

His jaw tightening, he stepped closer, until the ends of his shoes touched her pretty toes. He ran the tip of his finger in a light caress from her mouth, over her chin and down the long line of her slender throat.

Her voice trembling now, she asked, "Then what?"

He didn't reply at first, just stared down at her, watching the way her skin reacted to the ever-so-delicate scrape of his fingertip. She was rosy and flushed, tiny goose bumps of anticipation appearing on her skin, all the way down to the soft crevice of cleavage rising from her ruby-red gown.

He loved her breasts. Loved toying with them and tasting those perfect brown nipples as he had during a few of their more intimate moments. He'd known that when the time came, he'd have her on top of him, thrusting up into her in rhythm with each powerful suck and that image had kept him hard and desperate during many long, sleepless nights in Japan.

"Brandon, answer me. What is it you think I owe you?"

"What you owe me, Mia," he murmured, moving even closer so the smell of her hair and her body overwhelmed his senses, "is a night in your bed."

2
_____

THE EARTH STOPPED TURNING. At least, the little piece of it on which Mia stood. And her heart stopped with it. Because of all the things she'd expected to hear from Brandon Young, the idea that he'd tracked her down in Chicago to demand that she sleep with him wasn't even in the realm of possibility.

She should have been shocked. Offended. Instead, a warm drizzle of hunger, which had started coursing in her blood the moment she'd set eyes on his incredibly handsome face, roared through her like a tsunami.

"My bed?" she whispered, unable to tear her stare from the strong jaw, prominent nose and the curved lips she'd once loved to nibble on when they'd kiss good-night in his car or hers after a dinner date.

He might not have been her usual type, but from the moment they'd met, she'd seen past the nonthreatening, easygoing demeanor to the stunningly handsome man beneath. His green eyes had always been dreamy, his brown hair usually tousled, but the body had been pure, mouth-watering male from day one.

"Your bed, my bed, any bed," he replied, his tone even,

his form still, as if he had enough patience to track her to eternity to get what he wanted.

Her breath emerging choppily from her mouth, she stared at him, wondering what, exactly, had changed about him in six weeks. He was still, of course, very tall, built like someone who broke rocks for a living rather than a man who fiddled with computers. But he was dressed differently. The suit he'd worn to court on the day they'd met hadn't fit well, as if he couldn't be bothered to wear one very often. It had clung to his broad shoulders and hung baggily over what she'd come to learn were a very lean waist and hips.

Tonight, though, wearing a black turtleneck and soft, faded jeans, his incredible form was highlighted to perfection. The shoulders were broader—stronger. The arms beneath the tight black cotton thick and flexing with muscle. His chest was hard and huge, and Mia was suddenly struck by the memory of one of their last conversations, on the phone, before he'd gone away.

They'd spent at least an hour sharing whispered fantasies, growing a little—okay, a *lot*—more outrageous as the call wound on. Particularly since Mia had been drinking rich red wine and lying in a bubbly bath while talking. Even now, weeks later, her panties grew wet at the memory of his gravelly voice, telling her how much he wanted her to sit on his chest, spread her legs for him and let him devour her into a screaming orgasm.

It was a fantasy she'd had for a while and she'd promised to let him during their sex date. Especially since she'd fulfilled one of *his* fantasies in the car outside the airport the night he'd left. Now, it appeared, he was here to collect on that promise.

Swallowing, she closed her eyes for a second, wondering if she was really crazy enough—brave enough—to say yes.

He bent toward her, brushing the stubbled cheek—so unlike his usual clean-shaven look—against her face. His thick hair was longer than it had been, as if he'd had no time to get it cut. It was now sleek and straight, falling past his collar in a look no nice boy next door would ever wear.

But the eyes…those green eyes still mirrored a warm, romantic soul. He might change the rest, but those emerald-green eyes could never be anything but open, honest and beautiful.

"You promised to greet me at the door ready for sin when I got back. Imagine my disappointment when you weren't there."

She shivered, wondering how she could keep her thoughts together enough to deal with this when the man was brushing his lips ever so lightly against her neck. She felt his warm exhalations flowing on her skin and moaned at the contact. When he scraped his teeth on the fragile lobe of her ear, she actually began to shake. "Brandon—"

"Give me tonight, Mia. Give it to me not because you promised, but because you want it just as much as I do."

She did. God help her, she absolutely did.

"We take the pleasure we've *both* been looking forward to, then tomorrow we walk away. No questions asked."

That should have cinched it, since it was what Mia had wished could have happened the first time around. She'd regretted not having lain naked in Brandon Young's arms, at least once, every single day since he'd left.

But she'd also been long telling herself that having sex with him before leaving Pittsburgh would have complicated things—that he'd never have let her go, never have admitted how wrong she was for him, if they'd gone to bed together.

Now he was offering her what she'd been dying for with

absolutely no expectations. No fears that he'd fall deeper in love with her and set himself up for an even deeper hurt later on when he came to see her as the rest of the world did.

So why did the words *tomorrow we walk away* sound so stark—almost painful—as they hung in the warm, sensual air of her room?

"Come to me, Mia."

She didn't understand at first, since she was separated from him by only a sliver of night air, until Brandon released her. Without waiting for her answer, without allowing her to say a word, he moved away, giving her space, taking his warmth with him. With a slow smile that promised delights she'd never dreamed possible, he walked to the door, opened it and stepped into the corridor.

"My door will be unlocked."

And then he was gone.

WHAT IF SHE DOESN'T COME?

"She will," he murmured in the quiet of his room. He knew it. In fact, he was so confident of it, he kicked off his shoes and took off his shirt, knowing he wouldn't have to walk back across that hallway tonight.

They might not have dated long, but during the month they'd spent together, Brandon had come to understand Mia Natale in a way he doubted even *she* did. She wouldn't be able to resist, if only out of her innate curiosity.

Mia didn't like being wrong about anything. And if she sensed she'd misread *him,* she'd have to find out the truth. He could predict the thoughts going through her head and all would inevitably lead her to his room in less than five minutes.

The only thing he had never been able to comprehend

about Mia was why she'd dumped him before being absolutely *sure* he couldn't give her the wild, sexual affair she craved. For that, he was certain, was why she'd ended things the way she had. They'd built toward something explosive; she'd decided he couldn't deliver and had cut her losses and run without even giving him a chance.

She'd liked the guy the world knew, he didn't doubt that. But, he strongly suspected, she'd just never really believed he could be the right match for her sexually, since she was a brash, untamed woman and believed him a nice, conservative man.

Oh, how sad for her. She'd mistaken nice for unadventurous. Because when it came to sex, Brandon was up for just about anything. There wasn't much he hadn't done. There wasn't much he wouldn't do.

Especially tonight.

And once he'd shown her just how foolish she'd been to underestimate him—to never realize that the nice guy the world knew was *not* the one who would have shared her bed—he'd be the one walking away.

Thrusting away a stab of regret that thought caused him, he lifted his glass in a silent toast to the night. But he hadn't even had time to bring it to his lips before a soft knock intruded. Glancing at his watch, he murmured, "*Two* minutes," and laughed softly.

As he opened the door, seeing Mia's almost nervous half smile, he had to wonder something. If she knew what he *really* had in store for her tonight…would she still have had the nerve to show up here?

Didn't matter. She was here now and it was much too late for her to back out.

So, reaching for her, he took her hand. Then Brandon

drew her into his room for what he vowed would be the most erotic night the woman had ever experienced.

She might not remember the fantasies she'd once whispered to him during a long, sensual telephone call.

But Brandon most certainly did.

MIA HAD KNOWN there was something different about Brandon from the moment he'd pushed his way into her room earlier. The anticipation in his eyes and his lazy, almost jaded smile reiterated that. But somehow, she didn't care. Because at the sight of that huge, bare chest, rippling with muscle and covered with miles of glorious golden skin, she was stripped of all rational thought.

She wanted. She simply *wanted.*

"Drink?" he asked, walking over to the bar, which was positioned in mirror image to the one in her room across the hall.

"No, thank you," she whispered, as she dropped her purse. She had to wonder why he'd let go of her hand and stepped away. Was he going to make this difficult on her? Make her work for him after all he'd done to get her here?

Well…she could do that, she immediately realized. She could most certainly do that. "Brandon?"

Glancing back at her, he remained a picture of ambivalence, as if she were an acquaintance, rather than the woman he'd lured over here with promises of incredible sex and eroticism.

Not for long.

Mia reached for the zipper at the back of her neck and slowly began to tug it down. Her red velvet gown parted, gapping away until it finally fell off her body onto the floor.

Brandon devoured her with those glittering green eyes. His stare burned her. Every place it landed—her throat, her breasts, her hard nipples thrusting against the lace of her bra—silently pleaded for attention from his hands. His mouth. That magnificent erection straining hard against the zipper of his jeans.

He was not at *all* ambivalent about what was happening here.

The stare dropped to her waist, small and snugly wrapped in a red garter belt, then went farther. A tiny uptilt of one brow noted her lack of panties, which were right now on the floor of her room where she'd dropped them a moment ago.

Then he noticed the *rest* and he froze. His lips parted as he breathed over them. Because only the tiniest little tuft of curls remained above Mia's recently plucked sex. Her lips were silky smooth, already glistening with her arousal, he suspected.

She could hide absolutely nothing.

Some men got off on it, she knew. Frankly, though, Mia just liked the way it felt—liked the erotic wickedness of it beneath the conservative lawyer persona she played on a daily basis. Not having had a lover in a very long time, she'd never much cared what anyone thought. Until now.

"I can't wait to eat you," he murmured matter-of-factly.

That made her legs tremble, but she put a hand on the back of a chair to remain upright.

As if he hadn't just said something so blatantly sexual, Brandon continued surveying her, noting the silky stockings rising high on her thighs. The longer he stared, the tighter his jeans grew, highlighting the erection that would soon be buried deep inside her.

She licked her lips, knowing what was to come and hungering for it. Because while she'd never taken him fully, she had pleasured him in other ways and knew exactly why that bulge seemed so powerful.

On the night she drove him to the airport for his trip, Mia had demanded the right to take the edge off before his long journey. Brandon had tried to resist, swearing he wouldn't be able to keep his hands off *her* if hers were on *him,* and they'd already agreed to wait until his return to fully consummate their relationship.

But some devil had pushed her on, so she hadn't listened. Maybe because he'd told her it was one of his fantasies. Maybe because she wanted him to remember her—to long for her—when he was far away, surrounded by beautiful, exotic women. Or maybe even because something deep inside her had already known there would never be a consummation.

Whatever the reason, she'd been relentless. Right there in the airport parking lot, she'd unfastened his pants and released his sex. She'd pleasured him with her hand, stroking that thick, smooth member, toying with the vulnerable sacs beneath. Then, hearing his groans as his control fled, she'd shocked him by bending over and finishing him with her mouth, sucking him right through his powerful orgasm.

It wasn't something she'd ever particularly enjoyed before. Oh, she liked oral sex, she just preferred to finish things off the usual way. But exploding into the back of her throat was something Brandon had whispered about that night on the phone.

And she'd loved making it happen.

"Must have been cold today like that," he murmured with a half smile as he zoomed in again on the V between her thighs.

"It's very warm," she replied in a purr. She reached for the front hook of her bra, unfastened it, and let it fall to the floor. "As I'm sure you'll find out. *Soon.*"

"Uh-huh." He stepped closer. But rather than taking her

in his arms, Brandon shocked her by immediately dropping to his knees. Before she even had time to prepare herself, his mouth was *on* her, licking deep. Devouring her, as he'd once promised to do.

Mia howled, then shoved her fist in her mouth to try to control the sounds. He hadn't kissed her, hadn't touched her, but in under a minute, he'd pleasured her throbbing clit so thoroughly an explosive orgasm rocketed through her.

She was still shaking from it as he rose, nibbling his way up her body, pausing to nip a hip or sample her belly. The pause was a bit longer when he reached her breasts. He sucked one nipple into his mouth while reaching for the other and tweaking it between his fingers. The pressure with just the tiniest hint of pain had her ready to come all over again, and if he dropped his hand between her legs, she knew she would.

He didn't. Instead, he kissed his way up to her neck, whispering, "I have a surprise for you in the bedroom."

She quivered, wondering how his hands could be everywhere on her at once. "You do?"

"Something you once told me you wanted."

Mia wasn't sure what he meant, but since the bed was where she most wanted to be with him, she was definitely ready to follow him into the bedroom. "Take me there."

He entwined his fingers with hers, then led her across the small living area of the suite. Mia's curiosity grew, until she was almost holding her breath in anticipation.

When Brandon pushed the door open, she let the breath out in a quick exhalation, now remembering what she'd said. And when she'd said it. "You remember that conversation?" she asked, seeing and understanding the lengths he'd gone to in order to fulfill her fantasy. What else, she wondered, did he remember about that long, erotic phone call?

He nodded and led her to the massage table standing at the foot of the bed. On a small table beside it stood an array of lotions, as well as some candles, which he quickly lit. Soft, melodic music played in the background, setting a scene of pure relaxation. "You wanted a sensual massage. To be stroked everywhere, every muscle soothed with silky lotion and an expert touch."

She remembered uttering those words, exactly.

"To start slowly," he added, his words whispered, adding to the drugging mood, "like any other professional massage. Then to gradually be seduced into eroticism by a pair of powerful hands going *far* beyond the boundaries of a normal session."

Mia's whole body went soft, almost boneless, at the thought of his big, male hands kneading away all her tension. She loved massages, as she'd told him, and had long wondered what it would be like to get one from a lover. One whose touches would start firmly, professionally, then segue into wickedly seductive caresses.

"I can't believe you got a table," she said, almost stalling for time as she stepped closer and touched the fluffy white towel he'd draped across the top. She was dying for him to do as he'd said, but almost nervous. What if, having voiced the fantasy, the reality wasn't as good?

Then she glanced back, saw his confident smile and the powerful muscles flexing in his arms and hands, and knew it would be *very* good.

"Get on," he told her, holding out a hand to help her.

Mia did. But she didn't lie down right away, instead extending one leg straight out, silently ordering him to remove her stocking. Brandon reached for the front clasp, deftly unfastened it, then did the same with the back. He rolled the silky material down slowly—with infinite patience, touching her only with the slightest brushes of his finger-tips.

By the time he'd removed the second one, she was already a quivering mess. She didn't know how much of the massage she'd be able to stand before begging him to fill her.

"Lie down, Mia," he ordered as he removed the garter belt.

She did, rolling into her stomach. The table was a portable one, with no opening for the face, which was fine with her. She didn't want to remain removed and separated from the experience—she wanted to watch, to savor whatever he did to her. So she turned her head to the side, following every move he made.

"Now, ma'am, you requested our full-service package," he said as he moved to the door and flicked down the light switch. The room didn't plunge into darkness, it was still lit by the half-dozen candles. The shadowy lighting, the music, the smells and the anticipation all combined to build her senses to their highest peak. "Yes, I believe I did," she replied, playing along, wondering how a man as laid-back and friendly as this one could so easily fall into fantasy play-acting with a lover.

She'd *never* have suspected it. And it delighted her.

"As you wish." He retrieved another of those towels, a smaller one folded into a long, slender strip. Just as if he were a professional, he carefully draped it across her bottom, covering her curves. He took his time about it, trailing his fingers across her skin in a way no massage therapist ever had.

"Close your eyes," he murmured. "Relax and enjoy this. Remember, you said it was what you fantasized about."

She did, letting everything fill her head. She remained entirely relaxed as Brandon drew out the moment, not touching her right away as she'd expected him to. Then, finally, she felt a drizzle of silky liquid on the soles of her feet…followed by a pair of warm, strong hands. "Mmm, finally."

He worked them thoroughly, rubbing away the pain of the wicked bridesmaid shoes before slowly moving up to her ankles and giving them equally delicious attention.

"Wow," Mia said, "you are very good at this."

She wasn't really expecting an answer, but she got one. "He's paid to be very good," a voice whispered, close to her ear. Very close to her ear.

Which was physically impossible, since Brandon's hands were on her calves.

Not understanding, still a little drugged by the sensations battering her every pore, Mia opened her eyes, wondering how Brandon was able to take this fantasy so very far.

She became more confused when she realized she was face-to-face with him. He was sitting on a chair, bare chested, sprawled back, just a foot or two in *front* of her.

Meanwhile, the delicious strokes continued on the *back* of her calves, at the opposite end of her body. And suddenly the truth washed over her.

They were not alone.

3

BRANDON GAVE MIA a second to grasp the implications of what she was feeling. When shock caused her whole form to stiffen and her mouth to open, he leaned forward in his chair. Dropping his elbows onto his knees and staring into her beautiful, confused eyes, he murmured, "I want you to enjoy yourself. Just the way you talked about that night on the phone."

If he concentrated, he could still hear her whispers during that sultry call. The way her throaty voice had almost purred during the revelation of her most *secret* fantasy—which she'd said she'd never told to anyone before that night—had emphasized to him just what a chance she was taking by revealing so much of herself.

She'd be taking a much bigger chance tonight…by letting it happen.

Disbelief continued to hold her in silence. He saw the physical effort she made to remain calm, to hold still, while she analyzed the situation. Mia was trying desperately to figure out exactly *which* fantasy he intended to fulfill. He could almost hear her thoughts: *Did he hire a professional masseuse just for the massage? Or is he planning to fulfill the other—even more wicked—desire?*

He also saw one more thing—a touch of fear, and that immediately concerned him. He didn't want her afraid. He wanted her drowning in pleasure.

"It's okay, Mia," he murmured, as if trying to gentle a wild animal, "it's just a massage. You can enjoy it or stop it right here and now. Your choice."

The man he'd invited to join them paused, lifting his hands off Mia's beautiful legs, waiting for her response. More proof, in Brandon's mind, that he'd engaged the right person to assist him in this complete seduction of Mia Natale.

There was no listing in the yellow pages under "gigolo" and Brandon wouldn't have trusted a complete stranger, anyway. So it was very fortunate that, while in Japan, he'd met Sean Murphy. The expat had been charming his way around every bored wife of every American executive staying in their upscale hotel and he and Brandon had hit it off right away. Murphy had been a perfect escort-for-hire, squiring the wives to functions their husbands were too busy to attend, serving as interpreter, as well as, occasionally, bodyguard.

Whether he serviced them in their bedrooms, Brandon had no idea. But the guy certainly knew how to treat a woman. And he'd accepted Brandon's proposition with a firm handshake and a promise to treat the lady exactly as she wanted to be treated.

Whatever that entailed.

They'd also set one more boundary. The entire focus of the night would be on Mia…just Mia. Brandon was a free-thinker, but he was most definitely *not* into anything homoerotic. Nor did he in any way suspect Sean was up for it. The man appeared to be addicted to sensual women. And right now, Mia was the most sensual woman Brandon had ever set eyes on.

"I'd be happy to go if you want me to. Just say the word," Murphy murmured softly, his brogue hardly noticeable. He, too, had recognized this as a make-or-break moment.

Brandon hadn't been sure until this crazy thing had gotten underway a few minutes ago how he'd take seeing another man touch a woman he'd wanted for so long. But so far, he was fine. Murphy was a professional, there to service her, to please her. And while Brandon didn't know how he'd respond if Mia let things go a lot further—or *all* the way— for now, it was okay.

Because, as he'd often reminded himself, he didn't have any claim on her or any future with her. Tonight was about driving her insane with pleasure before walking away tomorrow. Teaching her a lesson. Making sure she never forgot this night…or him.

"Mia?" He still waited for her answer. "It's your call."

Her lips were parted, her breaths ragged. He didn't think he'd ever seen her looking so disconcerted—confused. Yet there was excitement in the movement of her mouth and the wildness of her eyes. Best of all, there was no more trace of fear.

Her body slowly relaxed, though not to the level of boneless contentment she'd achieved earlier. That was probably under-standable—a faceless, completely unknown man had his hands on her bare legs. And she still wasn't exactly certain which fantasy was about to be played out here.

"Okay," she whispered with a nod. "It's just a massage?"

Brandon leaned closer, rising to brush his lips against the

corner of her mouth. Putting his hand on her back he stroked the tender, vulnerable flesh there, knowing he wouldn't be able to watch for long—he'd have to be in on this massage in very short order. "It's just a massage."

She sighed in relief. At least until Brandon added, even more softly, "Unless you *want* it to be more."

OH, GOD. Mia closed her eyes, gulping, as everything that was happening sank into her consciousness. Rather than being naked in the arms of the man she'd been dying for over the past two months, she was being touched by someone else altogether. Someone she had never even seen but whose silky, oil-coated hands were doing lovely things to her legs. And could do lovely things to the rest of her. *If she wanted him to.*

"You remember everything I said that night, don't you?" she whispered, hearing accusation *and* anticipation in her voice.

It came as no surprise when Brandon nodded. That was the *only* thing that had come as no surprise tonight. Everything else—from the moment he'd pushed his way into her room, until right now when he was laying an incredibly sensual offer at her feet—had come as a complete shock.

"You remember that one particular fantasy," she said, still wanting to be absolutely sure.

Because it seemed almost impossible to believe he was offering her the wicked eroticism she'd almost been too embarrassed to admit to him during that long sultry call: a night with two men in her bed.

What she would do with both men, she'd never quite figured out. Oh, she knew the possibilities, knew the slots and tabs of the human body. But she wasn't sure just how far she'd let herself go, how much she'd dare.

It was shocking. Outrageous. Incredibly titillating.

And now, it looked like it might actually be happening. "Yes, Mia, I do."

Honestly, if Mia had time to consider this whole thing, she probably wouldn't have the guts to go through with it. No matter how far things went—whether she stopped Mr. Sexy Voice at a typical relaxing rubdown or invited him to perform the *erotic* part of the massage—this whole setup required a serious element of trust. She wasn't sure she'd have been able to muster that trust if given the time to consider it.

But she *didn't* have time to think, she had to go on instinct. And her instincts told her—had always told her—that she could trust Brandon Young. No matter what his motives for setting up this elaborate fantasy scene, she *did* trust him.

More, she wanted him. And whether or not she had the nerve to go all the way through this night, fulfilling fantasy after fantasy, she was at least willing to follow his lead and see how far they went. Because he wouldn't let anything happen to her that she didn't *want* to let happen.

It just remained to see how much she wanted to let happen.

She sucked in and released a quivery breath, already wondering if she was making a mistake. But finally she offered him a sultry smile and settled back down for more treatment from the man with the magnificent hands and the sexy voice.

"Good," Brandon whispered. Glancing past her, he added, "I think you can proceed, Sean."

Sean. That was as much as she knew about the man who could very well be doing some pretty intimate things to her tonight.

So be it.

"You are going to get involved with this at some point, aren't you?" she asked, wondering why Brandon was content to sit there, rather than using his hands on all the parts of her body not already being attended to.

"Don't you remember everything you said that night?"

Distracted by the particularly delicious stroke of a strong knuckle on the back of her calf, she didn't answer at first.

"You wanted to be watched," he reminded her. "You swore there was an untapped exhibitionist inside you."

She remembered. And she also recalled something else. "You had the same fantasy. And as I recall, you were part voyeur." Challenging him to deny it, she added, "So we're not just fulfilling *my* fantasies tonight, are we?"

He shook his head, settling back in his chair. His legs were sprawled apart, entirely relaxed. His incredibly broad, bare torso glowed in the low light of the candles and Mia licked her lips as she stared at him, her fingers itching to stroke all that firm, supple male skin.

Brandon's stare slowly shifted from her face, studying her naked body, lingering on the curve of her shoulder and the line of her back. His eyes narrowed in intensity and he appeared unable to tear his gaze away when he beheld the masseur working on the aching muscles of her upper thighs.

He seemed fascinated by the sight of another man's hands stroking her into pure physical contentment. "Oh, yes, we are definitely fulfilling a few of my fantasies, too," he admitted.

She didn't ask about participant number three, Sean, and what he expected out of this evening. Brandon had called him a professional—whether that meant he was a professional masseur or a male escort, she honestly didn't know. Nor was she certain she *wanted* to know.

She wanted faceless eroticism. Anonymous pleasure. The other man didn't matter so much and she wasn't entirely sure she wanted to see him clearly. It was enough to feel the long, firm stroke of his hand down her thigh and the brush of his fingertips across the sensitive skin behind her knee, wondering—always wondering—where he'd touch next and whether she'd *really* be ready for it.

"Mmm," she groaned as he worked his hand between her legs and gently pushed them apart so he could access the inner thigh muscles. He remained close to her knees, working her skillfully, still well within the bounds of any other massage she'd received. But Mia remained on edge, every nerve ending anticipating the next move, knowing that eventually one would cross that boundary.

Brandon's hungry stare made her want that touch to come soon. She wanted to see him as insanely excited as she was. Wanted him driven beyond control, until he had to push the stranger out of the way and be the only man touching, experiencing, loving her.

But he doesn't love you.

The thought came rapidly, unexpectedly, and she couldn't force it away. Brandon had *thought* he was falling in love with her. That, however, had been before she'd run out on him with nothing but an easy lie for an explanation. Any fragile, early feelings had to have been crushed by her actions.

It was far too late to regret pushing away any chance of a future—of love—with Brandon, because tonight wasn't about love. It was about lust and unkept promises and unfulfilled desire. It was about eroticism and pleasure. And, she strongly suspected, it was probably also a little bit about revenge.

Mia wasn't stupid. She'd sensed Brandon's anger and knew his taunts about having one sexual night with her before they parted forever had been partially inspired by payback. He wanted to show her what she was missing out on.

His plan would work. She wouldn't soon forget this night, though not for the reasons he might expect.

It wasn't just the sensuality she'd remember…it was the realization that she might have made a horrible mistake. She'd refused to *let* him love her, pushing him away, without realizing that maybe—just maybe—Brandon was strong enough for her after all. Perhaps he *wasn't* too good or too nice. Tonight had shown her he was real and unpredictable and open to absolutely anything. Maybe even handling a relationship with a cold, bitchy woman like the Mia the world knew.

And she'd tossed him away.

"How far, Mia? How far do you want to go?" Brandon asked, still watching through heavy-lidded, half-closed eyes.

Thrusting off her cloak of sadness for the mistakes she could not unmake, she forced herself back to the moment. She had one night…damned if she'd waste it on regret.

"Mmm…further."

He smiled in approval and Mia licked her lips, wondering why it was so exciting to watch him watch her. Something wicked deep within her wanted to push him, to drive him to insane lust. So she arched her back slightly—two inches at most. Lifting her bottom, she silently invited the stranger massaging her legs to move his attention higher.

He did so. Immediately. When Mia felt his hands slide high enough to brush the cotton towel and the vulnerable curve where her cheeks met the backs of her thighs, she groaned in sensual response. He soothed her, caressed her…but moved no further.

"God, I need another drink," Brandon whispered hoarsely. He slowly moved out of the room, still watching, as if loath to miss a moment of what was happening.

When he disappeared from sight, Mia tensed. She had a stranger's hands on her—a faceless stranger's. She suddenly realized that Brandon's presence was the *only* thing that had given her the courage to do this. And that watching his pleasure and excitement had made this interlude a warmly erotic one. Now, with him gone, what had been so damned exciting seemed incredibly risky.

The man seemed to know it because he immediately moved back down her legs, massaging places he'd already covered. Safe places. Non-intimate places.

A very intuitive one, this Sean.

When Brandon reentered the room, he was carrying something in his hand. Something that was ringing. "Hmm, Bridget Donahue, that's your cousin, isn't it?" he asked.

Mia sucked in a shocked breath, realizing he held *her* cell phone. "Brandon, don't you dare answer that…"

But he did. "Hello?"

Mia swung her arm out, trying to grab for it as he passed by her. She missed, of course.

Brandon held the phone out of reach, grinned and sat back down where he'd been before. "You've got the right number."

What her cousin must be thinking, Mia had no idea. Especially when Brandon leaned close to her, pressing a kiss on her bare shoulder and saying into the phone, "I'm sorry. Mia's in the…*middle* of something."

She heard a low chuckle from the man behind her and closed her eyes in shock. Hopefully her sweet little book-keeper cousin would never realize that the very wicked Brandon Young meant Mia was in the *middle* of *two* men.

"I'm going to get you for that," she vowed after

Brandon disconnected the call and tossed the phone onto another chair.

"Give it your best shot." He leaned back, lifting one leg and draping it over the arm of the plush chair. "I'm completely at your mercy."

His green eyes sparkled with amusement, but Brandon wasn't the only one who could tease. In fact, Mia knew exactly how to tease him into losing that confident smile.

She parted her legs bit. "Um, my thighs could definitely use some more attention."

The invitation was immediately accepted. Big hands encircled her thighs and strong male thumbs slid close—achingly close—to the bare lips of her sex. Mia hissed, dying for the completion of the caress, not giving a damn that she'd never even seen the person doing the caressing because all that mattered was the tension rising between her and her one-man audience.

Across from her, Brandon reacted. His laughter faded and he ran one hand through his thick, tousled hair. With a hiss of approval at the show she was providing, he dropped his hand onto his lap, as if to control his physical response.

She didn't want him controlling it. "More," she murmured, to both men in the room.

She was rewarded with the removal of two things: the towel covering her bottom. And Brandon's last bit of control.

Because as he watched a pair of strong hands move over her cheeks and begin stroking—the touch sliding dangerously close to the seam between them—Brandon slowly unfastened and unzipped his pants. Mia gasped as she watched him release himself, his powerful member fully engorged. He stroked it, obviously needing to pleasure himself as he watched her being pleasured.

The sight sent hot, liquid desire flooding to her sex. She swelled so much she had to part her legs even further, which, to the man doing wild and wonderful things to her backside, must have seemed an invitation to go further.

And he did.

She cried out when those wickedly fast hands moved again. Before she could even comprehend it, powerful fingers were sliding between her cheeks. The massage oil smoothed the way as he slid past the sensitive opening of her bottom, which he teased lightly before moving on, as if reminding her of the kinds of games they could get up to this night.

Before she even comprehended the fact that it was happening, she felt his touch gently sliding between the folds of her sex. "Oh, yes," she groaned, urging him on.

When her masseur slowly slid one finger into her wet channel, she let out a quivery sigh of delight. The man used his other hand to tug her up a bit more, then reached around to toy with her sensitive, swollen clit, until she shook and trembled.

Her eyes locked with Brandon's and she saw he was stroking himself harder, obviously in no way turned off by seeing what was happening. He appeared as aroused as she was.

"You're incredible," Brandon muttered.

It *felt* incredible, but Mia needed more. Needed to see more, feel more, experience more. "Brandon," she groaned, begging him without even knowing what it was she begged for.

He rose, kicking off his pants. His throbbing sex was a few inches away and she wished she could bend far enough off the table to cover it with her mouth. She wanted to suck him in a steady rhythm matching the deep strokes of the other man's fingers inside her, until all three of them were connected.

"How far do you want to go, Mia?" Brandon whispered, repeating his earlier query. He bent until eye level with her, then, before she could answer, covered her mouth with his and plunged his tongue deep. He was warm and delicious and Mia cried out against his lips as the sensations continued to build. They were still kissing as her climax rolled over her, making her gasp and shake against his mouth and against Sean's slowing hand.

When Brandon lifted away and she was finally able to speak—or breathe—she whispered, "Further."

His answering smile was positively wicked. "You got it."

4

EVERY TIME HE ASKED Mia how much further she wanted to go, Brandon held his breath until she answered. The truth was, he didn't *know* how he wanted her to answer. He was waiting for that moment when something inside him would rebel at watching someone else touch her so intimately, but so far, all he felt was out-of-his-mind excited.

One thing he knew, he could no longer remain an impartial observer. He had to touch, to taste, to savor. So, with a nod of warning at Murphy, he reached for Mia's shoulders and helped her sit up. The other man remained behind her, between the table and the bed, still stroking her hips, continuing the massage as if he hadn't just fingered her to a rocking orgasm.

"Kiss me, Brandon," she begged. She reached for him, grabbing his hair, twining her fingers in it.

"Nothing I'd rather do." He came down to her, covering her mouth in another breathless kiss. When it ended, he tasted his way down her neck, wanting to sample those puckered nipples, roll his tongue across them. "You have the most beautiful breasts," he muttered before licking one tip. It was as delicious as he'd expected, and hearing her cries of delight made it taste even better.

Sean remained behind her. He was stroking her shoulders now, digging his fingers into the tight muscles there. He probably needn't have. Any remnants of Mia's tension appeared to be long gone, replaced by pure sensual pleasure.

"I still can't believe this is happening," she whispered.

"Are you all right?" Brandon asked.

She nodded.

"Good," Murphy whispered, and Brandon completely understood the reaction. Because watching Mia experience what they were doing to her had to be driving the other man as wild as it was him.

Seeing her so into it made him curious about just how much further she meant. So he nibbled and kissed his way down her body. He breathed in the essence of her skin and the remnants of the heady massage oil, knowing her intrinsic scent was much more heady. Especially as he got closer to her quivering sex, pink and luscious and swollen for him.

She'd allowed another man to use his hands on her while Brandon watched. How would she feel about intense oral pleasure under the watchful eyes of a stranger?

"Please, Brandon," she cried, which gave him his answer.

He didn't hesitate, licking into her folds, mumbling, "I love the way you taste."

She answered by arching toward him, groaning when he covered her pretty clit with his tongue and played with it.

Mia gasped and sagged back…into another man's arms. Brandon watched for a second as another strong pair of hands moved across her shoulders and down, covering her breasts and tweaking the nipples Brandon had just been sucking.

That was when the queasiness started.

He ignored it, focused on her little cries of pleasure as he loved her with his mouth. But even as he brought her to another shattering orgasm, he wondered what would come next. If he asked her again how much further she wanted to go…what would be her response?

Whether they'd go all the way—whether she'd actually take the other man into her body, he didn't know. A quick tightening of his chest and the unconscious clenching of his fingers told him he probably didn't want to consider that yet.

He'd set some ground rules with Sean and one of them was that he'd stop short of actual penetration, unless Mia *really* wanted it. When he'd said that, he'd intended merely to protect her, in case things got too carried away too quickly. He hadn't considered how *he* would feel about it.

Well, he *told* himself he hadn't.

Because tonight wasn't supposed to be about finally having the woman he'd been crazy about six weeks ago. It was supposed to just be about having wild, dirty sex with a woman he was hot for…giving her a night she'd never forget, then walking away without ever looking back.

That woman he could take in any number of wicked ways. And the idea of being inside her while she was being pleasured by another man, too, was at the very least intriguing.

But this wasn't that woman. This was Mia. The sharp-edged lawyer who had an adorably sweet giggle that she almost never let anyone hear. The brown-eyed beauty who'd cried in his arms one night over a particularly brutal case she'd had to try. The great cook who'd single-handedly prepared an entire Thanksgiving feast for all their friends.

The woman he'd fallen in love with.

Brandon stopped what he was doing, having to close his eyes to mentally acknowledge the truth. What she'd done hadn't stopped his feelings for her…he loved her more now than he had the day he'd left. And he absolutely did not want anyone else making love to her, having sex with her or fucking her.

Not while he was in the room. Not while he wasn't. He wanted to be the only man plunging into her. *Ever.*

Which was pretty bad considering he had *handed* her to another man.

"What are you thinking?" she whispered.

Brandon looked up at her, lost himself in her big brown eyes, and knew he couldn't be the one to make the choice. "I'm thinking of how badly I want to be inside you."

She smiled down at him, sighing lightly in anticipation. Reaching for his shoulders and tugging him up, she touched her mouth to his and murmured, "Then be inside me, Brandon."

He deepened the kiss, tasting her fully, telling her silently everything that he hadn't been able to say out loud. And she kissed him back, languorously meeting the thrusts of his tongue, wrapping her arms tightly around his neck and her legs around his hips as if not wanting an inch to separate them.

But there remained one question to ask. "How much further, Mia?" he whispered.

She nibbled his earlobe. Then, casting a quick, apologetic look over her shoulder at Murphy—who she was actually *seeing* for the very first time—replied, "As far as *two* people can possibly go."

BRANDON MADE EXQUISITE love to her for the rest of the night. There was nowhere on her body he didn't caress, no inch of skin left unkissed. His stamina amazed her—because though he had seemed insane with need by the time the *very* handsome, black-haired Mr. Murphy had left them, he still managed to fill her for hours. And within minutes of coming inside her, he'd picked her up, carried her into the bathroom and started all over again in the shower.

She'd never experienced a night like it in her life.

And she almost had trouble believing it had all really taken place.

"Did we really do those things?" she whispered to the ceiling early the next morning. Brandon was sound asleep beside her, one arm resting in casual possession across her middle. "Did it truly happen?"

Glancing at the massage table, now collapsed and leaning against the wall, she sighed and acknowledged that yes, it had really happened. Brandon had brought an incredibly sexy stranger into their bedroom. Had watched while that man had brought her to orgasm with his hands. Had dropped his mouth to her lap and licked her to ecstasy while another man toyed with her breasts and watched every move they made.

Women went their entire lives fantasizing about the eroticism of such a night. Now Mia knew exactly what was possible. How far she could go, how much she would demand. And when, exactly, she would stop.

Murphy had pleasured her…but when it had come right down to it, she just couldn't go that final step. Maybe if she hadn't realized that she still loved Brandon, she'd have been able to do it. God knows when she'd seen the Irishman's incredible body and ruggedly handsome face, she'd had a mental flash of what could have been.

But she didn't regret it. Any wicked, erotic delights she'd gained from the two of them couldn't come close to what she'd experienced later. Brandon had thrust into her, over and over, whispering sweet, sexy words in her ear as he drowned her in pleasure. Mia was already certain she'd never be able to get used to the emptiness of not having him inside her.

Especially not a lifetime of that emptiness.

"You're awake," he whispered beside her.

Startled, she glanced over and saw him watching her. Mia quite honestly didn't know what to say. She'd had mornings after before, but never ones that had involved not one man but *two*.

In the light of day, would he regret what he'd started or judge her for going along with it? Now that he'd done what she suspected he'd set out to do—gotten even with her— would he casually toss her aside, thinking less of her for her wanton behavior of the night before?

"You okay?"

She nodded. "You?"

"I don't know," he admitted.

Oh, God. She sat up, shifted her legs to the side of the bed and prepared to stand, needing the floor beneath her and clothes on her body for the conversation she suspected was to come.

"Mia—" he ran a hand through his already bed-and-sex tousled hair "—wait."

She hesitated.

"I *know* I won't be okay if you get up and leave. Last night…"

"Was a fantasy come true," she whispered. When he opened his mouth to interrupt, she added, "I know why you came here, I know why you set this whole thing up. And believe me, it worked. I won't ever forget it and I know no man will ever make me feel what you made me feel last night."

As if he heard the sadness in her voice, he slowly sat up. "That's a bad thing?"

"Revenge is never a *good* thing."

He opened his mouth, then closed it, unable to deny what she already knew was true.

"But neither is cowardice," she added. "And me leaving Pittsburgh the way I did was pure cowardice."

His beautiful lips twisted into a frown. "Because I was too tame for you. Too nice, I think your voice mail said."

Hearing the bitterness in his tone, Mia immediately reached for him, putting one hand on his arm. He allowed the contact. "I am *so* sorry. I know you think that's why I left and what I meant. But it wasn't."

He remained motionless. "Then why?"

How to explain? How to tell him that she'd been trying to do what was best for him? That she'd misjudged him so completely as to think he'd end up with a broken heart—or worse, hating her—if they stayed together?

It was the ultimate irony. Because at that moment, knowing it was one of their last, Mia's was the heart that felt utterly pulverized.

"You were better off without me because I'm a heartless bitch," she finally admitted in a shaky whisper.

"Like hell…"

She held a hand up to stop him. "It's true. I'm ambitious and cold and I often trample over other people's feelings."

A twinkle appeared in those green eyes. "I would agree with two of those. But cold? No. Definitely not. I'm still on fire for you."

"I don't mean sexually."

"Neither do I," he insisted.

"Brandon, the last man who loved me ended up *hating*

me when all was said and done because he couldn't keep up with me and I always had to be in control."

"Then he was no man."

She blinked.

"Relationships aren't about control. And anyone who demands control doesn't understand the beauty of occasionally surrendering it." He bent and kissed her fingertips. "Like you did, last night."

Oh, she'd most definitely surrendered control last night, let herself be pleasured in as many ways as she could.

"Loving someone is about trusting them enough to not be in a constant state of struggle. Who gives a damn about who decides which restaurant to go to or who pays for the popcorn or what color the new curtains should be? That's not control, that's pettiness."

Good lord, it was as if he'd looked into a crystal ball and seen her past. The arguments he'd mentioned exactly described the final months she'd lived with her former lover.

"Couples who let the small shit tear them apart weren't meant to be together, anyway. And they play the I Want/ You Want game to escape a relationship they know isn't going to work."

The man had a future as a therapist. Or a seer.

"People who are meant to be together rise above pettiness every single time, Mia." He pulled her back down onto him, running his fingers through her hair, then cupping her face. "It's yin and yang, give and take. Offering control and accepting pleasure. Compromise."

She could say nothing, so she answered by brushing her lips across his. For the first time since last night, she began to sense that perhaps it wasn't too late for her to fix the mistake she'd made in pushing him away for his own good.

But he didn't respond by kissing her back. Instead, he frowned lightly and added, "I don't need you protecting me."

It was as if he'd read her thoughts.

The frown softened as he trailed his fingers across her bare shoulder, gently caressing the tender skin at her nape. "And I won't let you try to stop me from loving you."

Feeling moisture prick her eyes, she asked, "You really love me?"

"I do."

"Even after last night?" She needed to know for sure whether what had happened last night might ever come back to haunt them. Better to know now. Her voice quivering, she added, "After everything I let someone else do to me?"

Brandon rubbed his thumb across her bottom lip. "I loved watching that…."

"But?"

"But I'm glad it stopped when it did."

"So am I. There's a fine line between fantasy and regret. I'm glad we didn't cross it."

He shrugged. "I know. Because if it had gone much further I would have had to rip that guy's dick off."

Mia couldn't help it, she threw her head back and laughed. "You're the one who started it!"

"And I'm glad I was the only man who finished it."

So was she.

"I love you, Brandon," she whispered, knowing he had to be waiting for the words. His smile told her how much he treasured them. "Thank you for coming after me, even if it was just to teach me a lesson."

"I think I'm the one who got the lesson."

"I think we both did. You definitely don't have to prove anything else to me ever again."

"Like that I'm your match in bed? That I can go toe to toe with you on anything you come up with?"

Stretching like a cat, Mia slowly rose, straddling his lean hips, feeling him already hard and ready between her thighs. "Hmm…as I recall, you said something on the phone that night about gentle restraint." She wrapped her fingers around his wrists and pushed his hands over his head, holding them there, pretending he was trapped. "I've got you now. You can't move a muscle, can you?"

He played along with the fantasy, the latest they'd fulfill. But he couldn't help thrusting up and groaning, "I'm pretty sure I was talking about tying *you* up, sweetheart."

"I don't remember that at all."

Laughing in helpless desperation, he nipped at her breast, but Mia remained just out of reach. "Okay, okay, I give up. I'm willing to lie here and let you…"

He hesitated over the final unspoken words that echoed in the silent bedroom: *be in control.* But as if already determined to prove everything he'd said earlier, about give and take, yin and yang, he instead finished, "…have your wicked way with me."

She giggled at the old-fashioned term and at the helpless expression on his handsome face.

"Just be warned. When it's my turn? We'll be using real silk scarves."

Mia shivered, physically aroused and so happy she didn't know what to do. So she ended the game, collapsing on his chest and catching his mouth in a slow, sweet kiss.

Then catching the rest of his body in slow, sweet love.

As they rocked and swayed together, Mia couldn't help murmuring, "I'm so glad I didn't go back to my place last night."

"Mmm, me, too. Think they'll let us keep this room another day or two?"

A wicked laugh spilled out of her mouth. "If they knew the kinds of naughty things that had taken place in here, I'm sure they'd have ordered us out already."

"Are you saying nobody else in this hotel got lucky last night?"

"Brandon," she replied, going very still to look down at him with pure love in her eyes, "I don't think anybody in the whole world was as lucky as we were last night."

* * * * *

No Way Out

1

THERE WAS NO WAY in hell Vanessa McKee was going to stand outside in the cold with a crowd of rowdy drunks who'd had to evacuate a bar because of a fire alarm. And she said so. Loudly. "Forget this, let's hit it. The hotel's gotta have a bar...with heat. And drinks. And no fire."

The two remaining bridesmaids who'd stuck it out with her for the evening immediately agreed, though they bickered their way into the car. As she joined them inside, Vanessa wondered, yet again, how sisters could be so dissimilar.

In her mind, growing up in her grandmother's house in South Carolina with her two sisters and two brothers, she'd figured people raised together would inevitably be alike. No, her sisters weren't professional dancers like she was. But damn, they were *strong* like she was. As were the boys. They'd all been forged in the same fire of hardship and poverty after Mama and Daddy had died and their grandmother had taken them all in.

But the Natale sisters? Well, they'd once had the same last name, but there it ended. They had about as much in common as Vanessa did with one of those skinny white girls who pirouetted for the New York City Ballet. Both dancers… but that was about it.

"Jeez, it's cold. Even my hair's like a block of ice," Gloria complained as she huddled in a corner of the limo.

"Maybe it has something to do with the gallon of hair-spray you dump on it every day," said her sister Mia, sounding snarky. "Do you buy that stuff by the gross?"

"No. My *husband* buys it for me," Gloria sniped back.

Vanessa hid a laugh, having pegged these two right off. The oldest sister was the crazy, bossy one. The middle the hard-ass. And Izzie, Vanessa's best friend since they'd both landed spots with the Rockettes, was the self-confident sexpot.

The funny thing was, Vanessa could have become close friends with *any* of them. Because, in truth, they were all a little like her.

Some men had called her crazy. Especially the one she'd thrown a vase at when he'd shown up backstage to bring flowers to his *new* girlfriend. Vanessa being the old one.

Some had called her a hard-ass. Like that same guy.

And quite a few considered her a self-confident sexpot. Though, to be honest, not lately. It'd been a long stretch between men and she was definitely feeling a little…antsy.

"So where are all the hot men in this city, anyway?"

"If you find them, be sure to let me know," Mia replied.

Gloria rolled her eyes. "Come to *my* neighborhood. We got so many Italian studs walkin' the streets, a girl needs panty liners just to keep herself dry between home and the market."

Vanessa snorted. Even tough, somber Mia's lips twitched.

"Unless…" the oldest sister scrunched her brow.

Vanessa knew the unvoiced question, as every white friend inevitably asked it. "Unless I don't date white dudes?"

"Jeez, Gloria," Mia muttered.

"It's okay. It's a legitimate question. And the answer is, if the boy is *fine* and doesn't judge me by my skin color, I'm not going to judge him by his."

"I imagine most men judge you by those legs," Mia said.

She chuckled. "I haven't broken a man's hips yet."

When they reached the hotel, Vanessa hoped the three of them could continue their party in the hotel bar. She was a stranger in town, after all, and she had one last night before heading back to New York tomorrow.

But they both bailed on her. Gloria due to her family, and Mia because…well, Mia because she wasn't nearly as into this whole wedding thing as a typical sister of the bride would be. That was okay. Vanessa liked her anyway and she appreciated the effort the feisty woman had made. From conversations she'd had with Izzie, she knew the bride had appreciated it, too.

After the other women had gone, she decided to can the bar idea and head up to her room. But as she crossed the lobby, one of the hotel managers hurried out from behind the registration desk, calling her name. "I'm so sorry to inconvenience you, Miss McKee, but we've had a bit of an…incident this evening."

Great. First a bar fire, now what?

"One of the rooms on your floor was broken into." The man grew red in the face, hurrying to add, "Not a robbery, the hotel wasn't the target, apparently the guest was. Still, the authorities have blocked off that section of the corridor."

"Okay. So?"

"I'm sorry, they're not allowing guests access to that area, including…your room."

She sighed heavily. "So, what, I sleep on a lobby sofa?"

"Oh, no, indeed! We have arranged for you to be moved to one of our finest suites. If that is acceptable to you, we'll have your luggage moved and you can go up in short order."

"Whatever," she muttered, not particularly impressed at the whole "finest suites" thing. She'd traveled all over the country performing. A hotel room was a hotel room, no matter how much fancy crap they shoved into it.

"While you wait, please enjoy complimentary refreshments in the bar. I'll have someone bring your new key to you shortly."

Hmm…free drinks and an excuse to hang out in the bar without looking all single and pathetic. That *did* sound okay.

Entering the bar, she spotted a table in a corner, shadowy and separate. Perfect. She didn't feel like getting hit on tonight, not unless a superhot bad boy did the hitting. And the chances of that happening in this swanky, snobbish hotel were slim. Superhot bad boys didn't hang out at places like this.

At least she *thought* they didn't. But a few minutes later, while she sipped her chocolate martini, she saw a man walk in. A man who filled up the whole place with heat and simmering intensity and who instantaneously silenced every conversation and caught the attention of the entire room.

Like everyone else, she recognized him immediately. And Vanessa realized she'd been wrong. Because the baddest boy of them all had just walked back into her life. Not twenty feet away was the person she'd once so despised: the boy who'd made her fall in love with him, taken her virginity, then abandoned her, leaving her alone to face humiliation and scorn.

She wondered just how bad he was going to look after she greeted him the way she'd fantasized about doing for many years.

With a punch in his face.

STAN JACKSON always stayed in this particular hotel when he visited Chicago. Not just because the staff was equipped to deal with celebrities—and offered privacy and anonymity. But also because his mother had once worked as a maid at a hotel from the same chain down in Atlanta. That appealed to him the same way it appealed to him to know she now had a maid of her own, even though she insisted she didn't need one.

He didn't care if the woman did nothing but play cards with his mother…for the first time in his life, he had the money to take care of those he loved. And he intended to do it. Whether it was putting his little bother through med school or buying his elderly grandfather a new fishing boat even bigger than the last one, he'd give as much as he could for as long as he could.

"Excuse me," he said to the bartender.

The guy's eyes went wide and he slowly lowered the glass he'd been wiping out. "You're…you're Stan the Man."

"Yeah. Hey, listen, I'm trying to find the owner of this." He held up the unusual item he'd found in the hotel elevator, grinning as the bartender scrunched his brow. Stan added, "The guy at the front desk said a woman in a red gown just came in here. You happen to know where she is?"

"Sure, Stan." The bartender pointed to the corner of the room. "Can I have an…"

"You bet." Stan pulled a pen out of his pocket and scrawled his signature across the paper menu the other man shoved at him. He'd been playing in the NFL for six years and yet he still hadn't gotten used to that—to people acting like him signing his name on a piece of paper was some huge deal.

He never refused them. He knew how quickly all of it—the fame, the money, the magazine covers, the major deals—could

be yanked away with one bad season or one blown knee. He'd
learned that lesson very early on and it had stuck. Hard.

Nodding at a few people who lifted their glasses in silent
salute, he made his way through the bar. Chicago was a friendly
place…even to members of a rival team. He got several offers
of free beer and a few more requests for autographs.

He stopped for every one.

He also got suggestive looks from several of the women
in the place, some without men by their side. Some with.

He ignored all of them, focused only on the woman he'd
come in here to find. The one who'd left something behind
in the elevator.

As he neared the table in the corner, Stan took note of the
mysterious woman in red. Sister was tall…no doubt about
that, sitting higher in her seat than any other female in the
place, shoulders straight, head held up. For a second, he felt
a flash of trepidation—as if she might actually be too much
woman for him. He hadn't felt that way about anyone in a
very long time.

He liked his own reaction. It was different…and in these
jaded days, different was a good thing.

The stranger's soft, curly black hair was cropped close
to her head, emphasizing the perfectly shaped face and the
incredible bone structure. She looked regal, from the high
forehead to the huge brown eyes framed by thick lashes on
down to her jutting chin.

And that mouth… Lord have mercy, was it made for
sinning.

Feeling better about his decision to find her with every
step he made, Stan smiled. He'd come in here on a gentlemanly errand and was *very* glad he'd given in to the impulse.
Having found a woman's wickedly sexy red shoe in the

elevator, he'd tried turning it in at the front desk, only to be told the owner might well be in here. The guy had said a tall, beautiful woman in a red gown had just entered and speculated the shoe could be hers. Refusing the clerk's offer to take it, Stan had sought her out himself, wanting to see the owner, wondering if she was as hot as her footwear.

She wasn't just hot, the lady was on *fire.*

Finally reaching the table, he met her stare directly, liking that she made no effort to look away.

"Excuse me," he said with a smile, the same one women had swooned over in the Jockey commercial he'd done last year. "Does this belong to you?"

He reached into his pocket and drew out the spiky heeled sandal, holding it toward her. He waited for her to lick her lips, thank him, smile, ask him to sit down.

What he absolutely did *not* expect was the reaction he got.

"What do I look like to you, Cinder-freakin'-ella?" She stood up, thrusting an index finger toward his chest. "'Cause you sure ain't no Prince Charming."

His jaw falling open, Stan dropped the shoe. It bounced on the floor, landing beside the hem of the angry woman's red dress. He didn't *even* bend over to pick it up—she looked ready to bash him in the head.

"Okay," he said, holding his hands up, palms out. "No harm, no foul." As he started to back away, he scanned her features, wondering if he knew her. He *had* to know her— had to have come across her, maybe in his younger, wilder period. When he'd, uh, been a little less of a gentleman. There was no way a complete stranger would react so angrily.

"Sit your sorry ass down," she snapped. "Before you make a bigger fool of yourself."

"I don't think so...."

"You don't recognize me, do you." Her eyes were narrowed, that chin up higher, those crazy-sexy lips pursed.

"I meet a lot of people," he explained, wondering if he could possibly have picked up this stunning woman somewhere, had a wild night with her and then walked away. As he used to do.

Often.

"How many of 'em whupped your butt at T-ball every single game?"

And that was when he realized the truth. When the eyes became familiar and the cheeks as recognizable as his own. When he remembered that sassy voice, those lips—always curled up in laughter—and that stubborn jaw as she struggled to keep up with the boys in the small southern town where he'd spent a large part of his childhood.

All the memories of all the long, lazy days and the sweet summer nights poured into his brain and his heart took a hit harder than any he'd ever taken on the field.

"Vanessa McKee," he whispered, breathing the words more than saying them, as if her name was something sacred, something too painful to voice out loud for all the regrets and could-have-beens that would come with it.

"That's right," she said. "And now that you remember... *this* is for taking my virginity, humiliating me and then disappearing out of my life forever."

Giving him not one second to prepare, she swung her arm back, fisted her hand and slammed it right into his jaw.

2

VANESSA HADN'T REALLY thought about the fact that she was assaulting someone until she felt her knuckles connect with the block of granite disguised as Stan Jackson's handsome head. But once it did, once the crack sounded in the bar—sending the whole place into utter silence after one quick, shocked gasp from a nearby table—she had to admit it felt good. Damn good.

She'd been wanting to do that for twelve years.

"You *hit* me," he said, sounding completely astonished.

Too bad he wasn't saying it from the floor, all bloody and stuff. Landing a punch like that on almost any other man would have sent him down. But not this one. He simply stared at her in disbelief, rubbed his jaw and shook his head. "I can't believe you hit me."

"You're lucky I'm not armed."

"That's gonna bruise."

"Good." Banging up that strong face would serve another purpose, beyond causing him a few minutes' worth of pain.

Maybe it would bring him down a peg. Because no man should be *that* handsome and *that* sexy and a rich, gifted athlete on top of it.

Stan Jackson was a six-foot-two solid wall of muscle wrapped in creamy chocolate skin that every hot-blooded woman in America wanted to taste. His soulful brown eyes usually held laughter—at least when he wasn't in pain, like he was now. And the man had a killer smile, as many billboards around the country could prove. His high cheekbones and square jaw would have made him just as suited to a modeling career as to one in sports and the completely bald head just emphasized the stark, masculine beauty of his face.

Too bad all that prettiness was wasted on one lying, cowardly bastard.

The bartender, who'd come running over, huffed and puffed as he grabbed Stan's arm. "Mr. Jackson…do you want me to call the cops?" He swung his attention toward Vanessa. "What's your problem, lady, are you crazy? Don't you know who this is?"

"Hell, yes, I know who this is," she snapped back. "And if you knew him as well as I do, you'd want to punch him in the face, too."

"You're looney!"

"It's okay, I'm fine," Stan said, waving the bartender away. He focused all his attention on Vanessa, adding, "She hits like a girl."

Vanessa's fingers clenched again, until she saw Stan's body tense in preparation for it. He'd intentionally egged her on, like he'd always done when they were kids. If she went after him again, he'd be ready for her. And his piercing stare said his retribution would be swift.

He'd never hit her. Oh, no. He'd do something *worse*.

Like kiss her and prove to the world—and to Vanessa—that when it came to this brown-eyed boy, she had absolutely no willpower at all. Never had, and, judging by the way her heart was pounding her eardrums out at just the thought of him kissing her, never would.

The bartender walked away, shaking his head and mumbling under his breath. Once he was gone, Stan tilted his head and cocked a brow. "Nice to see you, too."

Oh, she'd like to say it was not nice for her, but she had to admit, some parts of her—not her brain, of course—thought it was very nice indeed. God, the man had gotten even more handsome with age, if that was possible.

As a boy, he'd been gangly and cute, all arms and legs like a puppy dog. He'd started growing into them as a teenager, his body filling out, growing wiry and powerful. She almost shivered when she thought about the way that long, lean form had felt pressed against hers, naked and wet from the secret swim they'd taken at a local pond. Back when they were lovers. Back when they were young. Back when she'd still believed in promises and true love.

"So how have you been, V?"

"Don't call me that," she snapped. "Only people I like get to call me that."

"I called you that all the time," he said softly. "Every day of every summer I'd come to spend with the old folks."

Yes, he had. From the time she was a child, Stan Jackson had been a part of her summer life—and had definitely been someone she liked enough to let him call her by her nickname.

He and his brother would come to their grandparents'

house every July, sent away from Atlanta by their hard-working parents to enjoy the sweet-smelling air of the South Carolina countryside. And from the very first time Vanessa's older brother had brought his new friend around—when both boys were about ten years old to Vanessa's nine—she had been *wild* about Stan. Wild enough to stalk him like a cat going after a canary, licking her chops right up until the minute she'd caught him.

He hadn't minded.

"I talked to Frank a few weeks ago," he had the audacity to say. "He and his wife caught a game when they were on the West Coast."

She sneered. "Just goes to show my brother has a short memory and no taste in friends."

"*We* were friends once, you and I," he said softly.

"Yeah. Right. Until you got what you wanted. You scored your touchdown, didn't even wait to see if you made the extra point, then skipped out of town forever."

Leaving his grandmother to clean up any possible messes he'd left behind. Lord, it infuriated her to this day.

He shook his head. "You've got a long memory, but not what I'd call an accurate one."

She rolled her eyes, not wanting to hear his excuses and lies. "Just go away."

"You really been hatin' on me for twelve years?"

She crossed her arms over her chest, noting the way Stan's eyes zoned in there. This was a man who liked beautiful women; he was probably with a different one every week.

While she had her faults, her looks weren't one of them. Vanessa was beautiful and she knew it. There was something rather nice about seeing the want in his eyes, especially since there was no way in hell the man would ever touch her again.

"Watch that ego," she replied. "I just saw the chance to pay a debt that was owed."

"You owed me a sock in the jaw? Wouldn't a letter have done the trick to get your feelings across?"

A letter. Sure. One final letter to ask him how he could have humiliated her the way he had. It hadn't seemed nearly enough. All the paper in the world couldn't have held the raging emotions—fury, abandonment, humiliation—she'd felt.

She'd written plenty of letters to him after that last summer, when she'd been fifteen and he a year older and they'd been playing some *very* grown-up games during his annual visit.

He'd stopped responding. And she'd soon found out why.

The day his grandmother had shown up at her door to confront her own grandmother about whether Stan had put a baby in Vanessa's belly that summer had been the most humiliating moment of V's life. She'd had to admit to the woman she most admired and most respected in the entire world that while she was *not* pregnant, she had ignored all her advice, all her cautionary tales, all her pleas and had given herself to a boy she might never see again.

That had proved prophetic, up until now. Tonight was the first time she'd set eyes on Stan Jackson—in person—since that last night at the lake.

She honestly didn't think she'd ever forget the sad disappointment in Granny's eyes. Not because Vanessa had proved herself human…but because she'd lied. And broken so many promises.

"Excuse me," a voice said, intruding on the tension hanging as thick as a quilt between them.

"What?" Vanessa growled. Then she saw the wide, hopeful eyes of a young boy standing beside his father and felt like a shrew. Normally, she'd question a parent for bringing a kid into a bar, but it was obvious this one had come in here for one reason only: to meet the man she'd just decked. "I'm sorry, I assume you'd like…"

Stan had already squatted down in front of the boy, who was probably about ten, and was engaging him in conversation. The father hovered over them, looking every bit as eager as the son, especially when Stan agreed to pose for a couple of pictures.

Vanessa would have taken the opportunity to make a dash for it, but she had nowhere to go. She didn't have a room.

Considering heading to the front desk and asking for anything they had available, she breathed a huge sigh of relief when she saw a bellman walking toward her table. "I was asked to bring this key—"

She didn't even give him a chance to finish his sentence. Plucking the small, white envelope from his hands, she muttered, offering him a big smile, "You're a lifesaver. Thanks so much." Then she reached into her purse, dug out a twenty and offered him a big tip.

"Wow, thanks!"

It was worth it. Getting out of here with a little of her pride and dignity intact was *so* worth it.

Fortunately, Stan's interaction with the father and son, and her own with the bellman, had given her a few minutes to calm down. Why her nerves should still be so frazzled, she didn't know. It was over, she'd gotten the anger that she didn't even realize she still felt off her chest. That punch should be the end of it, the punctuation mark as she said goodbye to the lousy memories: the look on her granny's face—and on *his* grandmother's; the pain and humiliation when she'd never even heard from Stan again; the heartbreak when she'd read about the young, hotshot football player being drafted into the NFL right after college, soon becoming a tabloid staple for the women always surrounding him.

All those things had exploded to the surface when she'd seen him and her fist had done her talking for her. Having gotten it off her chest, all the negative thoughts should now dissipate into her history again, where they belonged. She should already have returned to her normal, confident, cocky, slightly jaded self.

But she couldn't deny it. She was still incredibly wound up, her heart thudding wildly, her breath was jagged and uneven. She felt wild, ready to do something—hit him again or push him down onto the table and kiss his face off.

Not that. No way, girl. Get to your room.

She straightened her back, because there was not a chance in the world she would let Stan know she was still attracted to him. She'd sooner break her own dancing legs.

About to walk away, she was forced to stop when Stan stepped directly in her path. The father and son were already walking out the door, she just hadn't noticed.

"Where are you going?"

"Away from here."

"Without another word?"

"I would say I'm sorry for hitting you, but it would be a lie," she admitted.

"And I *know* you never lie."

"Not if I can help it."

His jaw tightened. "Neither do I."

She snorted. "Right."

"I didn't lie to you," he insisted, his voice husky. "I'm sorry I fell out of touch. I was a kid and, well, my life kind of…went to hell later that summer."

"Yeah, well, thanks to your grandmother, mine did, too."

His eyes scrunched in confusion.

"Oh, didn't she tell you about her visit to my granny's house? Where she outed me as the little whore who tried to trap her grandson by getting herself knocked up?"

"V, that did *not* happen." He frowned deeply, appearing astonished by the accusation. "That could *not* have happened."

"Oh, yeah, I'm a liar," she spat, seeing his stunned disbelief. The man lived in his own world and had obviously grown used to forgetting the truth and justifying his actions. "I guess I imagined it, huh?" Shaking her head in disgust, she turned to head for the exit.

"V…" He reached out and put a hand on her arm, just a light touch, but Vanessa flinched like she'd been grabbed.

"Don't. Just don't. We're done."

Without letting another foolish word leave her mouth or traitorous sensation wrest control of her body from her brain, she brushed past him, heading for the exit. As she left, she never once looked back at the boy from her past, completely confident she'd removed all thoughts of him from her future.

STAN STAYED IN THE BAR for a half hour after Vanessa left. Thinking. Wondering. Remembering.

Fortunately, everyone left him alone. There'd been plenty of witnesses to his confrontation with Vanessa and he imagined all of them were dying to tell their Chicago Bears-loving friends how the big-shot California quarterback got socked by a woman.

The pain in his jaw had faded right away, but the pain caused by the memories Vanessa had forced him to confront did not. Damn, maybe she had the right to hate his guts. He had done exactly what she said—taken her virginity, then left, promising to come back the next summer for a whole month of romance. Promising to keep in touch, to call, to write.

He hadn't. Not after a couple of weeks.

He'd like to say there was a big misunderstanding, that he'd lost the address, forgotten how to dial a telephone. But it wouldn't be true.

When Vanessa had stopped writing, he hadn't made any effort to find out why. He'd pushed her out of his thoughts and his mind intentionally, just as his father had asked him to.

But what she'd said about his grandmother…was it possible? Could that actually have happened?

Thinking back on that time, he realized that yes, it was definitely possible. God, no wonder she hated his guts.

Though he'd been too screwed up in the head to think straight at the time, he knew now that he'd made some pretty serious mistakes. What he'd done to Vanessa was the greatest one. And, oh, did he regret it.

Especially now, having seen her again. Because the feisty, tomboyish girl had become one incredibly beautiful, sensuous woman. Even now, sitting alone at the table she'd vacated, he was still aroused by her. Still kept picturing her flashing eyes, that wicked mouth. And, oh, the body. She was no longer the skinny girl with the pretty little breasts he'd have about *died* to taste when he was a teenager. Those beautiful curves would overflow his big hands as he plumped them and sucked on her sensitive brown nipples.

And Lord have mercy, judging by the slit in that dress, she had legs that went *all* the way up.

Not that he'd ever find out.

"She put you in your place," he muttered as he sipped his beer. "Smart thing to do is stay there." *Let her go.*

It wasn't like he could track her down and try to get her to change her mind about him, anyway. She could be in one of a thousand rooms in this hotel and he had not a clue where she was living these days.

He'd kept in touch with her brother Frank, though only sporadically. But Frank's younger sister was a subject that had remained off-limits. Stan had never asked what Vanessa was doing with herself and Frank had never offered to tell him.

He wondered just how much Vanessa's brother knew about what had happened between them. And what had happened to change everything when Stan had gone back to Atlanta that summer.

Didn't matter. Like she said, it was done. They were done. And he'd never set eyes on her again. As he left the bar, he tried very hard to convince himself that was a good thing.

"Hello there, Mr. Jackson, have a good evening?" a voice asked as he walked by the front desk.

He forced a smile at the night manager, an efficient, if obsequious, guy. "Interesting. It was…interesting."

"I assume you got your key?"

Stan paused, lifting a curious brow.

"When you came by earlier—with the shoe—you left your key on the counter. I sent it to you with one of the bellmen."

Stan checked his pockets, realizing his key was, indeed, missing. "He must not have found me."

The man's face reddened. "That's unacceptable. I am terribly sorry." He strode to one of the computer terminals. "I will rekey your room this *instant,* Mr. Jackson. Please accept my apologies. You may be assured the employee will be dealt with."

"Hey, it was my fault for losing the thing." He'd obviously had other things on his mind—like finding the owner of that sexy shoe. "As long as the guy didn't use it to break into my room and steal my drawers, I'm not gonna pitch a fit about it."

The relief on the other man's face said some other, more pampered guests might indeed have "pitched a fit" about it. He smiled weakly. "Thank you, very much."

Pocketing the new key, Stan headed for the elevator. No sexy red shoe waited inside it. No sexy black woman, either.

Forget her. You can't undo the past. There are plenty of other women out there just as sexy, just as exciting.

He was still telling himself that—still forcing himself to believe he could put Vanessa McKee out of his heart and his lustful thoughts for good—when he walked into the bedroom of his suite a few minutes later. But when he glanced toward the open bathroom door, and saw an utterly amazing sight, he began to doubt it was true.

He wasn't going to be able to put Vanessa McKee out of his lustful thoughts anytime soon. If ever.

Because the woman was standing in his bathroom, wide-eyed with shock, dripping wet and completely, *gloriously* naked.

3

VANESSA COULDN'T MAKE a sound, couldn't move, couldn't even breathe. Because standing a few feet away, looking like he'd stumbled into a *Penthouse* fantasy, was Stan Jackson. The very man she'd been thinking about—*intimately*—as she washed her body with slippery soap in the luxurious shower of her suite.

Remaining in the bedroom, he didn't move, either. Well, not *much*. The man definitely moved his eyes. His hot gaze traveled from Vanessa's head, clear down to her toes, with a few pauses for deep murmurs of appreciation in between.

Even from here she could see the way his soft, expensive-looking trousers tented over what she remembered was a very generous package. Why the realization that he wanted her should send every bit of feminine moisture in her body rushing between her legs, she didn't know. Especially since she hated the man.

Especially since he'd *invaded her room*.

"What in the holy hell do you think you're doing?" Snapping out of her daze, she grabbed a white, fluffy towel off a rack—the one she'd forgotten to move closer to the shower when she got in it—and wrapped it around her body. "Get out before I call the cops."

His brow shot up. "Excuse me?"

"You might be Mr. Rich Superstar, but you can't just bribe your way into a woman's room. Whoever let you in here is going to be short a job tomorrow."

"You've got it wrong…"

"Get out!" she repeated.

"Vanessa…"

She stalked out of the bathroom, dripping water on the carpet, but not caring. Carried on by righteous anger, she got right in his face. "You might be Mr. Superstar to everyone else, though God only knows why, it's not like you cure cancer or fight for world peace."

His eyes narrowed.

"You play a *game* for a living and people pay you millions of dollars for it."

The jaw clenched.

"But just because everyone else is used to giving you whatever you want, that does *not* give you the right to buy your way into the room of a woman who hates you."

She saw the exact moment he lost it, the very instant she'd pushed too far. It was at that word. *Hate.* Because without a sound, Stan hauled her into his arms, ignoring the wetness of her skin. He captured her mouth, forcing her lips apart, plunging his tongue against hers in as deep and carnal a kiss as she'd ever experienced. As if to prove she was the biggest liar the world had ever seen.

She was going to punch him again. After she pulled away. Then she was going to call the cops. Any second now.

Only, none of those things happened. Inflamed by the feel

of that tough, masculine body against hers and the wild, wonderful flavor of his mouth, she wrapped her arms around his neck. Tilting her head, she invited him deeper, tangling her tongue with his, filling all her senses with hot, irresistible man.

Her towel dropped. By accident.

Or maybe not. Maybe she let it go. Who could say?

Didn't matter, the end result was she finally got to feel him. Feel the heat of his skin through his expensive, silky dress shirt. Feel those big, strong hands on her hips. He squeezed her backside, hoisting her up on her tiptoes until their bodies perfectly aligned. That long ridge of arousal was pressed from her pelvis to her belly and Vanessa's legs shook as she remembered what it had been like to have him inside her.

She didn't think, she certainly didn't resist. Vanessa just soaked in all the sensations battering her body, wondering how in the name of God she'd ever considered herself a sexual being between the last moment she'd been in his arms and this one.

But even as she began to wonder if he was going to push her the few feet to the big, king-size bed, to finish this wild interlude the way they were both dying to finish it, Stan pulled his mouth away from hers. He released his grip on her butt, let her down and staggered back two steps.

"Woman, you are crazy," he muttered between choppy breaths.

"*You* kissed *me*," she reminded him, her voice just as ragged. The haze began to leave her and she bent down to grab the nearly forgotten towel, wishing her heart didn't do a little happy dance because of the way he kept staring at her body, as if he'd never seen anything as glorious in his entire life.

She was a professional dancer and she knew she looked damn fine. So maybe he *hadn't* seen anything as good, especially from any of those simpering sports groupies who followed professional players around, giving it up to any one who'd look at them twice.

Maybe it had been a long time since he'd seen a *real* woman. One with pride and confidence and power.

Well, wasn't that just too bad for him.

Too bad for you, stupid. You know *you want to see that man without his clothes.*

"Crazy," he repeated, now rubbing his jaw, right where she'd punched it earlier. As if he were trying to remind himself that she was dangerous to know.

Good. She hoped he never forgot it. Even if she did still tingle all over, every bit of her body sensitized by the completely unexpected kiss.

She forced the sensations away, struggling to find the white-hot anger she'd felt before she'd so foolishly let his embrace suck her dry of all feelings but *want.* "And you are the one who finagled your way into my room."

"It's *my* room," he snapped back.

She snorted in disbelief. "That's a lame excuse, even for a sorry fool like you."

"Vanessa," he said, his tone warning, his jaw rock hard, *"you are in my room."*

"Oh, please. You told me a half hour ago that you never lie. Yet here you are lying like a cheap toupee on a fat man's head."

Though his lips twitched a bit, he remained stiff. "Then what's my suitcase doing over there in the corner?"

Still scoffing, Vanessa glanced in the direction he pointed. "That's *my* suitcase. The hotel brought it up for me when they moved me from my other room."

"Uh-huh," he muttered, walking over to the standard black piece of luggage lying on a portable luggage rack. He unzipped it, and before Vanessa could even demand that he get his hands out of her panties, so to speak, he held up a pair of briefs.

These were *not* the boy briefs she wore when she was feeling a little bloated. These were men's.

"What…" she hurried over, pushing him out of the way, digging into the suitcase.

Men's socks. Men's shirts. Men's trousers.

The suitcase, she realized, looked very much like hers, but it most definitely was not. "How did you pull this off?"

"It's my room."

Vanessa stared at him, hard. "This is a joke, right?"

He slowly shook his head. "You *are* in my room. So maybe I should be asking…how did *you* pull this off?" He stepped closer, all his hot man aura washing over her like a heady breeze. Lifting his fingers to her face, he carefully rubbed her cheek, letting the side of his thumb pass across her lips. "You were waiting for me, naked, wet…should I be flattered or afraid?"

Vanessa trembled. The man actually made her *tremble*. She told herself it was out of pure embarrassment— humiliation that he thought she'd set him up for a sexy seduction.

In truth, she knew, it was the brush of his fingers on her lips and that knowing, sultry look in his eyes that had her whole body quivering. Not to mention that deep, sultry voice—that bedroom voice that women around the world went crazy over even if they only ever heard it through their TV screens.

Where would he touch next? What would he whisper if

he leaned close to her ear? When would he stop? Oh, Lord, was he going to kiss her again?

Swallowing hard, she managed a few words. "There was obviously some kind of mix-up. I swear to you, Stan, I had no idea this wasn't my room."

"Uh-huh." He didn't sound convinced. But he did sound amused—as if he liked making her sweat.

"Honestly," she insisted, wishing he'd stop touching her since she couldn't think with his hands on her. Yet knowing she'd cry if he took them away. "There was some problem on my floor, the manager told me they had to move me, and they sent a bellman into the bar with my new key."

He finally paused, tugging his fingers away from her cheek a scant centimeter. She missed the contact as if there was an ocean between them. "A bellman?"

She nodded. "He came in the bar and gave it to me while you were talking to that boy and his father."

No verbal reaction, but he moved back again, his whole body this time, not just his hand. "Oh."

"The front desk just messed up, put me in an occupied room." Shaking her head, knowing how bizarre that sounded, she muttered, "Of all the rooms in the hotel…I guess this was about as coincidental as something can get."

Clearing his throat, Stan shook his head. "No, it wasn't. I left my key at the front desk and the bellman was bringing it to me. I guess he thought we were…together."

Oh. She stopped defending herself, stopped blaming him, just thought about it. What he said made perfect sense. And considering Stan was about the sexiest man on earth and the two of them shot sparks off each other that a blind person could see, she could understand why the bellman had assumed they were a couple. It was pretty careless, but understandable.

"Wow," she whispered, feeling awkward and self-conscious for the first time since he'd walked in on her naked. "I guess I should get dressed and go find out where my real room is."

A tiny smile widened those sensuous lips of his. "Don't feel like you have to on my account."

"What, go to my own room?" she asked, surprised.

"I mean," he whispered, glancing down at the towel, "you don't have to get dressed."

VANESSA'S BIG, BEAUTIFUL eyes went wide with shock, but Stan saw something else in them, as well. Something she'd probably sooner slit her throat than admit: excitement. Titillation.

Possibility.

Well, he was excited, too. Had been from the minute he'd seen her, standing there so stunningly naked.

She was every fantasy woman rolled into one and he'd been unable to think one coherent thought when he'd first seen her. Tall, slim, with a tiny waist and curvy hips just perfect for a man to fit his hands around. As he'd discovered.

Vanessa's legs went on forever and her lush breasts had driven him crazy when she'd been pressed against his body. He'd wanted to lick off every bit of moisture on them. If he had one regret in pulling away from her when he had, since he knew he'd been driven by anger when he'd started the kiss, it was that he hadn't had at least one little taste of those sweet nipples.

She rolled her eyes. "You're a dog," she said, as if she'd read his thoughts.

"No, just a man." His good humor disappearing, he added, "One who apparently owes you an apology. Vanessa, I swear, I had no idea about what my grandmother did."

He *hoped* she believed him, wondering why it mattered so much after all these years, but knowing it did. Not just to her, but to him, too. She wasn't the only one who had regrets.

Vanessa sucked her bottom lip into her mouth, as if, of all the things she'd expected him to say, that was not one of them.

"I didn't tell anyone what happened between us," he swore, reaching out and taking her arm. "Not a soul."

"Then how…"

"My brother found one of your letters. The one where you said you were, uh…late."

She closed her eyes briefly, moaning as she brought a hand to her face. "Oh, Lord, what a fool I was. Two days late and I panicked. I should never have written that to you."

"I'm glad you did. I loved your letters. Hell, all my other friends had computers and e-mail and barely even knew how to write a sentence." He smiled, trying to tease her out of her sadness. "We were good practice for each other, with our writing."

"And with other things," she admitted, her voice husky.

Oh, yeah, they'd definitely helped each other learn other things. Things he'd only ever fantasized about in his young life until Vanessa McKee had made them a reality.

As if wishing she hadn't said it, she quickly returned to the subject at hand, "I can still remember being in such a panic about being late. But there was also this silly girl's dream…"

"Of?"

She turned away, shaking her head in reminiscence. "Of you, me, creating a new little family that would be just like the one I grew up in, only the parents would be there." She trembled slightly and he saw the tiny movement of the sleek muscles in her back. "They wouldn't have died."

"Amen to that," he murmured, knowing from experience

how hard it was to lose a parent. He couldn't imagine losing both in an accident, the way Vanessa had when she was only six.

She quickly shook off the sad mood. "It was obviously a false alarm." She watched him through half-lowered lashes. "So, what about your brother?"

"He took the letter to my father."

"That little shit," Vanessa muttered, making him laugh. Because it was the truth, his brother, even younger than Vanessa, had been a complete pest.

"He's in med school, can you believe it?"

"Probably needed to learn how to heal his wounds from getting his butt kicked over and over for being such a tattle-tale brat."

The words held no heat. She was, in fact, smiling as they left her mouth. He smiled back, unable to resist her. As if they were friends. As if she hadn't punched him an hour ago.

As if she wasn't standing here in a towel making him nearly break out in a sweat with the need to tear it off her and taste every inch of her womanly body.

But his apology wasn't finished. Afterward, well, maybe after he'd said what needed to be said, he'd see about that towel. See whether her skin would taste as sweet on his tongue as he remembered.

"I had no idea Dad sent my grandmother around to check on you. That must have been hell."

She nodded once.

"Then you didn't hear from me anymore…." He didn't say anything else, didn't continue, because he wasn't sure how much to say without sounding like some whiner looking for sympathy, especially after what *she'd* gone through in her childhood.

Vanessa had stiffened, how could she not? But then she admitted something he'd long ago realized. "You were every bit as much a kid as I was. We were playing games we weren't ready for, neither of us."

"True."

"And both of us went on to do some good things."

He wondered what she'd done, but didn't ask. There wasn't a ring on her finger and there wasn't one on his. That was all he needed to know right at this moment.

Maybe there would be time for more later. But for right now, he'd had enough of talking. It was all he could do to hold himself together while standing a foot away from her, smelling the sweetness of her skin, seeing the curls drying around her beautiful face. Smelling the musky scent of woman that told him she was still just as aroused by their kiss as he was.

That towel wasn't meant for a woman as tall as Vanessa. It hung low on her breasts and high on her mile-long thighs. And they could talk from now till tomorrow but he wouldn't be able to concentrate on one word because the need to touch her—to have her—was sending him out of his mind.

So he shoved everything else aside. The past. Her anger. Even his pride. And he laid it on the line.

"Come to my bed, V. Be my woman tonight."

4

FOR THE SECOND TIME in minutes, Stan Jackson sent Vanessa into complete shock. Because things had been going along so normally…they'd been talking, dealing with old wounds, saying sorrys. And then he'd hit her where she was most vulnerable.

Right in her quivering libido.

How the man *knew* she'd been standing here an oversexed mess, she'd never know. Maybe she hadn't done as good a job as she'd thought of hiding her reaction to his suggestion that she didn't "have to get dressed."

They'd talked for a few minutes beyond that, but the words had kept bouncing around in her head. Through the explanations. Through the apologies.

Until now, when this sex-on-a-stick man had asked her into his bed.

"V?" He reached for her, touching her cheek with his fingers, then cupping it.

She couldn't resist turning into that touch, pressing her lips to the palm, shivering at the strength of that calloused hand. "That would be crazier than anything else I've done tonight," she whispered.

"Aren't you curious?" he asked, stepping closer, so his arm brushed hers, his shirt scraped the towel. So his breath drifted against her skin and his handsome face filled her vision. "Don't you want to see, for just one night, how it could be, now that we're both older and know how to make it…mmm…*good*."

"So good," she mumbled, knowing it would be.

"I've been dying to lick my way from your toes all the way up to the top of those thighs."

The thighs in question wobbled.

"Press my face into your stomach and breathe you in."

The stomach quivered.

"Suck your nipples hard, until you beg me to stop *and* threaten to hurt me if I do."

Oh, she was so there already. Her breasts grew heavy, her nipples scraping against the terry cloth, which was soft and yet rough enough to give her a wicked thrill.

Stan bent to kiss her temple. "I could kiss you for hours."

"Stan…"

"Starting with your lips. Then on down your body until I get to do one thing you and I were too inexperienced to try."

She knew exactly what he was talking about and her pussy clenched reflexively, knowing this man's tongue would be as magical as his hands…his voice.

"You will let me taste you, baby, won't you? Don't turn a starving man away."

She sagged against him and he caught her hips, holding her steady. This time, when the towel fell, there was no doubt how it came down. He unfastened the twist above her right breast with two fingers and sent the thing plunging to the floor.

"I'll make you feel things you never dreamed possible."

"Right back at you," she whispered, finally accepting the inevitable. They were going to spend the night in Stan's bed. She had not one twinge of regret at the realization. Whatever had happened before, whatever happened next, for *now* she was going to make love to the man she wanted…who had once been the boy she'd loved.

He smiled at her confidence, glancing down at her. She was no longer wet from her shower, her whole body was smooth and supple. He couldn't tear his eyes away.

Reaching for the top button of his shirt, she slowly unfastened it. "Let me see what you got, big man."

"If I look half as good to you as you do to me, V, we are both gonna be very happy people."

She laughed softly at the compliment cloaked in arrogance, then finished unbuttoning the shirt and pushed it off his shoulders. Then she had to stop. Just stop. And look at the glory of the male body revealed before her.

"My, have you grown up," she muttered, stunned at the amount of muscle on the man. His arms were massive, his pecs so well defined she simply had to reach out and touch. To scrape her finger across his rippling torso, around one flat male nipple, then down the lean, hard stomach.

She was breathing hard when she unfastened his belt and panting when he helped her push the pants and his briefs down.

"Oh, *my*," she whispered, a little shocked, and *very* pleased. "I *wasn't* imagining it just because you were my first."

He smiled proudly, all cocky and confident, kicking the rest of his clothes away to stand naked in front of her. She felt like a kid in a buffet line, not sure whether to go for the macaroni and cheese or head straight for the creamy ice cream.

He didn't give her the chance to decide. Bending, he

picked her up, like she was one of those little ballerina chicks instead of the dancer dubbed the Amazon woman of Radio City. Tossing her onto his big bed, he came right down with her, pressing that hot, muscular body against hers.

"I want everything," she said matter-of-factly. "Just so you know. Absolutely everything. And then I want it again."

"As many times as you can take it," he promised, his eyes glittering. "As long as I'm breathing, I'll be loving you."

Loving her in the physical sense. She knew that's what he meant. But still, the words jabbed. Because he'd once said them to her in the emotional sense.

Forget about it. Take tonight and run with it.

Stan hadn't noticed her hesitation. He'd begun to kiss her, sweetly on the mouth, then slowly moving his way down her throat to her collarbone. He tasted her there, as if it were the most erogenous spot on her body and, suddenly, she suspected it was. *Every* spot his mouth touched was.

Especially when he went there…and, oh, *there.* She gasped as his stubbled jaw brushed against the side of her breast. "Please," she begged, arching toward him, knowing if he didn't use that mouth on her nipple soon she'd die.

He teased her some more, licking the bottom of each breast, tasting around the areolas. Then, finally, when she was wishing he had hair so she could yank his mouth to where she wanted it, he covered one nipple and suckled her, deep and strong.

She cried out, glad his room was a big suite. If there were neighbors nearby, they'd be hearing some noise tonight. Because Vanessa was loud in bed and she had a feeling this man would be making her scream before too long.

"You sure grew up," he muttered as he licked one nipple, then the other. "How'd you get to be so big and womanly?"

She rolled her head back and forth on the pillow. "They're real, if that's what you're asking."

He laughed softly, looking up at her. Cupping one breast in his hand, he replied, "Oh, no doubt about that. I know the real thing when I'm tasting it."

The hunger in his chocolate-brown eyes melted any mild annoyance and she smiled down at him. "You're going to find some other real parts of me to taste soon, aren't you?" she asked, shifting restlessly. She wanted more of him. More of his hands, his mouth. That big, powerful body.

"We're getting there," he said with a chuckle.

By the time he was done with her breasts, Vanessa was digging her heels into the bed, trying to stay still but needing to thrust and writhe. Needing *more.*

He understood, moving down her body, soothing every nibble with his hands, kissing every crevice and indentation he could find. Until he came to the juncture of her thighs, and pushed her legs apart to stare appreciatively at her sex.

"So pretty," he muttered hoarsely before lowering his mouth to her clit, rolling it against his tongue.

Wild flames of pleasure roared through her. "Oh, yes."

He kept tasting her, teasing her, licking then moving away to bite on her inner thigh, only to return for more madness. Finally, Vanessa could take no more, no more of lying there, being feasted upon. She wanted to do some feasting, too. So giving him no time to elude her, she scooted around on the bed, kissing her way down his side, to his lean hip.

"V?"

"Don't stop," she whispered, tilting her hips toward his mouth again. "And don't stop *me.*"

"Not on your life," he replied, his voice thick.

That was all the permission she needed. As he buried his

face between her thighs, Vanessa finally gained her prize, too, covering the thick, bulbous head of his sex with her lips. He hissed against her slick folds as she took more of him, sucking him into her mouth, taking as much as she could until he hit the back of her throat.

"Oh, Lord have mercy," he grunted, pausing to enjoy what she was doing to him. She didn't mind. She liked giving oral sex almost as much as she liked getting it. If they were both happening at the same time...so much the better.

Reaching between his legs, she toyed with those vulnerable sacs between, feeling him flinch in response. Relentless, she moved her head up and down, making love to him with her mouth, still tenderly holding him in her hand. Stan quickly returned to what he'd been doing. It was only a minute or so before everything—the spicy tastes, the rich smells, the sighs and moans and, oh, heavens, the *feelings*— all exploded into a cacophony of pleasure and she climaxed against his lips.

She shuddered from it, giving her body over to it, barely noticing as Stan pulled away only long enough to turn around. She was still shaking when he moved over her.

"Look at me," he ordered.

She opened her eyes, doing it, seeing his self-satisfied smile and the glisten of her own body's moisture on his lips.

"You taste amazing."

"I feel even better, just wait and see" she boasted, arching up toward him. They'd played enough. Now she wanted him inside her, filling her up, pounding into her until her head blew off.

Stan reached for the pocket of the pants he'd tossed onto the end of his bed, retrieving a condom from it. Vanessa would have offered to help, but she was shaking and feared she'd drop the thing, prolonging the agony. Because waiting *was* agony. She was twisting, thrusting up toward him, begging him for it. She was almost ready to cry in frustration, needing him so badly.

"You are the most beautiful woman I have ever seen," Stan said, sounding almost reverent. He lowered himself back between her thighs, his face close to hers so he could press a languorous kiss on her mouth. And as he kissed her, as his tongue played gently with hers, he slowly slid into her body.

Vanessa emitted a tiny gasp, in the very back of her throat, her breath hitching. He was moving so gently, taking such care, as if afraid to hurt her. Though she had been wanting it wild and hard and fast, the tenderness of the man hit her harder than any booty-rocking sex ever could.

"Beautiful," he repeated, cupping her head in his hand.

She stared into his eyes, wondering why, though the frenzy was gone and she was getting what she wanted, tears still tried to spill from her eyes. Maybe it was the expression on his handsome face. The warmth in his gaze. The sweet smile on his lips. That smooth voice and tender tone.

She had never felt like this with another man. Never. She wanted to wrap herself around him and thank him for making her feel so cherished. And, as he drove home, stretching her to her limit, for making her feel so…damn…*good.*

LATER, after Vanessa had finally tumbled into an exhausted sleep, Stan found himself lying on his side of the bed, propped up on one elbow, staring at her face. Her lips were parted as she breathed lightly, and they were still red and swollen from his kisses.

He didn't think he'd ever tire of kissing this woman.

He'd sure done a lot of it tonight. They'd made love for over an hour until his body had finally had enough of him putting off his climax and had simply taken over. She'd fallen right to sleep afterward, their legs still entwined.

He hadn't been able to follow her. He was too keyed up. The sex had merely taken the edge off his energetic mood, it hadn't killed it. Though he'd like to wake her up for another round, he figured the woman could use an hour or two of sleep first.

Then he'd wake her up.

Glancing at the clock, he saw it was midnight. Late here, but not too late on the West Coast. He had a nightly call to make. So he slipped out of bed, padding naked into the next room. Quietly shutting the door behind him, he picked up the phone in the living room and dialed a familiar number.

When the sweetest female voice on earth answered, he couldn't help smiling. "Hey, baby."

"Daddy! You're late. I had to hide my Hello Kitty phone under my pillow so Granny wouldn't take it."

He laughed softly. His baby girl might only be four, but she was already a bossy thing. Funny, she reminded him of the female sleeping in his bed. "I'm sorry, sugar, you know I'm in the middle of the country where the clocks are different."

"The clocks are *different?* You mean they tell different times? Is it thirty-eighty o'clock there?"

He chuckled again, liking the wonder in her voice. Telling her what he'd meant, he asked about her day and listened intently as she related all the important stuff happening in her little-girl world. She probably could have gone on for an hour, but he knew it was way past her bedtime. Promising to call earlier the next night and telling her to be good for Granny, he whispered, "I love you, sugar-baby."

He was just hanging up the phone when he heard a noise and looked up to see Vanessa watching him, wide-eyed. Tight-lipped.

"V, I'm sorry, did I wake you?"

"No. Did you wake your *sugar-baby?*"

Was that…it couldn't be jealousy on her face, right? The woman had been swearing she hated him a few hours ago. Despite the wild loving they'd shared, she couldn't have strong enough feelings to be jealous, could she?

The deep frown said that yes, she could. Which, for some reason, brought a smile to his lips.

"If you're married, I am going to string you up by that thing you so prize between your legs."

He reacted like any man. He scooted back and crossed his legs a little. Instinct. "I'm not married."

"But you have a girlfriend." Not waiting for his answer, she swung around as if to march back into the other room and get dressed for her big dramatic exit. "Why did I ever trust you?"

"I was saying good-night to my daughter," he murmured.

Vanessa froze, slowly turning back toward him. "Your what?"

"I have a four-year-old daughter. Her name's Kendra and I was calling to say good-night. It's not so late in L.A."

That seemed to take all the energy out of her. Vanessa slowly sank onto the edge of a chair, still naked. Still…oh, *so* nice.

"A daughter? How did I not know this?"

"I like my privacy. There's some crazy folks out there."

She nodded, understanding immediately. "But the mother?"

"We were married for about five minutes right after I got drafted into the NFL. She's not around anymore."

"Oh?"

"She wasn't interested in Kendra—ever—and lost all interest in me when I was injured during my rookie year and it looked like I'd never play again."

Vanessa's jaw dropped and that fire sparked again in her eyes. He wondered if she had any idea that she was shaking—in indignation, and on his behalf, he had no doubt. "She walked out on you when you were *hurt?*"

"Best thing that could have happened. I found out early what she wanted from me and was able to get custody easily."

"What happened when you came back to the game?"

"She tried to come back, too." He couldn't prevent a slightly evil smile.

"Bet I know how that turned out."

"Bet you do." He hesitated, then added, "If you've been wondering, about the news stories…"

"The women," she said drily.

"Yeah. I went a little crazy after the breakup. But I wised up quick, I wouldn't do anything to hurt Kendra."

"I know. You're too good a man to be a bad father."

He wondered why that quiet confidence warmed him as if he'd just been named player of the year. Funny how much her opinion mattered to him…still.

"Now, if you're satisfied, and I don't have to worry about you punching me again, how about we go back to bed?"

She rose, slowly approaching him. "How about we stay here?"

Right here sounded fine. Just fine. Especially when Vanessa crawled onto his lap, straddling him. She was already wet and creamy, and she slid up and down on his hard cock, mimicking the way they'd made love just a little while ago.

He grabbed her face and tugged her to him so he could kiss her, deeply, then whispered, "I don't have…"

"I dug through your suitcase and found them. Brought one with me," she replied. "Only, I dropped it in the doorway when I overheard part of your conversation."

She hopped off his lap, jogged over to the bedroom door and bent over to pick up the condom. Stan groaned at the sight. "Woman, you're gonna give me a heart attack."

The witch didn't straighten up. She remained right as she was, bent over at the waist, wagging that beautiful ass and that sweet, wet sex at him like a honey pot at a bear. Glancing back toward him, she licked her lips and murmured, "Gee, I can't find it. I could have sworn it was right here. Maybe you should help."

Stan didn't hesitate, knowing exactly what she wanted and more than happy to give it to her. He got up and stepped behind her, dropping his hands onto her hips, squeezing that soft, womanly flesh, rocking against her. His cock slid against her cheeks, and she rode him up and down a little, just to drive him out of his ever-loving mind.

"Oh, look. Found it," she said with a giggle that was just damn cute.

"Maybe you better keep looking. Might find something else down there."

She laughed again, straightening a tiny bit, enough to hand him the condom. Once he'd put it on, she pushed back against him, those round cheeks jiggling. Grabbing the door frame with both hands, she arched her back, watching him over her shoulder. "You like what you see?"

He liked what he saw more than anything else in the world. And he knew he was going to like what he'd feel. Sliding into her heat from behind, never loosening his hold on her hips, he groaned at how good it was. Tight and hot, she gripped him inside, sliding back to meet his slow, forward thrusts.

"We definitely didn't dream about things like this when we were young, did we?" she whispered, sounding dreamy and erotic.

"I don't think I ever imagined anything this good in my entire life," he admitted, throwing his head back as he continued to rock. Until finally, the rocking grew wilder, the thrusts grew frantic, and he came inside her with an explosion of pure pleasure.

5

THEY TALKED long into the night. Stupid stuff. *How are your sisters?* and *What do you do for a living anyway?* He seemed to like the idea of her being a Rockette. A lot. He made several comments about her long-enough-to-wrap-around-him-twice legs, eventually begging her to do a private, pantiless kick-line dance.

She did it.

That had led to another wild round of sex at around four o'clock in the morning.

It was now nine and Vanessa was wide-awake, watching the beautiful man sleeping beside her. "I wish I could keep you," she whispered.

Even as she said it, she knew that was crazy talk. Stan was a superstar with women dogging his every step. Last night had been about…last night. Seeing, as he'd said, how it would be now that they were older.

He didn't love her. Certainly not, that was ridiculous. He hadn't really loved her in the old days, either. And while she'd forgiven him for that—for being a typical teenage boy, panicking and giving her the brush-off after that pregnancy scare—she couldn't help but be hurt by it, even now.

Because she *had* loved him. Loved him enough that she'd punched him in the face last night, after carrying rejection and sadness and humiliation around in her heart for twelve years, even after she'd had a dozen other lovers and lived a full, rich life.

Which meant only one thing: she could not afford to get any more emotionally involved with Stan Jackson now. Uh-uh. No way.

Her decision made, Vanessa moved quickly and quietly. She had a plane to catch in a few hours, back to New York, back to her life. Time to say goodbye to the old one forever.

If he woke up, he'd stop her. She already knew it. Maybe not forever, but for at least a day, which meant she'd have another day to fall deeper under his spell. Another day to build upon the feelings that had been welling up inside her since she'd seen him enter the bar the night before.

She didn't make a sound. Tiptoeing, she grabbed her clothes from the bathroom hook where she'd hung them before her shower last night. Stan sighed in his sleep, rolling over, and she froze, praying she wouldn't be caught. When he settled back down into the pillows, she drifted out of the room, into the living area, where she dressed. But she couldn't just leave once her body was covered, for two reasons. First, her shoes and stockings were still in the bathroom, and second, she owed him some kind of goodbye.

The goodbye was tough. She agonized over it for several long minutes, finally writing him a friendly note—thanking him for the night before, telling him how glad she was that they'd rediscovered one another as adults and wishing him well.

Warm. Affectionate. Not gushy. Not pathetic.

The shoes actually turned out to be a bigger trick. Because as she tried to go back into the bedroom, the door squeaked. Stan made a few sounds, mumbling her name; Vanessa froze in indecision. But he didn't wake up.

Once he'd rolled back over, she realized the shoes weren't worth it. They'd killed her feet, anyway. So, grabbing her purse and tiptoeing out the front door of his suite, she cast one more look at the closed bedroom door behind which the man of her dreams slumbered, and walked out of his life.

STAN KNEW as soon as he woke up that she was gone. The air was still, the room silent, the sheets cool. He sat straight up in the bed, hoping he was wrong, but a quick glance around confirmed it. She was not in his bedroom nor in his bathroom. And a search of the rest of the suite proved futile, as well.

He found her note. "Oh, V," he mumbled as he read it, easily able to read between the lines.

Last night had been incredible for *both* of them. But the woman just didn't know, couldn't trust in his feelings for her. Had he ever given her reason to?

Those feelings were hard to describe this morning. Elation, satisfaction, desire, yes, all of those. But there was more. He'd loved her when they were kids. Really *loved* her.

And last night had showed him something: nothing had changed.

How he could know, after just one night in twelve years,

that she was the woman he'd always wanted and the one he would always want, he didn't know. But it was true.

"Uh-uh, girl, you're not getting away this time," he swore as he headed to the bathroom to shower. Spying her sparkly red shoes—just like the one he'd asked her about at the start of their very unusual evening—on the floor, he had to laugh.

"You might not think I'm Prince Charming, but I'm coming after you, anyway."

He got ready quickly, not sure when checkout time was. But he knew Vanessa would have some obstacles today... such as finding her room. The right room. The one with her luggage.

After he'd dressed, he grabbed her shoes and stockings, stuck them into his coat pockets and headed for the desk. The same manager was on duty and it took Stan one smile and a single mention of the key mix-up to get the room number of a Miss Vanessa McKee.

He was at her door five minutes later.

"Yes?" she asked when she opened it, appearing flustered and distracted, not even looking at him.

"Hey, V."

That got her attention. Though she'd been bent over, tugging a shoe on her foot when she pulled the door open, now she shot straight up and stared into his face. "Stan..."

"You weren't really going to leave without saying good-bye."

"I left you a note."

"I got it."

She swallowed visibly. "I think it said all I had to say."

Shaking his head, he lowered his voice, noticing a few people coming out of their rooms to check out early on this

Sunday morning. "No, there's more to say. I need to tell you something. Then, if you still want to tell me goodbye, you go ahead and do it."

Vanessa's trepidation was outweighed by her curiosity, as he'd known it would be. Though she practically gnawed her bottom lip off in indecision, finally she backed out of the way, opening the door for him.

He entered a suite that was much like his own, refused her offer of coffee, then sat down on the plush sofa. "I stopped writing to you that summer."

Blowing onto the steaming top of her own cup of coffee, she waved an airy hand, as if that didn't matter at all.

It mattered.

"I didn't want to."

"Stan, that's ancient history."

"Not ancient enough." He rubbed his jaw where she'd punched it the previous night. He didn't get any sympathy, just a scowl that said she didn't buy his ploy.

"Okay. Say what you have to say."

He made it fast, blunt. "My father died."

Whatever she'd been expecting, it wasn't that. Vanessa's eyes widened and she leapt out of her seat, rushing to his side. Dropping to her knees in front of him, she put her hands on his legs. "Oh, my God, Stan, when? Last night? Do you need to get home?"

He took her hands, shaking his head, hard. "No, no, I meant, he died that summer."

She jerked away, sitting on her heels, still wide-eyed, but now more wary. "What?"

He sighed heavily, remembering that awful time. "You can't know how it was."

"I might understand more than you think."

Hell. Of course she would. "I'm sorry." Wondering if he could get through this without making any more stupid verbal mistakes, he sighed, then started again. "He came to me about the letter. *Your* letter. And he was so disappointed, V, I can't tell you."

Her mouth twisted. "Like my granny, I suppose."

Grabbing her hands again, he clenched them. "Just like that. Only, he also told me something else: he'd been diagnosed with colon cancer and it didn't look good. He…"

She waited, saying nothing, letting him get it out in his own way.

Stan pulled himself together, squaring his shoulders, shoving away the waves of grief that sometimes threatened to drown him, *still*. It crushed him to realize his father had never seen just how far he had come. "He told me he was counting on me to take care of my mother and my brother. Told me how it had been for him—how he'd had a chance, how good he'd been at baseball. He'd always envisioned himself in the major leagues. Then he'd been careless."

"And had you?" she whispered.

He nodded. "He didn't make me feel unwanted, V," he said, wanting to be sure she understood. "Never that. He made it clear how much he loved me and my mother and brother."

"I'm glad."

"But he also swore that I had a gift, a God-given talent and not only was it my ticket to a better future, but it was the door to a good life for the rest of my family. And that I needed to focus only on that gift and on the family who needed me. Not on any girls, not on sex, not on *anything* else."

She squeezed his hands. "That's quite a load on a sixteen-year-old's shoulders."

Yes. It most definitely had been.

"What happened?" she whispered.

"Exactly what you think happened. I promised him I wouldn't ever be stupid again, would never take a risk and get myself tied down with a wife and a kid. That I'd finish school, make it in the majors, take care of Mama."

"That wasn't all though," she whispered. Her eyes grew moist and he knew she understood. All of it.

"And I begged him not to die," he admitted, his throat so tight he could barely manage the words.

Tears spilled out of those eyes and her full lips quivered. It would probably have been impossible for anyone who hadn't gone through it to understand. But she did. *She did.* "But he died anyway."

"Yeah. That September."

"You kept your promise."

He nodded. "I worked hard, practiced twelve hours a day. Never looked at girls, made money where I could. Jeez, Vanessa, I never even had sex again until I was twenty-one years old and I had to *propose* to the girl to make it right with myself."

She was sniffling, the tears spilling down her beautiful cheeks. Damn, he had not meant to make her cry, not meant to make her feel sorry for him.

He only wanted her to understand.

"I loved you, Vanessa."

She froze, blinking, her lips parting in a shocked gasp.

"I loved you," he repeated. "I was young and inexperienced and stupid. But I loved you and it about killed me to have to do as my father asked and put you out of my head…and my heart."

It was true. It had about killed him. The only thing that had gotten through was the sadness on his mother's face and the fear on his little brother's. And the promise he'd made to his father.

"I thought about you every day, until I had convinced myself that you'd forgotten about me. Every girl I met was you, every woman I met could only ever *hope* to be you."

"Stan, that's crazy talk."

Maybe. True, though.

He dropped to his knees, kneeling on the floor in front of her. "Vanessa, I'm not saying I know for certain that we're going to be together forever. What I'm saying is I *did* love you once, I've never loved anybody else." Wondering if she could hear the tremor in his voice, the uncertainty in his soul, he added, "And last night was the most amazing night in my life."

She leaned closer, her body moving as if drawn by his warmth, until the tips of her breasts touched his chest and her sweet, womanly scent filled his brain. "For me, too."

"Tell me it won't be our last," he urged.

"How? We live—"

"We'll figure out how. I have a plane."

"You also have a child," she pointed out.

Stan stiffened, for the first time wondering if it was true, if they were too late. Because the one thing he would not unbend on was his relationship with his daughter.

"What if she doesn't like me?" Vanessa asked, her voice small, unsure, lacking in confidence for the first time since he'd met her.

Stan broke into a smile, then into a laugh. He chuckled, long and hard, unable to help it. Because his daughter and his woman were so much alike, it was impossible to think they wouldn't immediately become lifelong companions. Or mother and daughter.

She didn't get mad at his laughter. Instead, she smiled back at him, as if reading his thoughts. "She's like me, huh?"

He nodded. "*Exactly* like you."

"You sure you can handle that? *Two* tough, feisty females like us?"

There was absolutely nothing he'd rather try. "I can handle anything you can give me, lady."

Then, even though he knew it was corny as hell, he couldn't resist reaching into the pockets of his sport coat, drawing out the two sexy red shoes, just like the one he'd offered her in the bar…only bigger. Big enough for *his* beautiful, powerful woman.

"I think these are yours," he murmured.

Her bottom lip trembled. "You know, when I'm around you, Stan Jackson, I do feel a little like Cinderella." She took the shoes from his hands, glanced at them for a second, then tossed them over her shoulders. "But these things hurt like hell. So I think I'm just gonna have to leave them off."

Throwing his head back, Stan laughed heartily, finally agreeing, "Okay. But only if you take everything else off, too."

She nodded in agreement, already unbuttoning her shirt. Her eyes alight with anticipation and happiness—so much happiness—she reached for him and twined her hands behind his neck.

"I always loved you, Stan My Man."

He covered her mouth with his, kissing her, undressing her, telling her everything that needed to be said.

Then he gave her the actual words. "I always loved you, too, V."

And somehow, Stan already knew that he and Vanessa would fall in love with each other again.

If, indeed, they'd ever stopped.

* * * * *

All the Way

1

BEING MARRIED had its advantages.

Gloria Santori could list a dozen of them right off the top of her head. The list included such things as never having to worry about changing the oil in her car, not sweating what she was going to do every Saturday night, not having a freaking heart attack because she'd gained ten pounds over the last few years. It also meant never competing with other women over men.

Getting laid every so often wasn't bad, either.

Though, since she'd given birth to James, her third son, last spring, getting laid wasn't exactly the way to describe it. More like getting rubbed against between bouts of fatigue and breast-feeding. And kind of enjoying it, even while wondering if the twenty minutes would have been better spent paying the bills or washing the kitchen floor.

Frankly, with the baby, the two older boys and Tony working his ass off at his family pizzeria, Gloria was just as likely to have a sexual experience from eating a pint of Ben & Jerry's as she was from getting naked with her hubby.

That, she supposed, was one of the disadvantages of being a nice, thirtysomething Italian housewife.

As was this. "You sure you can't come hang out a little while longer?" said Vanessa, one of the other bridesmaids. The striking woman was only in town for one more night and obviously wanted company.

"I can't. Tony and the brats are waiting."

Brats being meant in only the most affectionate sense, of course. Though, if little Anthony got into her lipstick and drew one more battle map for his dragon warriors on the wall of his room, she was, at least mentally, going to call him worse than that. Like *demon child sent to torment her.*

"Yeah, she has to make sure the big lug didn't stop to pick up milk and forget one of them in the store," Mia said with a deep chuckle.

Gloria responded in her typical fashion. She gave her sister the finger. Oh, not the middle one, the ring one. On her left hand.

"Yeah, yeah, bite me," Mia mumbled.

"So sad, you need your sister to bite you. If only you had a man."

"Bite me twice."

Her caustic younger sister smiled as she said it. A little. So did Gloria. The exchange was a typical one between them. Outsiders might think they didn't even like one another, but that wasn't true at all. They loved each other... they just had nothing in common.

While there were moments when Gloria wondered what it would have been like to go to college and be out in the workplace, she wouldn't trade her life for Mia's. Especially knowing tonight her sister would, once again, sleep alone. Mia hadn't dated since she'd returned to Chicago and she would wake up tomorrow morning having spent yet another night all by herself.

Gloria, on the other hand, would probably wake up with four males in her bed. Three of whom had come out of her vagina and one of whom had put them there.

One of these days, she was going to tell the older boys that she'd installed a motion alarm in the house so they'd stop sneaking out of their own rooms and into hers. Their midnight adventures creeping in to sleep with her and Tony were another reason she'd had almost no sex in months. The one time little Anthony's head had popped up beside the bed, asking Tony why he was "playing leapfrog" with Mommy in the middle of the night had been quite enough. So it was pretty much quick up-against-the-wall shower sex or nothing these days.

Man, what she wouldn't give to play a nice long game of leapfrog. Or even traditional, conservative, face-to-face boy on girl wrestling. *Anything.*

"Well, good night, then," Vanessa said after Mia had left, heading for her suite. "You be careful."

"I'll be fine," Gloria insisted. "I'm going up to the room to change before heading home."

It had seemed a waste to keep the hotel suite another night when nobody would be sleeping in it, but at least she didn't have to drive home in this gown. She only wished she and Tony could have gotten somebody to take the boys for the night—God, wouldn't she love a full night out with her husband in a lovely hotel. But since both her family and his were involved in this big wedding, there'd been nobody to do it.

Upstairs in her suite, she reached for her jeans—still one size bigger than she'd like, even though she'd lost much of the baby weight—and headed toward the bathroom. But she hadn't taken two steps when her cell phone rang. "Hello?"

"Hey, babe."

"Hey, Tone. Kids okay?"

"They're fine. Mikey's down for the night. James is ready to go, too."

"He did okay with the bottle?"

"Yep."

"Good." She'd been trying to wean him for weeks. That child had been as stubborn about staying stuck to her boobs as his father used to be.

"You made it back to the hotel okay?"

"Uh-huh. Just getting ready to change and head home now."

He mumbled something.

"What?"

"Nothing, Anthony wanted a glass of milk."

She glanced at the clock on the table by the bed. "No milk. Just water. It's too late."

"It's too late," he repeated, and she assumed he was talking to their son.

Then she registered the apologetic tone and realized he'd been talking to *her*. "Oh, great, you know how he is. Welcome to a midnight visit from the My Tummy Hurts, Can I Sleep with You? monster." She ran a weary hand over her eyes, rubbing them in the corners. Another sleepless night ahead. Oh, joy.

She glanced at the big, king-size bed in the suite. It had proved incredibly comfortable the night before, even with Tony in it beside her and the boys eventually leaving the foldout in the next room and crowding in between them. The whole family would have stayed here again tonight if not for the baby's fussiness in the port-a-crib.

Oh, how she would love to just fall into this bed and sleep for twelve hours straight. Or maybe have hot, wild monkey sex and then sleep for eight hours straight.

"Listen, Glo, things are covered here. Why don't you stay there for the night."

Sucking in a surprised breath, she instantly demurred. "I can't do that…"

"Yes, you can," he insisted. "You've had a hell of a week."

Hell of a *winter*.

"And I don't want you out driving in this weather, anyway. So just stay, okay? Get a good night's sleep for a change, enjoy yourself." He chuckled, that warm, deep chuckle that had told her from their first date that the mountainous, rock-hard guy had a gentle nature. "It's not like I gotta worry that you're gonna be down in the bar picking up some stranger for a hot, wild night, right?"

Gloria laughed, too. Because the idea that she, a harried mom and wife and hippy thirty-four-year-old would have a one-night stand with a stranger was so utterly ridiculous. Then she glanced at the bed, that big, wasted bed, and sighed. Because while it was ridiculous, it was also just a tiny bit titillating. What, she wondered, would it be like to feel like a desirable woman again, rather than the maternal, exhausted, sexless being she'd been lately? To be Gloria, the sexy brunette who still had a great ass, rather than mommy of Anthony, Michael and James and wife of that guy who ran the pizzeria?

She'd never know. Never. Which on most days was okay. But right now was feeling just a little bit like a prison sentence.

"Not that you couldn't," he quickly added, as if fearing

he'd insulted her. "You are about the hottest mom I've ever seen. My number one MILF."

"What's a milf?" came a little voice, talking to Tony in the kitchen of their townhouse.

Gloria snorted, wondering how her lunkhead husband was going to answer that one. Because she knew the slang, knew *exactly* what the acronym stood for.

"It stands for Mother I'd Like to...have Fun with," he replied, stumbling over the last words.

"Good save," she murmured when he returned his attention to their call. She only hoped her precocious five-year-old didn't start repeating the expression to all his pals at kindergarten.

"Jeez, that kid's as quiet as a cat. I thought he went back to bed."

"Tell me about it."

"Now, where were we..."

She smiled in anticipation. *Talking about me being a mother you'd like to f—*

"Oh, yeah. Talking about you staying there, having fun and enjoying one night of freedom."

That, too.

"I couldn't do that. Baby James is cutting a tooth, he'll drive you nuts tonight."

"Worrying about you making it home in this weather will drive me more nuts," he insisted. "Besides, he's sitting right here in his high chair, gnawing on a frozen bagel, loving life."

"Oh, great, my baby's first word is going to be *milf*."

He chuckled deeply. "Everybody'll think he's saying milk. Besides, he wouldn't be the first of our kids to spit out unexpected first words. Remember Anthony..."

She did. Her eldest son had spent a lot of time in the kitchen of the restaurant as a baby. The kitchen where her father-in-law, a blustery little old Italian man, often used colorful language. *"Madone,"* she muttered. Just as her son had every other minute until he was three.

"Exactly. Now, don't sweat the baby. I'm watching every second and won't let him keep the bagel once it starts getting soft."

Gloria sighed and shook her head, but knew better than to criticize. Tony might not be the most textbook father, but he adored their boys and would never let anything happen to them. She had to let him parent in his own way.

And she kind of wished she'd thought of the bagel idea last month when the first two teeth broke through!

"So do it," he insisted. "Stay there. Take a night for yourself. You know you need it."

She had to admit it, the idea was very tempting. But she still felt guilty about it and tried to refuse.

At least until Tony cajoled her a little more. Convincing her with every word he said.

Until, finally, with a smile on her face, Gloria very happily agreed. She'd stay the night at the hotel and come home to her family—and her real life as wife and mommy—in the morning. But for tonight?

Tonight she was entirely free to be the woman she'd once been.

THE HOTEL HAD TWO BARS, one crowded with chatty late-night patrons, the other a small piano lounge off the restaurant, nearly empty. Though there were more people—probably more single women—in the first one, he went to the piano lounge instead. It was more private, more intimate. A better fit for his mood tonight. After the evening he'd had, he could use a quiet place to get his brain functioning again.

Not to mention getting his full-throttle libido aimed in the right direction. Because right now, it was revved up and had had no release in far too long. And he was *dying* for release.

When he entered the room and saw the woman sitting alone at one of the small, round tables, he realized he'd made the right choice. His body reacted with predictable excitement as he noted the thick, shiny dark hair—his favorite. If she had big, brown eyes with long, thick lashes, he was going to think he'd died and gone to heaven.

One thing was sure, even from here—this was not one of those on-the-prowl single females probably lining the walls in the other, more crowded bar. This woman appeared introspective. Almost lonely as she listened to the soft background music provided by the bored-looking guy at the piano. There was a sadness in her posture, a weary slump in her shoulders that said she didn't often escape her regular world and didn't quite know what to do with herself now that she had.

His heart twisted in his chest. No woman that lovely should ever have such a lost look on her face, as if she truly didn't know what to do with her life. And any man who left her feeling as unsure about herself as this one looked didn't deserve to be called a man.

She wasn't too young, probably, in fact, around his age, in her midthirties. He counted that as a good thing. In his job, he met a lot of women. Young, vapid girls hanging with their girlfriends or hanging on their dates. Older, jaded women looking for a thrill even if they had to pay for it.

The young ones had no conversation, no allure. Nothing but white smiles and loud laughs. And the older ones had no emotions at all. Just entitlement.

This woman, though, had some substance. Real depth. Sipping a creamy-looking chick drink, she wore an aura of aloofness that said she wasn't interested in any attempts at conversation from a stranger. Especially a male stranger.

That very attitude posed a challenge that would intrigue any man. Especially one like him.

He didn't approach her right away, instead watching from the doorway. She sipped slowly, then lowered her drink to the table. Running the tip of one finger around the rim of her glass, she looked neither left nor right, oblivious to the few other people around her. Sad, almost, with the tiniest downturn of her full lips and a small frown on her brow.

Despite the somber mood, she had a beautiful profile—pretty nose, high cheekbones, beautiful olive-toned skin. Her dark hair was pulled up onto her head in a complicated mass of curls, like she'd gone someplace special today.

It would look better down around her face. Curling beside one delicate cheek, draping over those slender shoulders, across those full breasts. Oh, she definitely had some curves. The black dress she wore was low cut enough to reveal a hint of mouthwatering cleavage, yet not enough to say she was looking for company.

He wondered if she'd want some, anyway.

It was certainly worth a shot. So, with a nod toward the cocktail waitress, he picked his way around the empty tables and went straight to the brunette's. "Hello."

She looked up quickly, startled from her thoughts, and her pretty lips parted on a gasp.

"Sorry to bother you, miss. But do you mind if I join you?"

Those eyes—yes, brown, heavily lashed, big and sparkling, God help him—widened even more. As if she had no idea she was beautiful and exotic looking. Was it really possible, he wondered, his heart twisting again, that she did not?

He'd remedy that. Damned if he wouldn't.

"I, uh…"

"Look, I know I'm a complete stranger. I'm not going to try some sleazy line on you. I just thought you looked a little down and might like somebody to talk to."

Her lashes half lowered over those eyes and she tilted her head away, as if thinking about it. Trying to decide.

It was at that moment he realized she was probably married. A lonely wife drinking alone in a hotel bar. While her husband was…where? Traveling? Working? In the arms of a mistress?

Fool.

"Just a drink," he murmured. "I'm new in town, I don't know anybody and would rather not drink alone."

She nibbled on her full bottom lip for a second, then nodded. Clearing her throat, she said, "Suit yourself. It's a free country."

That wasn't exactly a rousing welcome, but he'd take what he could get. Sitting in a low, plush leather chair across the small table from her, he caught a whiff of her perfume. It was light but not flowery. Spicy. Unusual. He sensed it would only be the first unusual experience he'd have tonight.

"I'm…" He hesitated for a second, then came up with a name. "I'm Tom."

One brow went up in a fine arch, as if she knew damn well he was lying. Her lips twitched a tiny bit, her first hint of a smile. Then she replied. "Jennifer."

False, as well. He knew that. Just as sure as he knew she was not as aloof as she'd been trying to portray herself to be when he'd first come in.

The woman was interested in being a little wild tonight. She was just unsure, as if this was her first time even thinking about doing something as reckless as picking up a stranger in a bar. Not that he could be sure that's what she had planned…at least, not until he glanced at her left hand and saw the pale line of untanned skin on her ring finger.

Yes. That pale skin told him she was, indeed, considering a one-night stand. It also told him she was a first timer.

She'd taken off her wedding ring. Not because any guy in a bar with an ounce of testosterone would give a damn that she was married. But because she was *already* feeling guilty.

Well, she didn't have anything to feel guilty about. They were just having a friendly drink; she'd done absolutely nothing wrong. Not *yet,* anyway.

As for the rest of the night? Well, that remained to be seen.

2

GLORIA SANTORI knew the incredibly handsome, black-haired man's name wasn't Tom. Not any more than hers was really Jennifer.

She also knew she should be feeling a whole lot more nervous than she was. Nervous, guilty, afraid, guilty, self-conscious, *guilty*. But she didn't feel anything except excited.

How could she not? She was sitting in a hotel bar, late at night, chatting with a sexy man who'd given her a fake name and who couldn't take his hot, hungry eyes off her. Oh, yes, she'd seen the look in his dark eyes. He was definitely interested in her. She hadn't been married and procreating so long that she didn't recognize pure lust when she saw it.

Lust. She, the harried mommy who was the homeroom mom of her son's kindergarten class, had inspired heated desire in this big, tall, broad-shouldered hunk.

Nothing would come of it, she knew. She would never have the courage to act on the attraction. But oh, was it nice to feel like a desirable woman again. To be looked at in that way, to almost feel the man's stare on her face, her throat, the curves of her breasts.

To think, she'd almost missed out on this. She hadn't planned on coming back downstairs. In fact, she should probably have gone straight to bed to luxuriate in an uninterrupted night's sleep for a change.

But she hadn't. Instead, she'd slipped out of her red bridesmaid gown and put on the black dress she'd worn to the rehearsal dinner the night before. She'd come downstairs, heading not for the loud bar she'd seen Vanessa go into earlier, but for the more quiet one.

She'd just wanted one drink. One solitary, grown-up drink in a grown-up place. Wanted to be anonymous and unattached. Wanted to pretend, for just a while, that she wasn't going to have to express the milk out of her breasts and throw it away to make sure the baby didn't get himself a little Kahlúa and cream buzz tomorrow.

Then *he'd* sat down. And drinking alone had no longer been an acceptable option.

"So are you in town on business?" he asked after he'd ordered himself a drink from the waitress.

He'd offered her another one, but she'd refused. The mommy in her might be hiding, shoved out of sight for now, but she was still shouting from deep inside, protesting the thought of wasting all that breast milk.

"No. A wedding," she admitted, wondering what to be truthful about and when to lie. She was *so* not good at this game. But she was not ready to give it up yet. Because no matter what else, it was exciting. Her pulse was pounding wildly in her veins, her heart thumping in her chest.

She hadn't experienced anything like it in a very long time. "What about you?"

"Business. I travel around the world a lot."

She'd noticed the slight accent in his voice and almost asked if he was European. But she wasn't sure she wanted to know. This was just anonymous chitchat. It didn't have to get any more personal than that—no last names, no phone numbers, no background information.

"So, why didn't your husband come with you to this wedding?"

Gloria sucked in a surprised breath, immediately clenching her left hand. It felt so bare, so empty without her wedding ring. And she almost instinctively reached for it, on her right hand, to put it back where it belonged. But the warmth in the stranger's eyes kept her from doing it.

"Is it that obvious? That I'm married?"

"Only to someone with some experience."

"You have a lot of experience with women?"

He smiled a little, his lips curling up only on one side, flashing the tiniest dimple in his cheek. It made him look more boyish, less tough, not a bit dangerous. "I know a few things."

"Then you tell me why I'm sitting here in a hotel bar without my husband," she challenged.

He leaned forward in his chair, dropping his arms onto the table between them. Gloria couldn't help focusing on his hands, his big, strong hands. There was such power there and she shivered at the very thought of being stroked by him. Being touched, massaged, caressed.

It was wicked. It was also irresistible.

"You slipped out of your room, leaving him there,

asleep and oblivious. Once again, he fell into bed, brushed a lazy kiss good-night on your forehead, then rolled over and went to sleep."

She blinked, realizing he'd just described many of her recent nights.

"And you couldn't stand yet another night of lying there, unfulfilled beside him, your body aching to be touched, needing wild passion, sweet caresses and decadent pleasures."

"Oh, my God," she whispered, fascinated, even if against her own will.

"You love him…but you miss the excitement, the thrill. Life has become too normal. And while it's good, there are times when you long for something more."

"How did you…"

He smiled gently. "It's easy to see in your face. And it's a damn tragedy. You are too beautiful to feel that way about your life."

"Thank you," she whispered.

"It's not easy being misunderstood."

She frowned. Her husband understood her, all right. He just didn't do anything about it.

As if realizing he'd misstepped, he clarified. "I mean, being underappreciated."

Her frown faded.

"You're overworked and you have a lot of responsibilities."

"That's true," she murmured, reaching for her glass.

"You don't get enough help and you feel like you're on autopilot all the time. Struggling to get everything done for everybody else, without ever having one minute to do anything for yourself."

Gloria's mouth opened in surprise. Because that had been

one incredibly intuitive comment. One she wouldn't have expected to come out of this man's mouth.

"You don't feel like a beautiful, desirable woman. You feel like a boring housewife."

The open mouth now fell far enough that she could almost feel her chin on her chest. The handsome man—Tom—laughed softly, then reached across the table. Touching her face lightly, with just the tips of his fingers, he pushed her jaw closed. Her whole body tingled at the contact, as if he'd done something much more intimate than that quick brush of skin on skin.

"When was the last time your husband came up behind you, kissed the nape of your neck and whispered that you were the sexiest, most beautiful woman he'd ever seen?"

She shook her head slowly, swallowing at the very thought of something like that. If Tony did such a thing, one of the boys would invariably stick his little head between them, demanding a hug from Daddy, too.

"When did you last spend an entire day in bed, being worshipped and adored?"

"He works so hard," she whispered.

Tsking, he shook his head. "No man should ever work so hard that he can't take some time to show his wife how much he wants her." His hand slid across the table, until the tips of his fingers touched her bare forearm. Just that, yet she trembled at the contact. "Having an incredible woman in your life comes with a lot of responsibility and some men just aren't up to the task."

Swallowing hard, she asked, "Responsibility?"

He nodded. Those fingers moved, sliding up her arm, leaving sizzling heat and tension along the way. "Every woman needs to be touched."

Oh, God, yes, she did.

"Needs to be stroked, needs to have her soft skin appreciated and her sweet scent inhaled."

This time, when Gloria reached for the glass, she gulped a big mouthful of her creamy drink.

"Her thick, shiny hair needs to be wrapped around a man's hands, or draped across his chest so he can go out of his mind at how soft it is, how good it feels."

Her breaths were hitching in her throat. She used to love the way Tony would brush her hair, back when they were first married and alone. They would sometimes shower and he'd love to wash it for her, letting the soap slide down her body and his, so that when they rubbed against one another, there was no friction, only delicious slickness.

They had shower sex once in a while now, but only the fast someone-could-knock-at-any-moment kind. And he hadn't washed her hair in years.

"Her body *must* be caressed…every inch of it touched, every spot tasted."

Closing her eyes, she just sat there, letting the words—the possibilities—wash over her. She licked her lips, unable to help it, wanting to at least pretend she might end up in the arms of a handsome, worldly stranger who was seducing her with his every word.

"A woman who's loved should be kissed for hours. Everywhere. In every way. Sweetly, on the soft, full lips. Hotly in the hollow of her throat."

"Where else?" she whispered, unable to help it. Her whole body was warm with arousal, languid and awash with sensations. Just those whispered words—the sound of his voice and that maddeningly light touch on her arm—had her picturing the sorts of things she hadn't even thought about in months. Not with her husband…not with anyone.

Her nipples were thrust hard against her dress, her panties tight and uncomfortable against her moist sex. She was inching closer, her bare leg brushing his pants beneath the table, her face now close enough to feel the warmth of his breath falling on her hair. All because she wanted more. More whispers. More fantasy. More possibility…even if that possibility would be absolutely impossible to fulfill.

He finally answered her. "There are so many delicious places on a woman's body. I love the collarbone—delicate and fragile, leading from the soft shoulder to the vulnerable throat."

Lifting one hand, her elbow on the table, Gloria casually traced the tips of her fingers across her own collarbone, then let them rest at the base of her neck.

"The fingertips should be sampled, one at a time," he murmured. "The soft hands should be appreciated for everything she does."

That was all wonderful, but Gloria couldn't help holding her breath, as if he was actually kissing her—tasting all those places—rather than just talking about doing it. And there were a few *other* places in particular that would especially benefit from some in-depth kissing.

"The breasts."

That'd be two of them.

"Kissing a woman's breasts is one of the most perfect things in the world. The skin is so soft on the tongue, the nipples so amazing when they get hard against the lips. They beg for attention, thrusting up, demanding gentle *and* rough, sweet kisses *and* deep sucking."

She whimpered a little. Or a lot. Part of her wondered if she was a complete fool to have started this game, because it was going to be nearly impossible for her to get back to her room after this. Her legs were already quivering and weak; if she tried to stand now, she'd probably fall on her face.

Or right onto this sexy, dangerous man's lap.

"The stomach…I love to bury my face in her stomach, not only to savor the softness of her skin against my cheek, but also to drive myself mad with the warm scent of her building arousal."

She slammed her hand down on the table, unable to take another second of this verbal—very public—seduction. "That's enough."

His tiny half smile told her he knew exactly why she'd stopped him. "Something wrong?"

"I shouldn't have come down here. In fact, I should have gone home and not stayed here alone tonight at all."

The smile widened. "You're *alone* here tonight? Your husband's not upstairs?"

Oh, that had been stupid. A big tactical error. "Th-thanks for the company," she mumbled. "But I really should go."

He stood and at first she thought he was merely being a gentleman, rising as a lady exited the room. But instead of remaining behind and watching her go, he fell into step beside her, taking her arm.

"What are you…"

"You do know you invited me up to your room with every tiny sigh, every little gasp, every hungry stare, every lick of your lips."

If she was really a lady, she would have slapped his face and told him he'd imagined it.

But Gloria couldn't lie. Couldn't pretend. She had, indeed, done exactly what he accused her of.

She only wondered what in the name of heaven she was going to do about it.

3

As THEY WALKED through the hotel lobby toward the elevators, he could feel the trembling of her body. The beautiful woman at his side was nervous—uncertain. But the trembling was not caused by that nervousness.

Pure excitement poured off her. He could almost taste it in the warm, musky scent of excitement oozing out of her every pore. She might be the loving, dutiful housewife in her other life. But right now, she was the beautiful seductress whose uncertainty only made her more attractive.

"I can't…what if someone sees…"

"That makes it more exciting, doesn't it?" he whispered back, keeping his hand firmly on her elbow. Not controlling her, just lending her moral support for the battle that had to be raging inside her. "I'm just escorting you to your room," he added. "Giving you a chance to think about what you want to do when we get to your door."

Though, if he had his way, it wouldn't take that long. Because he was ready for her now—right now. And he knew by the tautness in her body, the way her nipples pressed against her dress and her skin was prickled with excitement, that she was ready, too.

At least her body was. Only her mind needed to fully engage…or else get out of the equation altogether. Honestly, he didn't care which way it happened. It just had to *happen*.

"I love my husband," she whispered.

"Never said you didn't."

"I don't *do* this kind of thing."

"Never said you did."

Another couple approached. Probably about the same age as they were, walking slowly, not touching. Their low voices hinted at a comfortable conversation, which matched the comfortable aura between them.

He knew for sure they were a married couple. Relaxed with each other, most of the sparks and excitement gone. He *almost* felt sorry for the guy, wondering if he had any idea his wife was probably having fantasies much like the brown-haired beauty beside him was having. That she wanted to be touched. Desired.

If the guy had any sense he'd have draped his arm over the woman's shoulders, have tucked in close beside her when they walked. Would have let their legs brush and their hips touch. Would have fingered her curls and leaned in close to laugh at something she said, letting her know he liked the way she smiled, liked the way she felt, liked everything about her.

He sensed the lesson would be wasted. Especially when the husband lifted a hand to his mouth and yawned loudly. He went on to complain about the prices in the bar and gripe over the maid service in the hotel, never once noticing the downward tilt of his wife's mouth and the slight slump in her shoulders.

Clueless.

And if they were on the same elevator, he was going to shoot himself.

"Good evening," the wife said, smiling impersonally at him and the beautiful brunette by his side. *Jennifer.*

That beautiful brunette stiffened, and he'd lay money she was about to erupt in a panic, as if everyone could look in her face and know she was planning a wild night of raucous sex.

He put a hand against the small of her back, lightly stroking her with his fingers, then he leaned close, brushing his cheek against her hair.

The other man's wife watched them closely and slowly flushed. She knew what they were doing and was excited by it. It was just a damn shame her husband hadn't figured it out.

As the elevator arrived, he held his breath, then blew it out, relieved, when the other couple stepped to the opposite side of the vestibule. They were apparently on a higher floor and were taking an express.

Meaning he and his beautiful stranger were completely alone.

Once inside, she lifted her hand and pushed the button for her floor, visibly trembling. He reached for it, brought it to his mouth and kissed the tips of her fingers.

Progress. She didn't yank her hand away.

"The sixty-ninth floor," he murmured, seeing the number she'd depressed. "How very…prophetic."

She groaned, long and low.

"We never got to that part of the conversation. Because if there's one thing a sexy, beautiful woman needs to make sure she knows she's wanted, it's some thorough tongue-work."

"Oh, enough already," she snapped, as if simply unable to take another second. He almost laughed at it, loving the way he'd pushed her buttons until she'd finally reacted exactly as he'd expected her to.

"Shut up and put your money where your mouth is." Thrusting aside her last bit of inhibition, she grabbed the front of his shirt in two fists. She shoved him back against the wall of the elevator, falling against his body to pin him there, one long, slim leg sliding between his.

His eyes widening in surprise, he could only savor the pleasure of it as the beautiful woman with the dark, flashing eyes covered his mouth with hers and thrust her tongue deep.

He dropped his hands lower, wrapping his arms around her. Easily managing her weight, he hoisted her up until their bodies lined up perfectly. She whimpered against his mouth at the feel of his cock pressed hard at the juncture of her thighs. And even through their clothes, he could feel her wetness and knew she was ready.

"Can't wait," she muttered against his lips. "I *can't*."

God, he wanted her. The excitement was catching—electric. So he took control, turning her around so she was the one with her back pressed against the wall. "I can't wait, either."

She reached frantically for his shirt, tugging it out of his waistband, then hesitated. Her face flushed, she glanced up. "Do you think there are security cameras?"

He followed her gaze and saw what he knew had to be a lens. His jaw tight, he thought quickly. "Only the one."

Smiling, he pushed her into the corner directly beneath it. "And it can't look straight down."

That seemed to eliminate her last fear. "Thank heaven."

Her fingers moved quickly, his even more so. She undid his belt and trousers, he pulled up her dress.

"Oh, yes," she groaned when she reached into his shorts and grabbed his thick, hard cock with her cool, soft fingers. "I want that. I want it so bad."

The elevator continued to move, the floors passing by in a series of slow dings, and at any time it could stop to let on more passengers.

He didn't give a damn. He just had to feel her. Shoving her panties to the side, he slid his fingers into her creamy sex, noting how ready she was—how hot she was—all for him.

"I want so much more than this," he said hoarsely as he sunk one finger inside her, mimicking what he'd soon be doing with his cock. "I want to do everything I said to you downstairs."

Her thighs clenched. "Later. This first."

She didn't have to ask him again. Even though they were now passing the fortieth floor, he freed himself from his clothes. She was whimpering, her eyes closed, her hair falling from its pins. He planned to wrap his fingers in that hair…to feel it on his hands, on his chest, on his balls.

But, as she said, it would have to be later. For now, he had about a minute to grab a taste of heaven and he wasn't going to pass it up.

"Just a taste," he whispered. Then he lifted her up, holding her thighs, which she quickly wrapped around his hips. She bucked toward him, pleading and whimpering, and he plunged into her, driving hard and deep. She screamed a little, holding on tight as he drove her into the wall, fucking her wildly for a few incredible seconds. Wrapped in her warm, tight channel, he almost lost it like some inexperienced kid. He gave himself over to it for as long as he could. Then he felt the elevator begin to slow.

"Hell," he muttered, immediately pulling out and lowering her to the floor, even though it nearly killed him to do it. He stuck his dick back into his pants, yanking the zipper up as his beautiful lover shifted and twisted to fix her panties and her dress.

He was just buttoning his pants when the door opened. Thankfully, they'd arrived at their own destination and hadn't stopped for passengers on another floor. Because there was no way anyone could have stepped into that elevator and not smelled the rich, unmistakable scent of raw, primal sex.

The thought that it was just the beginning was the only thing that enabled him to follow her out into the corridor, rather than pushing the button to close the door and driving right back into her.

But he hadn't been kidding about what he wanted to do to her. What he had in mind would require privacy. And a whole lot of time.

ANYBODY COULD HAVE BEEN WAITING on the other side of that elevator door. A knowing stranger, a curious kid…God, even one of her sisters!

Funny. Gloria couldn't bring herself to care. She was too wound up, too excited, too frenzied to give it anymore thought.

She'd just had wild, completely irresponsible sex in a

public elevator and her whole body was still shaking from the pleasure of it. He'd been huge and rock hard, thrusting into her like he had to take her or die.

She'd never in her life done something as provocative, as reckless, and she didn't know that she ever would again. But for tonight…well, for one night, she was going to be crazy and selfish and utterly insane.

"Give me the key. Your hand's shaking so much you'll probably drop it," he said.

The demanding tone in his voice thrilled her and she immediately did what he said. He strode to the door of her room. Pushing it open, he tugged her into the room with him.

They were on each other immediately. It was as if there'd been just a brief intermission and now they both needed to finish what they'd started in the elevator. They would get to the slow and steady stuff they'd talked about downstairs. But first…oh, first there was *this*.

"I've got to feel you. Gotta be in you, now," he muttered hoarsely as he kissed her neck and filled his hands with her breasts. He hadn't even bothered fastening his belt and quickly worked himself free of his trousers, pushing them down around his lean hips and taut butt.

Gloria lifted her dress, pushing her panties down with the tips of her fingers, letting them fall to the floor. She kicked them out of the way.

The bed was only a few feet away, but she didn't want it on the bed. Not yet. She wanted that wild, raw, sex-with-a-stranger feeling she'd had in the elevator.

"Finish it," she ordered, grabbing him by the hair, pulling his face to hers for a deep, thorough kiss. "Take me."

He didn't hesitate, lifting her again, positioning her just right, then thrusting up into her.

Gloria threw her head back and cried out. His possession was undeniable, complete. He filled her, stretched her, completely *owned* her at that moment.

She could only hold on to the thick shoulders, marveling over the power of his huge chest and the strength in those amazing arms. He held her like she weighed nothing, thrusting into her again and again until she was sobbing against his neck. When his groans signaled his climax, she milked him inside, squeezing him, urging him on.

She wasn't there yet, but she didn't care. She wanted him completely out of control, unable to stop himself from exploding in her, filling her with his essence. Afterward, she knew, they'd slow down and she'd get whatever she needed from him. After all, they had all night.

"I'm going to…"

"Do it," she ordered, covering his mouth with hers again, thrusting her tongue hard, thrusting her body harder.

He finally did, groaning loudly as he finished with a few long, shuddering strokes. Then, with his powerful sex still inside her and her legs still wrapped around his waist, he carried her to the bed. He lowered them both onto it, keeping his arms wrapped around her, pressing kiss after kiss into her hair. "You're so beautiful. You're so beautiful," he murmured, saying it over and over again.

Tears rose in her eyes. Tears of pleasure. Tears even of appreciation. Because he'd done it. He'd made her feel beautiful—absolutely irresistible, sexy, desirable. All the things she hadn't felt about herself for such a very long time.

"So beautiful," he whispered. "And I love you so much."

Smiling, keeping her arms around his shoulders and her legs around his waist, she kissed him back and replied, "I love you, too, Tony."

4

SO MUCH FOR making slow, sweet, erotic love to his wife for hours. They were finally alone, finally had some privacy and a great big bed to do it in, and he'd taken her up against a wall.

That wasn't what Tony Santori had planned to do tonight. He'd intended a slow fantasy, a slower seduction.

When his parents had showed up at his door this evening, demanding the right to babysit the boys so he and Gloria could have one night alone together at the hotel, he'd been ready to kiss their feet. Because God knew, he and Gloria needed it.

He might be a lunkhead, as she affectionately called him sometimes. But he wasn't stupid. It didn't take a genius to know that his sweet, sassy wife was unhappy. That she'd lost a bit of her sparkle and some of her self-confidence.

What he hadn't realized, until recently, was that she missed their sex life as much as he did.

"You know, I've been telling myself for a couple of months that I was a pig for wanting to jump on you every time we were out of the boys' sight," he admitted a short time later, as they lay, still entwined, on the hotel bed. "There you were being mother of the year to my three hellion sons and all I wanted to do was rip your clothes off and screw your brains out."

She tightened her arms around his neck, lightly kissing his nose. "That's one of the nicest things you've ever said to me."

He laughed and so did she. Because she was probably right. He wasn't exactly the poetic sort.

"It wasn't until I heard you cry last week, after we had a fast grope-and-go under the covers, that I realized you might not be any happier about the situation than I was."

"I haven't been," she admitted, confirming what he'd finally begun to figure out. "I've been feeling so disconnected. So…asexual, almost. Not to mention just plain horny."

He looked down at her, slowly unbuttoning her dress, uncovering the beautiful breasts, the soft curves of her body. "You are the most sexy, sexual woman I've ever laid eyes on. And I will take care of your every need, whenever you need me."

She lifted her shoulder, then a hip, to help him ease her clothes off her body. Reaching for his, she helped him, as well, until neither of them wore a thing. Except each other.

He reached up and touched her shoulder, running the tip of his finger across her collarbone, loving the softness of her skin.

"Those things you said downstairs…"

"They were easy to say," he admitted. "Because they were all true. Every damn one of them."

He meant it. A poet he was not, yet when clearing the air with his wife, who'd seemed so distant lately, everything he'd been thinking had come rushing out. From what he felt about her, to what he saw when he looked into her sad eyes and her weary smile, to how much he had taken her for granted…and oh, God, to what he wanted to do to her.

All of it true.

"And yet, with all of that, the first chance I got, I jumped on you," he said, hearing his own self-disgust.

She arched toward him, as if unable to help it. "That's what made it so…mmm…*good.* Do you know how much I needed to feel like you were absolutely out of control over me?"

He moved his hand, replacing it with his mouth, kissing her as he'd said he wanted to. "I was. I am." When he reached the hollow of her throat, he licked the skin there, tasting a tiny bit of sweat from their wild, sexual exertions.

"Oh, Tony," she groaned, tilting her head back, silently asking for more. He gave it to her, nibbling his way down her body so he could kiss the top slopes of her full breasts.

She twined her hands in his hair. "I couldn't believe it when you said on the phone that your parents were taking the kids, and you were coming here tonight."

"I wanted to surprise you, but I was afraid you'd head home."

"I probably would have." She giggled. "I also couldn't believe that you told me to wait for you downstairs in the lounge with no ring…or panties."

He chuckled softly against her skin. "You didn't obey that one, wife."

"No, I most certainly did not. What if someone had seen?"

That turned his chuckle into a belly laugh and he pulled away to look at her. "You mean like the guards monitoring the elevator security cameras?"

She jerked. "You said it was safe."

"I'm kidding. I'm sure they didn't see…much. Just a desperate man kissing a gorgeous woman."

And, perhaps, him slipping his hand under her dress before pushing her out of sight.

She seemed mollified. "Of all the things I pictured tonight, it was *not* you showing up with a sexy, fake accent, pretending to be a complete stranger who was trying to pick me up in a bar."

He had to admit, he was kind of proud of himself for that one. Even if he had gotten the initial idea from a men's magazine, not every guy in the world would actually do it. And he'd found himself really getting into the spirit of the thing, probably because his wife was still the sexiest woman he'd ever seen and she drove him crazy with want every time he laid eyes on her.

"You were very smooth. Like you had a lot of practice."

"You were very unsure. Like you didn't."

"Really? I thought I was too easy."

She sounded like she felt a little guilty, which made him laugh harder. "Don't worry, you're only easy for me."

And he liked it. A whole lot. That he had been her only lover…*ever,* and she his, was one of the foundations of their relationship. They'd loved each other forever—since high school. Neither of them had ever even dreamed of being with anyone else.

No other woman existed, as far as Tony Santori was concerned.

Returning his attention to the full breasts he loved, Tony rubbed his rough cheek against her skin, getting an excited hiss in response. Gloria had been beast-feeding their son for months, and part of him had felt like there had been a big Hands Off sign above these things of beauty. But now that he knew she wanted him just as much as he wanted her, he couldn't prevent himself from kissing, tasting, nibbling.

"Oh, babe," she groaned, tightening her fingers in his hair.

"I've missed this," he mumbled, licking her nipple while plumping the other breast in his hand. He teased her, sliding his lips back and forth, knowing by the way she arched toward his mouth that she needed a deeper caress.

"*Please,* Tony."

He gave her what she begged for, covering her nipple and sucking, not giving a damn that her body gave him a taste of the life-sustaining fluid his sons had so often consumed.

"Oh, Lord," she cried, writhing beneath him.

"I've been starving for you," he murmured as he continued to play with one breast, then moved to the other. He tweaked her nipple with his fingers, knowing exactly how much pressure she needed. He was entirely familiar with her likes and dislikes after sharing her bed for so many years. And yet, it was so good, so exciting. Like they really were strangers.

When they were on their game, he and Gloria had always been like this. There'd been a few bumps in the road, particularly after the birth of each baby. But they always found their way back to each other, back to the excitement and the passion that had drawn them together in the first place.

He couldn't get enough of her. Aside from loving her beyond all reason, he simply craved the physical pleasure he'd only ever found in her arms.

"Love you," she whispered, lying back in the bed, taking all the delights he desperately wanted to give her. He moved down from her breasts, tasting her stomach, breathing in her skin and her arousal, just as he said he wanted to when they'd been playing their sexy game.

He kept right on going, tenderly kissing the slight bulge in her belly where his sons had grown. Then farther, until he nuzzled into her curls, finding her sensitive clit and focusing all his efforts there.

She panted and gasped, rising up toward his mouth. Holding her hips, he kept her where he wanted her, knowing from experience that as she drew closer and closer to the highest peak, her body would helplessly try to twist away from the incredible intensity.

He wouldn't allow that. He held her steady until she was sobbing, not letting her go until she came in his mouth.

She was still whispering his name as he slid up her body, following the same familiar, well-loved trail he'd descended. "Amazing," she whispered when they were face-to-face. Then she couldn't say anything else because he was sliding into her, filling her.

He buried his face in her neck, smelling her hair, feeling her arms wrap around his shoulders. They were completely entwined, totally joined, blissfully alone. Just Tony and Gloria, the passionate couple they'd been at the beginning of their relationship, the adoring couple they would, please God, be at the end of it on his last day on this earth.

"Love you, babe," he whispered as he drew up to watch her face. "Thank you for marrying me. For being everything I ever wanted in a wife and in the mother of my kids."

She kissed him sweetly, moisture rising in her eyes. The emotion didn't diminish the physical pleasure, it only enhanced it. She was crying and laughing as they rocked together, each of his tender thrusts met with a welcoming one of her own.

"I love you, too, Tony," she whispered, touching his face, rubbing her thumb across his lips. "Thank you for reminding me that I'm *more* than your wife and the mother of your kids."

"My lover," he interjected, understanding immediately.
"Your lover. Tonight…and forever."

CHECKOUT TIME was at noon, but they got up to get ready to go by nine. Gloria would have loved to stay longer, to spend an entire blissful day in bed with her passionate husband. But her in-laws weren't getting any younger. And her sons were, as Tony had called them last night, little hellions.

They *did* linger over a long shower. She almost melted with pleasure when Tony insisted on washing her hair, gently massaging her scalp, delicately covering each long strand with shampoo. The shower was bigger than the one at home and this time the sex wasn't quick, frantic and furtive. It was slow, sultry. And very slippery.

Afterward, they left their room, heading for the elevator. One came right away, but her husband didn't step into it.

"Tony?"

"Let's wait," he murmured, glancing toward the next one down the line.

She laughed softly. "It's 11:00 a.m., not p.m. I don't think we're going to get away with that in the light of day."

"Guy can always hope," he said with a big grin.

Of course, the elevator wasn't empty. But that didn't stop her sexy man from copping a feel as they eased into one corner, pushed there by the crowd that grew with every stop on every floor. Gloria couldn't help casting a quick glance at the camera, wondering if Tony had been right about just how much of a show they'd given the security guard.

Then she smiled up toward it. A cocky smile. Not really giving a damn.

"I saw that," he murmured as he took her arm and led her off when they reached the lobby.

She feigned innocence. "Saw what?"

"You're a wicked woman, Gloria Santori."

Her chin went up, as did one brow. "I can't imagine what you're talking about. I'm a respectable wife and mother. A homeroom mom. A library volunteer."

He dropped the bags, right there in the lobby, and turned to face her. Sinking his hands in her hair to cup her head, he drew her close and pressed a long, openmouthed kiss on her mouth. Gloria gave herself one second to be shocked and worried about an audience before wrapping her arms around his neck and kissing him back with every ounce of love she felt for the man.

"*And* you're my woman," he reminded her when he finally let her go, both of them a little out of breath.

She couldn't get rid of the silly grin on her face as Tony picked up the bags with one hand, dropping his other arm across her shoulders to tug her against him. He might annoy her when he went all he-man on her sometimes, thinking he could actually boss her around or win an argument. But, oh, she liked it when he went a little he-man on her sexually.

"Tony?" she said as he led her out into the cold Chicago morning. The sky was bright blue, the ground blazingly white. Fresh and crisp and heartbreakingly beautiful.

"Yeah, babe?"

"Next time…I won't wear the panties."

Throwing his head back and laughing, he replied, "You better believe I'm gonna hold you to that."

A guy working the valet stand stared at them curiously. So did a couple of businessmen getting into a taxi.

She didn't care. Not one bit.

"One more thing."

"Yes?"

"Next time...*I'm* the traveling businesswoman and *you're* the misunderstood husband, okay?"

"Anything you want, love," he replied as they walked down the street. "Anything you want."

* * * * *

Epilogue

THEY NEARLY MISSED their flight.

After a long, full night of eroticism and tenderness, Izzie and Nick both overslept. By the time Izzie glanced at the clock through nearly lowered lashes, awakened by the slant of sunlight peeking through the slit in the heavy drapes, it was nearly ten. Their flight to Aruba left O'Hare at noon.

The two of them threw their things in their suitcases, washed and dressed frantically, and raced out of their room. The whole way down in the elevator, Izzie snuck glances at her watch, nibbling her lip in concern.

"There are other flights, if we miss it we'll catch the next one," Nick said, obviously noticing. Then he smiled slowly, that sexy, insatiable glimmer in his eyes. "We could always come back here. I sure wouldn't mind spending another night like the last one."

Oh, goodness, neither would she. Though she and Nick had been lovers for several months, nothing had prepared her for the intensity of being *married* lovers. It had taken all the physical pleasure and catapulted it beyond anything she'd ever known. She'd never suspected, never dreamed how much better things could get with the exchange of two rings and some vows.

"Wait, is that Gloria?" Nick said as they got off the elevator and strode toward the lobby.

Izzie glanced at the main hotel doors, seeing a dark-haired woman walk out them. Shaking her head, she replied, "I doubt it. She was going home last night. Lots of little boys to take care of."

Nick must have heard something in her voice. Because even though they were running terribly late, he stopped and put a hand on her shoulder. "We're not having kids for a long time, remember?"

She nodded. While she wanted Nick's babies, she didn't want them anytime soon. She and her new husband were having too much fun by themselves. "I know. But when we do? Promise we won't be like Gloria and Tony, doing nothing that doesn't involve the kids, never sparing a private moment for each other."

He put an arm across her shoulder and started walking again. "I promise."

Feeling better, since Nick would never break a promise, Izzie murmured, "I feel a little sorry for her. I know she loves your brother, but she's just so…maternal. Unadventurous."

"I think *you* got all the adventurous genes in your family," Nick said as he led her out the door into the cold Chicago morning. He slipped the doorman a big bill and the man stepped right out in traffic to hail them the next passing cab.

"Mia's tough, but you're right, she's not exactly adventurous when it comes to her personal life," Izzie admitted. "She never lets herself go, never takes chances. It's a shame." Thinking more about the topic, she added, "It seems as if *none* of my bridesmaids are terribly lucky in the romance department."

"Gloria and Tony love each other…."

She waved a hand. "Oh, of course they do, I'm not talking about that. I'm talking about wild, romantic, *fun* relationships." Her jaw tightening, she muttered, "I wish Bridget could get over that jerk FBI agent who strung her along last year. And that Leah would meet some rich doctor while she's going to nursing school, someone who'll pamper her and treat her right after all the garbage she went through in her childhood."

"I'm sure there are lots of rich doctors at the club," he offered, a tiny smile on his lips. "Just none who are looking for a wife."

She smirked. "*You* found one there."

"No, I think *you* found *me* on a table full of cookies at Gloria and Tony's wedding."

Izzie responded by swatting her new husband's arm. She'd long heard the snickers about how she'd fallen on top of Nick when she'd been a chubby teenager and he a sexy young Marine. He'd called her Cookie ever since. "You want to continue this honeymoon, don't mention that again."

He made a lips-zipped motion over his mouth.

But even the light banter with her sexy hubby couldn't distract Izzie from her thoughts of her sisters…and her friends. "Even Vanessa, as beautiful as she is, has no one special in her life and hasn't for as long as I've known her."

"That's a shame," Nick said, slipping an arm around her waist. "But it'll happen. Would you have pictured us being like this six months ago?"

Izzie shook her head. She most definitely had *not* envisioned this day even as recently as last summer. "You're right. Something wonderful could happen to any of them."

"Maybe it already did. Who's to say they didn't have as spectacular a night last night as we did?"

They looked into each other's eyes, both remembering the night before. And both of them burst into peals of laughter at the exact same moment.

Because that was absolutely *impossible*.

When the laughter faded, Izzie put her head on her husband's strong shoulder, noting the way he had turned his back to the wind to shield her from the cold. So protective. God, how she loved him.

The doorman quickly got them a cab and they hurried over to it, hopping into the backseat as the driver tossed their bags in the trunk.

"You okay?" Nick asked, once they were under way. "Not worried about your bridesmaids anymore?"

She shook her head. "No. Like you said, it'll happen, maybe even today. Who knows? This could be the first day of the rest of their lives."

Her new husband brushed his lips across her forehead, then her cheek. "Just like it is ours," he whispered.

Meeting his mouth for a tender kiss, Izzie could do nothing but agree. Because a lifetime of loving Nick Santori was all she'd ever dreamed of…and everything she'd ever wanted.

She only hoped that someday her bridesmaids would be equally as happy.

* * * * *

HARLEQUIN®

is proud to present

Because sex doesn't have to be serious!

Don't miss the next red-hot title...

PRIMAL INSTINCTS

by
Jill Monroe

Ava Simms's sexual instincts take over
as she puts her theories about mating
to the test with gorgeous globe-traveling
journalist Ian Cole. He's definitely up for
the challenge—but is she?

On sale February 2008 wherever books are sold.

You can lead a horse to water...

When Alyssa Barkley and Clint Westmoreland
found out that their "fake" marriage was never
rendered void, they are forced to live together
for thirty days. However, Clint loves the single
life and has no intention of being tamed, but
when Alyssa moves in, the sizzling attraction
between them is ignited and neither wants the
thirty days to end.

Look for

TAMING CLINT
WESTMORELAND

by

BRENDA
JACKSON

Available February wherever you buy books

REQUEST YOUR FREE BOOKS!

2 FREE NOVELS PLUS 2 FREE GIFTS!

HARLEQUIN®

Blaze

Red-hot reads!

Romantic
SUSPENSE

**Sparked by Danger,
Fueled by Passion.**

When Tech Sergeant Jacob "Mako" Stone opens
his door to a mysterious woman without a past,
he knows his time off is over. As threats to Dee's
life bring her and Jacob together, she must set
aside her pride and accept the help of the military
hero with too many secrets of his own.

Out of Uniform
by **Catherine Mann**

Available February wherever you buy books.

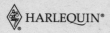

HARLEQUIN®
Blaze™

COMING NEXT MONTH

#375 TEX APPEAL Kimberly Raye, Alison Kent, Cara Summers
A sizzling Valentine collection—Texas-style!
Ride 'em, cowboys! Take a super-hot former rodeo star, a lust-worthy down-home boy and a randy Ranger, mix well with three Southern ladies who are each in need of a little action between the sheets, and what do you get? Tons of *Tex* appeal!

#376 MY WILDEST RIDE Isabel Sharpe
The Martini Dares, Bk. 4
Seduce the man you most desire? That's one tough dare for vulnerable Lindsay Beckham. But she can't resist hot bartender Denver Langston, a man known for serving up delicious cocktails…like Sex on the Beach.

#377 SHAMELESS Tori Carrington
Extreme
Torn between two lovers… Kevin Webster, Patrick Gauge and Nina Leonard are business partners and the best of friends. They share everything, including their sexual exploits. So when Nina complains about sleeping alone, Gauge and Kevin set her up with a stranger for a night of incredible anonymous sex. Only, the man in Nina's bed is no stranger….

#378 PRIMAL INSTINCTS Jill Monroe
Blush
Ava Simms's feminine instincts take over as she puts her theories about mating to the test with gorgeous journalist Ian Cole…who's definitely up for the challenge. But will he satisfy Ava's sexual curiosity?

#379 YOUR BED OR MINE? Kate Hoffmann
The Wrong Bed
Caley Lambert is making some changes. She's just dumped her boyfriend, and she's thinking about ditching her job. But she needs time to think, and attending a family wedding at the old lake house seems like the perfect solution. Only, waking up in bed with her first love isn't exactly what she was expecting….

#380 BURNING UP Sarah Mayberry
A month in a luxury location cooking for one man…it's the perfect job. But when Sophie Gallagher agrees to be actor Lucas Grant's chef, she's so not falling for his charm…until he pursues her with delicious intent, that is. And she discovers he is the hottest man alive!

www.eHarlequin.com